Android®

2nd Edition

by Dan Gookin

Android® For Dummies®, 2nd Edition

Published by: **John Wiley & Sons, Inc.,** 111 River Street, Hoboken, NJ 07030-5774, www.wiley.com

Copyright © 2020 by John Wiley & Sons, Inc., Hoboken, New Jersey

Published simultaneously in Canada

For general information on our other products and services, please contact our Customer Care Department within the U.S. at 877-762-2974, outside the U.S. at 317-572-3993, or fax 317-572-4002. For technical support, please visit www.wiley.com/techsupport.

Wiley publishes in a variety of print and electronic formats and by print-on-demand. Some material included with standard print versions of this book may not be included in e-books or in print-on-demand. If this book refers to media such as a CD or DVD that is not included in the version you purchased, you may download this material at http://booksupport.wiley.com. For more information about Wiley products, visit www.wiley.com.

Library of Congress Control Number: 2020942384

ISBN: 978-1-119-71135-3; 978-1-119-71136-0 (ebk); 978-1-119-71137-7 (ebk)

Manufactured in the United States of America

SKY10020249_080320

Contents at a Glance

Table of Contents

Introduction

You know it's intimidating when they call it a "smartphone." Worse, the supersize smartphone, the tablet, supposedly does everything your computer does but without a keyboard — or very many knobs or switches. Still, if you own one of these devices, don't you want to get all the features you paid for?

This book makes the complex subject of Android phones and tablets understandable. It's done with avuncular care and gentle handholding. The information is friendly and informative, without frightening you. And yes, ample humor is sprinkled throughout the text to keep the mood light. New technology can be frustrating enough without a touch of levity.

About This Book

Please don't read this book from cover to cover. This book is a reference. It's designed to be used as you need it. Look up a topic in the table of contents or the index. Find something about your Android mobile gizmo that vexes you or you're curious about. Look up the answer, and get on with your life.

Every chapter is written as its own, self-contained unit, covering a specific Android topic. The chapters are further divided into sections representing tasks you perform with the device or explaining how to get something done. Sample sections in this book include

>> Typing without lifting your finger

>> Making a conference call

>> Blocking calls

>> Sending email to a contact

>> Surfing the web on a mobile device

>> Helping others find your location

>> Recording video

» Creating a mobile hotspot

» Flying with an Android

» Extending battery life

You have nothing to memorize, no sacred utterances or animal sacrifices, and definitely no PowerPoint presentations. Instead, every section explains a topic as though it's the first thing you've read in this book. Nothing is assumed, and everything is cross-referenced. Technical terms and topics, when they come up, are neatly shoved to the side, where they're easily avoided. The idea here isn't to learn anything. This book's philosophy is to help you look it up, figure it out, and move on.

How to Use This Book

This book follows a few conventions for using your Android phone or tablet, so pay attention!

First of all, no matter what name your phone or tablet has, whether it's a manufacturer's name or a pet name you've devised on your own, this book refers to it as an *Android*. Sometimes the term *phone* or *tablet* is used, and sometimes *device* or, rarely, *gizmo*.

Because Samsung modifies the Android operating system, and because the company's gizmos sell more than other phones and tablets, its devices are often called out in the text — specifically, when a Samsung galactic gizmo does something different from a typical Android gizmo.

The main way to interact with an Android mobile device is to use its *touchscreen*, which is the glassy part of the device as it's facing you. The physical buttons on the device are called *keys*. These items are discussed and explained in Part 1 of this book.

The various ways to touch the screen are explained and named in Chapter 3.

Chapter 4 covers text input, which involves using an onscreen keyboard. When you tire of typing, you can dictate your text. It's all explained in Chapter 4.

This book directs you to do things by following numbered steps. Each step involves a specific activity, such as touching something on the screen; for example:

3. **Tap the Apps icon.**

This step directs you to tap or touch the graphical Apps icon on the screen. When a button is shown as text, the command reads:

3. **Tap the Download button.**

You might also be directed to choose an item, which means to tap it on the screen.

 Various settings can be turned off or on, as indicated by a master control, which looks like the on–off toggle, as shown in the margin. Tap the master control to enable or disable the feature, or slide its button to the right or left. When the feature is enabled, the Master Control icon appears in color.

Foolish Assumptions

Though this book is written with the gentle handholding required by anyone who is just starting out, or who is easily intimidated, I've made a few assumptions.

I'm assuming that you're still reading the introduction. That's great. It's much better than getting a snack right now or checking to ensure that the cat isn't chewing through the TV cable again.

My biggest assumption: You have or desire to own a phone or tablet that uses Google's Android operating system.

Your phone can be any Android phone from any manufacturer supported by any popular cellular service provider in the United States. Because Android is an operating system, the methods of doing things on one Android phone are similar, if not identical, to doing things on another Android phone. Therefore, one book can pretty much cover the gamut of Android phones.

If you have an Android tablet instead, it can be a Wi-Fi–only tablet or an LTE (Long-Term Evolution) tablet that uses the same mobile data network as an Android phone. This book covers both models.

Any differences between an Android phone and tablet are noted in the text. For the most part, the devices work similarly because they run the same Android operating system.

The Android operating system itself comes in versions, or flavors. This book covers current Android versions 8.0 through 10.0. To confirm which Android version your gizmo uses, follow these steps:

1. Open the Settings app.

Directions are found in Chapter 3 for accessing the Settings app.

2. Choose System.

If you see the About Phone or About Tablet item on the main Settings app screen, choose it. This item might be named About Device.

3. Look at the item titled System Update or Android Version.

Newer devices use System Update to disclose the current Android version. Older devices show a number by the Android operating system item. Also check for the item Software Information.

Don't fret if these steps confuse you: Check out Part 1 of this book, and then come back here. (I'll wait.)

More assumptions:

You don't need to own a computer to use your Android mobile thingy. If you have a computer, great. Your phone or tablet works well with both PC and Mac. When directions are specific to a PC or Mac, the book says so.

Programs that run on your Android are *apps*, which is short for *applications*. A single program is an *app*.

Finally, this book assumes that you have a Google account, but if you don't, Chapter 2 explains how to configure one. Do so. Having a Google account opens up a slew of useful features, information, and programs that make using your Android more productive.

Icons Used in This Book

This icon flags useful, helpful tips or shortcuts.

This icon marks a friendly reminder to do something.

WARNING

This icon marks a friendly reminder not to do something.

TECHNICAL STUFF

This icon alerts you to overly nerdy information and technical discussions of the topic at hand. Reading the information is optional, though it may win you the Daily Double on *Jeopardy!*

Contacting the Author

My email address is dgookin@wambooli.com. Yes, that's my real address. I reply to every email I receive, and more quickly when you keep your question short and specific to this book. Although I enjoy saying Hi, I cannot answer technical support questions, resolve billing issues, or help you troubleshoot your phone or tablet. Thanks for understanding.

My website is wambooli.com. This book has its own page on that site, which you can check for updates, new information, and all sorts of fun stuff. Visit often:

```
wambooli.com/help/android
```

Beyond the Book

Thank you for reading the introduction. Few people do, and it would save a lot of time and bother if they did. Consider yourself fortunate. No, consider yourself handsome, well-read, and worthy of praise, though you probably knew that.

Beyond my own website (see the preceding section), my beloved publisher also offers its own helpful site, which contains official updates and bonus information I'm forbidden by law to offer to you. Visit the publisher's official support page at www.dummies.com and then search for *Android For Dummies, 2nd Edition* — the whole thing! I'd offer more specific information, but I don't have it. The publisher told me that the actual address of the online material is held in one of 20 briefcases and that if I choose the right one, I get paid — something like that.

Your task now: Start reading the rest of the book — but not the whole thing, and especially not with the chapters in order. Observe the table of contents and find something that interests you. Or look up your puzzle in the index. When these suggestions don't cut it, just start reading Chapter 1.

Enjoy this book and your Android mobile gizmo!

1

Your Own Android

IN THIS PART . . .

Get started with your Android gizmo.

Work through configuration and setup.

Learn basic techniques and procedures.

Force yourself to enjoy the onscreen keyboard.

IN THIS CHAPTER

» **Unboxing your Android**

» **Charging the battery**

» **Locating important things**

» **Getting optional accessories**

» **Storing an Android**

Chapter **1**

An Out-of-the-Box Experience

Y ou begin your Android adventure by removing the device from its box. Yes, I know: You've already completed that task. I don't blame you; I removed my new Android from the box before I read this chapter. Yet you may consider a few helpful tips and suggestions before that out-of-the-box experience becomes a distant memory.

Liberation

Like most electronics, your new Android phone works fastest when you remove it from its box. Savor the moment. Breathe deep the scent of the industrial epoxy used to seal the box. Gingerly lift out the packaging. Marvel as you peel back the plastic sheeting.

Array before you the contents of the box. These useful items include

» **The device itself:** If further assembly is required, directions are found inside the box.

» **USB cable:** Use it to connect the device to a computer or a wall charger.

>> **Power adapter:** Use this thing with the USB cable to charge the Android's battery. The adapter may come in two pieces, both of which must be assembled.

>> **Earbud headset:** This item might be a simple headset, or you might find a microphone/controller gizmo on one of the earbud leads.

>> **Useless pamphlets:** It's odd that the safety and warranty information is far more extensive than the flimsy user guide. That shows the priority our culture places on lawyers over technology writers.

>> **The SIM card and removal tool:** You may find the card holder used to install the device's SIM card. If the SIM has already been installed, you can toss the holder, though I recommend keeping the SIM card removal tool.

ANDROID BUYING TIPS

The major things to look for when purchasing an Android gizmo are its cellular provider, storage, camera options, screen size, and overall design.

All phones have a cellular connection, but only some Android tablets use this feature. Most tablets use only the Wi-Fi connection for Internet access, which is fine. Cellular or LTE (Long-Term Evolution) tablets cost more and also incur monthly mobile data charges.

Some Androids feature removable storage, in the form of a microSD card. This feature allows you to expand the device's storage and more easily share files with a computer, though using removable storage isn't without its issues. See Chapter 19.

The device's camera has a maximum resolution, measured in megapixels (MP). The higher the value, the better the camera, though unless you plan to edit high resolution images, a zillion megapixels isn't worth the extra cost. Ensure that an Android tablet has both front and rear cameras. And confirm that the rear camera has a flash. It's not an important feature, but it's best to know before you buy the device.

Both screen size and design play together — specifically, with how the device feels in your hand. Some large format phones, often called *phablets* (for *phone/tablets*) are too big for some people — and pockets. Tablets come in two sizes: a smaller format, about the size of a paperback book, and a larger format, better suited for watching videos. The best way to know which size works best for you is to try out a few devices at the store.

Beyond these basic items, Android phones and tablets have only subtle software differences. Do ensure, however, that your device can access and use Google Play, the online store for the Android operating system. Some bargain phones and tablets restrict your purchases to the manufacturer's own app store. I would avoid those gizmos.

The important thing to do is confirm that nothing is missing or damaged. Ensure that you have all the parts you paid for, including any optional accessories. If anything is missing or appears to be damaged, immediately contact the folks who sold you the device.

TIP

>> I recommend keeping the packaging and its contents as long as you own the Android: The box makes an excellent storage place for that stuff — as well as for anything else you don't plan to use right away.

>> The process of transferring information from your old phone to a new one is covered in Chapter 2.

Android Assembly

Android devices come fully assembled. If not, directions that came with the device describe what to do. Even then, odds are that the nice people at the store assembled the gizmo for you. If not, well then, they weren't so nice, were they?

Peeling off the plastic sheeting

Like laser blasters and time travel pods, your Android ships with a clingy plastic sheeting adhering to its surface. The sheeting might describe various features, so look it over before you peel it off. And, yes, you must remove the sheeting; it's for shipping protection, not for long-term protection.

TIP

>> Check the device's rear camera to confirm that you've removed the plastic sheeting from its lens.

>> Feel free to discard the plastic sheeting.

Installing the SIM card

A *SIM card* identifies an Android device to the digital cellular network. Before you can use it on that network, the SIM card must be installed.

TECHNICAL STUFF

SIM stands for *subscriber identity module*, which should help you if you enjoy doing crossword puzzles.

Most of the time, the sales staff at the phone store install the SIM card. They pretend it's a task that requires a PhD in quantum mechanics, though it's really LEGO-brick simple.

If you've purchased your phone or cellular tablet outside the realm of the phone store and you have a SIM card to install (and you know how to obtain service for it and all that stuff), follow these steps when the device is turned off:

1. **Locate the SIM card cover on the device's outer edge.**

The cover features a dimple or hole on one end.

2. **Firmly insert the SIM card removal tool into the hole on the SIM card cover, and press to remove the SIM card tray.**

The SIM card cover pops up or the SIM card tray slides out.

3. **Pop the SIM card out of the credit-card-size holder.**

Push the card with your thumb and it pops out. Don't use scissors or else you may damage the card.

4. **Set the SIM card into the SIM card tray or otherwise insert it into the SIM card slot.**

The SIM card is shaped in such a way that it's impossible to insert improperly. If the card doesn't slide into the slot, reorient the card and try again.

5. **Insert the SIM card tray back into the slot or close the SIM card cover.**

You're done.

The good news is that you seldom, if ever, need to remove or replace a SIM card.

CHOOSING A CELLULAR CARRIER

You do have a choice when it comes to the cellular provider for your Android device. Most of the time this decision is made by where you buy the phone: The store that provides mobile data also sells you the device. However, you can buy an unlocked phone, which can be used with any compatible cellular service.

The key issue when choosing a carrier is coverage. Though its colorful coverage maps may look good, the best way to ensure that a cellular provider has the coverage you need is to ask your friends and associates who use that same provider. Does the signal work everywhere? Is the signal consistent?

Another option available to you, though unpopular, is to pay full price upfront for the phone. Buying the phone outright frees you from a long term contract (generally, two years). Though expensive, using the service without a contract makes it easier to switch carriers if you later choose to do so.

Charge the Battery

Manufacturers give your new phone enough charge to survive the setup process, but little more. Therefore, one of your first duties, and eventually a routine task, is to charge the Android's battery. You can wait in an old castle for a lightning storm or just abide by these steps:

1. **If necessary, assemble the charging cord.**

Connect the charger head (the wall adapter) to the USB cable that comes with the Android.

2. **Plug the charger head and cable into a wall socket.**

3. **Connect the Android to the USB cable.**

The charger cord plugs into the micro-USB connector, found at the device's bottom.

As the device charges, you may see a Charging Battery graphic on the touchscreen, or a notification lamp may glow. Such activity is normal.

When the device is fully charged, the icon is "full" or you see 100% on the battery indicator. At that point, you can remove the charging cord, though leaving the Android plugged in doesn't damage the device.

>> The phone or tablet may turn on when you plug it in for a charge. That's okay, but read Chapter 2 to find out what to do the first time the Android turns on.

>> Some tablets use their own charging cord, not the USB cable.

>> I recommend fully charging the gizmo. You can use it while it's charging, but give it a full charge before you disconnect the cord.

>> Older Androids feature a micro-A USB connector, which plugs in only one way. If the cable doesn't fit, flip it over and try again.

>> Newer USB Type-C cables and connectors plug in any-which-way.

>> Some Androids can charge wirelessly, but only when you purchase a special wireless charger: Place the phone or tablet on its charging pad or in the charging cradle. See the later section "Adding accessories."

>> If the battery charge is too low, the Android won't turn on. This is normal behavior. Let the device charge awhile before you turn it on.

>> The Android also charges itself whenever it's connected to a computer's USB port. The computer must be on for charging to work. The device may charge only when plugged into a powered USB port, such as one of those found directly on the computer console.

>> Androids charge more quickly when plugged into the wall than into a computer's USB port or a car adapter.

>> Unlike with the old NiCad batteries, you don't need to worry about fully discharging the battery before recharging it. If the phone or tablet needs a charge, even when the battery is just a little low, feel free to do so.

>> See Chapter 24 for battery and power management information.

Android Exploration

No one told the first person to ride a horse which direction to face. That's because some things just come naturally. If using your Android phone or tablet doesn't come naturally, refer to this section for help finding important items on the device and learning what those doodads are called.

Discovering what's what and where

Take a gander at Figure 1-1, which illustrates common items found on the front and back of a typical Android phone. Android tablets are similar, though larger.

Not every item shown in the figures may be in the exact same spot on your device. For example, the Power/Lock key might be found on the top edge, not on the side.

The terms used in Figure 1-1 are used throughout this book and found in whatever scant Android documentation exists. Here are the highlights:

Power/Lock key: This button, or key, turns the device on or off as well as locks or unlocks the device. Directions for performing these activities are found in Chapter 2.

Volume key: The volume control is two-buttons-in-one. Press one side of the key to set the volume higher, or the other side to set the volume lower.

Touchscreen: The biggest part of an Android gizmo is its touchscreen display, which occupies almost all the territory on the front of the device. The touchscreen is a look-touch gizmo: You look at it but also touch it with your fingers to control the Android.

Front camera: The front-facing camera, found above the touchscreen, is used for taking self-portraits as well as for video chat.

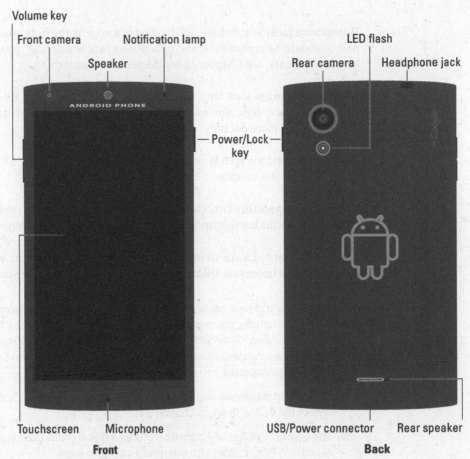

Volume key

Front camera

Speaker

Notification lamp

LED flash

Rear camera

Headphone jack

ANDROID PHONE

Power/Lock key

FIGURE 1-1:
Your phone's face
and rump

Touchscreen

Microphone

Front

USB/Power connector

Rear speaker

Back

Rear camera: The rear camera is found on the back (duh). Some devices feature multiple lenses for different focal lengths or special effects. The camera may be accompanied by one or more LED flash gizmos.

Speaker(s): The primary phone speaker is located top-center, above the touchscreen. One or more additional speakers might also be found on the phone's bottom edge or backside. Tablets feature stereo speakers on either side of the device, though some smaller tablets may have their speakers on the back.

Microphone: Somewhere below the touchscreen, you'll find the phone's microphone. It's tiny, about the diameter of a pin. Don't stick anything into the hole! A second, noise canceling microphone might also be found on the back of the phone. Android tablets put the microphone along the edge, typically on the bottom.

Headphone jack: Somewhere on the device's edge is the hole where you can connect standard headphones. If the headphone jack is missing, you must use wireless headphones; see Chapter 18 for details on Bluetooth.

Removable storage slot: Into this slot you insert a microSD card, which expands the device's storage. Not every Android features this expansion option. See Chapter 19 for more details.

SIM card cover: This spot is where you access a cellular device's SIM card, as covered earlier in this chapter.

USB/Power connector: This slot is where you connect the USB cable, which is used both to charge the battery and to connect your Android to a computer.

Take a moment to locate all items mentioned in this section, as well as shown in Figure 1-1. It's important that you know where these items are on your device.

>> As you might expect, some devices feature extra doodads, beyond the basics here. For example, you may find a row of navigation icons along the bottom of the touchscreen. Older Samsung devices feature a physical Home button. Newer Samsung devices have a Bixby button, used to summon Samsung's eager digital assistant.

>> The back of the phone may feature a fingerprint scanner, which is used to unlock the device. Refer to Chapter 22.

>> The Galaxy Note line of Androids features a digital stylus pointing device called an S Pen. It slides into the device's bottom edge.

>> It's common for some phones to feature controls on the back. You may find the power button (near the top-center on the back of the phone), a volume key, or a fingerprint scanner.

Using earphones

You can use your Android without earphones, but they're nice things to have. If you didn't find a set of earbuds in the box, I recommend that you buy a pair: The earbud-style earphone sets directly into your ear. The sharp, pointy end of the earphones, which you don't want to stick into your ear, plugs into the device's headphone jack.

Between the earbuds and the sharp, pointy thing, you might find a doodle button. The button is used to answer a call on an Android phone, mute the mic, or, on both a phone and tablet, start or stop the playback of music.

A teensy hole on the doodle serves as a microphone. The mic allows you to wear the earbuds and talk on the phone while keeping your hands free. If you gesture while you speak, you'll find this feature invaluable.

REMEMBER

>> The earphones must be inserted fully into the jack. If they aren't, you won't hear anything.

>> You can also use a Bluetooth headset with your phone, to listen to a call or some music. See Chapter 18 for more information on Bluetooth.

TIP

>> Fold the earphones when you put them away, as opposed to wrapping them in a loop. Put the earbuds and connector in one hand, and then pull the wire straight out with the other hand. Fold the wire in half and then in half again. You can then put the earphones in your pocket or on a tabletop. By folding the wires, you avoid creating something that looks like a wire ball of Christmas tree lights.

Adding accessories

Beyond earphones, you can find an entire phone store full of accessories and baubles for your Android. The variety is seemingly endless, and the prices, well, they ain't cheap. Here are some of your choices:

Phone case: Protect your phone by getting it a jacket, one that further expresses your individuality.

Pouches, sleeves, and keyboard covers: Android tablets have larger-format cases, almost like folios. Special pouches double as tablet stands. The fanciest tablet accessory is a keyboard cover, which features a wireless (Bluetooth) keyboard.

Keyboard: Speaking of keyboards, even if it isn't part of the case, a Bluetooth keyboard is a handy Android tablet accessory.

Screen protector: This clear, plastic sheet adheres to the touchscreen, protecting it from scratches, finger smudges, and sneeze globs while still allowing you to use the touchscreen. Ensure that you get a screen protector designed specifically for your device.

Belt clip: To sate your envy of Batman's utility belt, and demonstrate that you're definitely over 50, consider getting a fine leatherette or Naugahyde phone case that you can quickly attach to your belt.

Arm band: Demonstrate to the world that you're not only healthy but you're also under 50 by wearing your phone on your upper arm. Do so only while jogging or wearing such attire while standing in line at Starbucks.

Selfie stick: Cheaper than having friends and more trustworthy than handing your phone to a stranger, use the selfie stick to take a self portrait minus that awkward "I'm holding my own phone" posture. It's a must for tourists.

Vehicle charger: Use the vehicle charger to provide power to your phone or tablet for a long trip. This accessory is a must for older vehicles that lack USB ports.

Car mount: This device holds your Android phone so that you can easily see it while driving. It makes for easier access, although these things are forbidden in some states.

Wireless charger: Not every phone can be charged wirelessly, but if yours can, definitely get a wireless charger. Set your phone on the pad or prop it up in the dock. The phone's battery starts magically recharging.

Portable charger: Battery life isn't always what it's cracked up to be. These pocket-size power plants let you charge your phone anywhere power isn't otherwise available.

Screencasting dongle: This accessory connects to an HDTV or computer monitor. Once configured, it allows you to cast the Android's screen onto the larger-screen device. It's ideal for watching movies or Netflix or YouTube videos, or for enjoying music. Google's Chromecast is an example of a screencasting gizmo. See Chapter 19 for more information on screencasting.

Other exciting and nifty accessories might be available for your phone or tablet. Check frequently for new garnishes and frills at the location where you bought your Android. Your credit card company will love you.

>> Android devices generally don't recognize more than one button on the earphone doodle. For example, if you use earphones that feature a volume button or mute button, pressing that extra button does nothing.

>> Another useful accessory to get is a microfiber cloth to help clean the touchscreen, plus a special cleaning solution wipe. See Chapter 24 for more information about cleaning an Android's screen.

Where to Keep Your Digital Pal

The good news is that an Android combines multiple devices. So, rather than keep track of a clock, camera, phone, video recorder, game machine, tiny TV, and, possibly, other gizmos, you need to mind only one device. Of course, the panic is still there when you misplace the phone. This section offers hints on how to avoid that situation.

Toting an Android phone

The compactness of the modern smartphone makes it perfect for a pocket or even the teensiest of party purses. And its well-thought-out design means you can carry your phone in your pocket or handbag with no fear that something will accidentally turn it on, dial Mongolia, and run up a heck of a phone bill.

>> Most phones feature a proximity sensor. It keeps the touchscreen locked, which prevents a phone in a pocket or purse from waking up and making a call.

>> Don't forget that you've placed the phone in your pocket, especially in your coat or jacket. You might accidentally sit on the phone, or it can fly out when you peel off your coat. The worst fate for any smartphone is to take a trip through the wash. I'm sure your phone has nightmares about it.

WARNING

Taking an Android tablet with you

The ideal place for an Android tablet is in a specially designed case, pouch, or sleeve. The pouch keeps the device from being dinged, scratched, or even unexpectedly turned on while it's in your backpack, purse, or carry-on luggage or wherever you put the tablet when you're not using it. Further, the tablet cover may prop up the device for easy viewing in a coffee shop or in the middle seat during a long airplane trip.

Also see Chapter 23 for information on using an Android tablet on the road.

Making a home for the Android

It's best to keep your phone or tablet in the same place when you're not actively using it, especially a tablet. I prefer to keep my gizmos by my computer, where I can charge them and also refer to them as I work.

Another ideal location is on a nightstand. Especially if you get a dock for the phone or tablet, you can use it as your alarm clock. Ensure that you connect the Android to a power source so that it charges overnight.

Above all, keep the phone or tablet in the same spot. That's the key to not losing it. Always set it back in the same place. (This advice applies to anything you're prone to losing, not just a phone or tablet.)

>> Phones and tablets on coffee tables get buried under magazines and are often squished when rude people put their feet on the furniture.

>> Avoid putting your phone or tablet in direct sunlight; heat is bad news for any electronic gizmo.

IN THIS CHAPTER

» **Configuring the device**

» **Adding more accounts**

» **Upgrading to a new phone or tablet**

» **Turning on an Android**

» **Unlocking the screen**

» **Locking the screen**

» **Shutting down an Android**

Chapter **2**

The On–Off Chapter

Somewhere between *Pencils For Dummies* and *Home Surgery For Dummies* lies the complexity of the Android phone or tablet. For example, *Pencils For Dummies* lacks a chapter describing how to activate a pencil. *Home Surgery For Dummies* features an entire chapter on anesthesiology using items found under a kitchen sink.

For this book, the complexity of your phone or tablet mandates a chapter dedicated to turning the device on and off, as well as putting it to sleep, waking it up, and locking it. Further, you must endure Android setup, a one-time procedure, but quite important to start you off on the right foot.

New Android Setup

To thwart your excitement over getting a new phone or tablet, you must endure the ordeal of first-time setup. This process is a necessary rite of passage — therefore, it's important that you get it out of the way before further exploring your new Android pal.

Configuring your Android

The very first time you turn on an Android gizmo, you're required to work through the setup-and-configuration process. Various options are presented, from which you must make choices, fill in the blanks, and perform other tasks. The process is only mildly annoying: Some items can be skipped or postponed, but it's best to get it out of the way now.

The specifics of the setup and configuration differ subtly, depending on the device's manufacturer and cellular provider. If the people at the phone store helped you through the process, great! If they didn't, first read the generic steps presented in this section and then go back and work the steps with your phone or tablet:

1. **Press and hold the Power/Lock key to turn on your Android.**

You may have to press the key longer than you think; when you see the brand logo appear on the screen, release the key.

TIP

It's okay to turn on the device while it's plugged in and charging.

2. **Answer the questions presented.**

The Android assaults you with a series of questions and prompts. Here are the highlights:

- Select your language
- Activate the device on the mobile data network
- Connect to a Wi-Fi network
- Set the time zone
- Accept terms and conditions
- Sign in to (or create) your Google account
- Set location information
- Grant permissions
- Configure a screen lock

Two other steps include adding other online accounts and restoring your data from another Android mobile device or your Google account. The following two sections cover these steps in detail.

When in doubt, accept the choice presented. You can always change a setting later. Even so, choosing a Google account sets the default, or administrator, account for the device, which cannot be changed without a factory data reset.

The SKIP button is your friend. Even if you don't use it, you change a setting later. Details are offered throughout this book.

To fill in text fields, use the device's onscreen keyboard. See Chapter 4 for keyboard information.

3. **After each choice, tap the NEXT or SKIP button.**

The NEXT button might be labeled with the text or an icon, as shown in the margin. The SKIP button is always text, though it's sometimes difficult to find on the screen.

4. **Tap the FINISH button.**

The FINISH button appears on the last screen of the setup procedure.

After initial setup, starting your Android works as described elsewhere in this chapter. See the later sections "Turning on your Android" and "Unlocking the device."

>> During setup, as well as immediately after and as you explore your Android, you see prompts to try out or understand various phone or tablet features. Some of those prompts are helpful, but it's okay to skip them. To do so, tap the GOT IT or OK button. If it's present, select the Do Not Show Again check box so that you won't be bothered again.

>> Additional information on connecting your Android to a Wi-Fi network is found in Chapter 18.

>> Apps must ask permission to use certain features or device hardware. I recommend that you tap the ALLOW button for now. You can review app permissions later, which is a topic covered in Chapter 22.

>> Some apps request use of the device's GPS technology to obtain your location. As with other permissions, I recommend that you allow the apps to proceed. That way, you get the most from your Android.

>> It's not necessary to use any specific software provided by the device's manufacturer or your cellular provider. For example, if you don't want a Samsung account, you don't need to sign up for one; skip that step.

>> Your Google account provides for coordination between your Android and your Gmail messages, contacts, Google Calendar appointments, and information and data from other Google Internet applications.

>> See the nearby sidebar "Who is this Android person?" for more information about the Android operating system.

Adding your online accounts

Your Android serves as home to your various online incarnations. This list includes your email accounts, online services, social networking, subscriptions, and other digital personas. I recommended adding those accounts to your mobile gizmo to continue the setup-and-configuration process described in the preceding section.

With the device on and unlocked, follow these steps:

1. **View the apps drawer.**

   Swipe the screen from bottom to top, which displays the apps drawer. If your gizmo features an Apps icon, which looks like what's shown in the margin, tap it. Refer to Chapter 3 for specifics on accessing the apps drawer.

   The apps drawer lists all installed apps on your Android.

2. **Open the Settings app.**

   You may have to swipe the apps drawer screen a few times, paging through the various icons, to find the Settings app.

   After you tap the Settings icon, the Settings app runs. It's used to configure various device features.

3. Choose the Accounts category.

The category may be titled Accounts and Backup, Accounts and Sync, or something similar.

Upon success, you see all existing accounts on your Android, such as email accounts, social networking, cloud storage, and whatever else you may have already set up.

If you don't see the list of accounts, look for an Accounts item and choose it.

4. Tap the Add Account thingy.

You see a list of account types you can add. More or fewer items appear on the list, which is generated based on installed apps and settings made by the device manufacturer.

5. Choose an account type from the list.

For example, to add a Microsoft Exchange account, choose its item in the list.

Don't worry if you don't see the exact type of account you want to add. You may have to add a specific app before an account appears. Chapter 17 covers adding apps.

6. Follow the directions to sign in to your account.

The steps that follow depend on the account. For most, use your existing username and password to sign in.

 Repeat these steps to continue adding accounts. When you're done, return to the Home screen: Swipe the screen from bottom to top, or, if it's available, tap the Home navigation icon, as shown in the margin. Refer to Chapter 3 for details on accessing the Home screen.

>> See Chapter 9 for details on adding email accounts to your Android.

>> Chapter 11 covers social networking on your Android and offers advice on adding those types of accounts.

Upgrading from an older phone

Your new Android phone may not be your first Android. If so, welcome to the process of upgrading your phone. It's not the ordeal you might fear.

First, because you have a Google account, by signing in to the new device with that same account, your apps and cloud data are synchronized with the new device. So your Gmail, contacts, calendar, and other items are immediately copied. Photos and other data backed up to the cloud are also restored to the new device.

Second, some devices may allow you to synchronize more than cloud storage. For example, you may be prompted to connect your new device to your old one by using a cable or the local Wi-Fi connection. Items such as icon arrangement on the Home screen, wallpapers, photos, and music stored on the old device are duplicated. This type of transition to a new phone or tablet makes the upgrading process painless.

Finally, though most of the items transferred to the new device, you may still need further configuration. For example, alert sounds and app settings might not be duplicated. If so, you must venture into each app to make notifications, alerts, ringtones, and other settings manually.

» The term *cloud* refers to online storage, or files backed up and available from the Internet.

» Not all apps may be copied to the new device. That's fine: You can easily reinstall them. Paid apps need not be paid for a second time. See Chapter 17.

» See Chapter 26 for details on the various things you might need to do after you upgrade your Android to a new device.

» Samsung devices feature the Smart Switch app, which automagically moves data from an older device to a new one.

Greetings, Android

Your Android lacks an on–off switch. Nope, it's a Power/Lock key, though you can refer to it as "the power button" when you're short on time. The reason for the naming confusion is that turning on an Android is more complex than just flipping a switch.

Turning on your Android

To turn on your Android phone or tablet, press and hold the Power/Lock key. After a few seconds, you may feel the device vibrate slightly, and the start-up logo appears. You can release the Power/Lock key and enjoy the hypnotic animation and cringeworthy start-up music.

Eventually, you see the lock screen. See the later section "Working a screen lock" for information on what to do next.

» The lock screen always appears when the Android is first turned on or restarted, even after an upgrade.

» Android tablets lack the vibration feature. When turning on an Android tablet, press and hold the Power/Lock key until you see the device's touchscreen come to life.

» The device won't start unless the battery is charged. If the battery charge is too low, it may not start even when connected to a power source. In this situation, wait for the battery to charge. See Chapter 1.

Unlocking the device

Most of the time, you don't turn your Android off and on. Instead, you lock and unlock it. To unlock and use the device, press the Power/Lock key. A quick press is all that's needed. The touchscreen comes to life and you see the lock screen, illustrated in Figure 2-1.

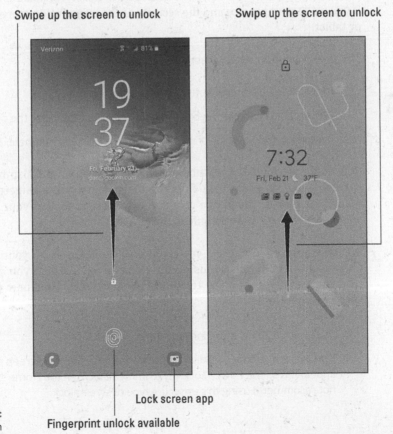

Swipe up the screen to unlock   Swipe up the screen to unlock

Lock screen app

FIGURE 2-1:
The lock screen

Fingerprint unlock available

To begin using the Android, swipe the screen as shown in the figure. If you have the screen lock applied, work the lock; see the next section for details. Eventually, you find yourself at the Home screen, where you can begin to use and interact with your phone or tablet. See Chapter 3.

>> Samsung devices with a physical Home key unlock when you press that key. The Home key is centered below the touchscreen.

>> On Samsung Galaxy Note gizmos, remove the S Pen to unlock the device.

>> Opening the cover on an Android tablet unlocks the device.

>> You can answer an Android phone, or decline an incoming call, without having to unlock the device. See Chapter 5 for more information.

Working a screen lock

If you've configured a screen lock for your Android (and I recommend that you do), after you unlock the screen you must work the screen lock. This step is a must if you value your privacy and the security of the information stored on your phone or tablet.

The three common types of screen lock include

Pattern: Trace a preset pattern over dots on the screen.

PIN: Use the onscreen keyboard to type a number to unlock the device.

Password: Type a password, which can include letters, numbers, and symbols.

Depending on your device, a biometric screen lock might also be available. For example, you can press your finger to the screen or on a fingerprint scanner to unlock the phone. The phone may use its camera to look at your face, called *face unlock*, which can instantly unlock the device.

Once the device is unlocked, you can use all the features on your Android device. Chapter 3 offers details on using the Home screen, which you probably should read right away, before the temptation to play with your new phone or tablet becomes unbearable.

>> See Chapter 22 for more information on screen locks.

>> If you've applied the dreadful "None" screen lock, the lock screen doesn't appear: Press the Power/Lock key to immediately see the Home screen. I do not recommend using this unsecure type of screen lock.

>> Some Android devices feature unusual or often wacky screen locks. For example, some Galaxy Note devices feature the signature unlock. This oddball screen lock works the same as the traditional locks: Press the Power/Lock key, and then work the wacky screen lock to gain access to your gizmo.

Unlocking and running an app

Your phone or tablet's lock screen may feature app icons, such as the Camera icon illustrated earlier, in Figure 2-1. To unlock the screen and run that app, drag its icon across the touchscreen. Though lock screen app icons, also called *launchers*, are convenient, using them doesn't unlock the device. To access more features, you must work the screen lock as covered in the preceding section.

See Chapter 21 for details on adding and managing lock screen apps.

Farewell, Android

You can dismiss your Android in several ways, only two of which involve using a steamroller or raging elephant. The other methods are documented in this section.

Locking the device

Locking the gizmo is cinchy: Press and release the Power/Lock key. The display goes dark; your Android is locked.

>> The device spends most of its time locked. The gizmo still works while locked; email comes in, music continues to play, alerts bleep, and alarms clang. Phone calls arrive. Yet while the device is locked, it doesn't use as much power as it does when the display on.

>> Some Androids may not turn off the display while they're locked. You may see the current time and notifications displayed, albeit on a very dim screen. This feature doesn't impact the device's battery life, and in many cases this setting can be changed if you don't like the always-on touchscreen. See Chapter 21 for details.

>> Press and release the Power/Lock key to lock an Android phone during a call. The call stays connected, but the touchscreen display is disabled.

>> Locking doesn't turn off your Android.

REMEMBER

>> The phone or tablet locks automatically after a period of inactivity, usually 30 seconds. You can set another timeout value, if you like. Refer to Chapter 21.

Turning off your Android

To turn off your mobile device, heed these steps:

1. Give the Power/Lock key a good, long press.

Release the key when you see the Device Options card, as illustrated in Figure 2-2. The variety of options and their presentation may differ from what's shown in the figure.

Pixel 4 Device Options card

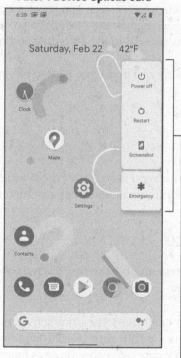

Samsung Device Options buttons

FIGURE 2-2:
The Device
Options card

Options card

2. Tap the Power Off item.

If a confirmation message appears, tap the OK button or otherwise verify your choice. The Android shuts itself off.

If you chicken out and don't want to turn off your Android, after Step 1 use the Back gesture to dismiss the Device Options card: Swipe the screen from the far right edge to the center of the screen. If the Back navigation icon is available, as shown in the margin, tap it to back out. Also, tapping elsewhere on the screen may dismiss the card.

REMEMBER

The Android doesn't run when it's off. You aren't reminded about appointments. Email stays on the server. Alarms don't trigger. Phone calls are routed to voice-mail. The device isn't angry with you for turning it off, though you may sense some resentment when you turn it on again.

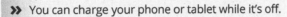

TIP

» You can charge your phone or tablet while it's off.

» Keep your Android in a safe place while it's turned off. Chapter 1 offers some suggestions.

IN THIS CHAPTER

» Getting around the touchscreen

» Changing the volume

» Working on the Home screen

» Checking notifications

» Getting at quick settings

» Running apps

» Accessing recently used apps

» Exploring common icons

Chapter **3**

Android Tour

Unlike the dress shirt industry, high-tech no longer values buttons as a sign of status. Gone are the many buttons and flashing lights of days gone by. Aside from the volume key and a few other token buttons, your Android phone or tablet is blissfully button-free. So how do you communicate with the gizmo, let alone look fashionably cool? By using the device's mysterious touchscreen.

Basic Operations

Your Android's capability to frustrate you is only as powerful as your fear of the touchscreen and how it works. After clearing that hurdle, as well as understanding some other basic operations, you'll be on your way toward mobile device contentment.

Manipulating the touchscreen

The touchscreen works in combination with one or two of your fingers. You can choose which fingers to use, or whether to be adventurous and try using the tip of your nose, but touch the screen you must. Here are some of the many ways you manipulate your Android's touchscreen:

Tap: The basic touchscreen technique is to touch it. You tap an object, an icon, a control, a menu item, a doodad, and so on. The tap operation is similar to a mouse click on a computer. It may also be referred to as a *touch* or a *press*.

Double-tap: Tap the screen twice in the same location. A double-tap can zoom in on an image or a map, but it can also zoom out. Because of the double-tap's dual nature, I recommend using the pinch and spread operations to zoom.

Long-press: Tap part of the screen and keep your finger down. Depending on what you're doing, a pop-up or card may appear, or the item you're long-pressing may get "picked up" so that you can drag (move) it around. The long-press might also be referred to as *tap and hold*.

Swipe: To swipe, tap your finger on one spot and then move your finger to another spot. Swipes can go up, down, left, or right; the touchscreen content moves in the direction in which you swipe your finger, similar to the way scrolling works on a computer. A swipe can be fast or slow. It's also called a *flick* or *slide*.

Drag: A combination of long-press and then swipe, the drag operation moves items on the screen. Start with the long press, and then keep your finger on the screen to swipe. Lift your finger to complete the action.

Pinch: A pinch involves two fingers, which start out separated and then are brought together. The effect is used to zoom out, to reduce the size of an image or see more of a map. This move may also be called a *pinch close*.

Spread: In the opposite of the pinch, you start out with your fingers together and then spread them. The spread is used to zoom in, to enlarge an image or see more detail on a map. It's also known as *pinch open*.

Rotate: Use two fingers to twist around a central point on the touchscreen, which has the effect of rotating an object on the screen. If you have trouble with this operation, pretend that you're turning the dial on a safe.

Variations on these techniques are used in several ways. For example, you swipe down from the top of the screen using two fingers to access the Quick Settings drawer. A short swipe, or tug, from the top-center of the screen downward refreshes a web page as well as the contents of other apps. A short upward swipe followed by a quick stop displays the Overview or list of running apps.

REMEMBER

You can't manipulate the touchscreen while wearing gloves unless the gloves are specially designed for using electronic touchscreens, such as the gloves that Batman wears.

Selecting a group of items

A common touchscreen technique that might be new to you is selecting a group of items. On a computer, you drag the mouse over the lot. On a touchscreen, you perform these steps:

1. Long-press the first item, such as a photo thumbnail in an album or another item in a list.

The item is selected. It appears highlighted, is adorned with a tiny check mark, or features a filled-in circle. An action bar appears atop the screen, like the one shown in Figure 3-1. It lists icons such as Share and Delete, which manipulate the group of selected items.

2. Tap additional items to select them.

The action bar lists the total number of selected items, as illustrated in Figure 3-1.

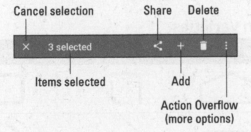

FIGURE 3-1:
A typical
action bar

3. Do something with the group.

Choose an icon from the action bar.

To cancel the selection, tap the Close (X) icon on the action bar, which deselects all items.

Navigating

Your Android device offers common and consistent ways to move around the Home screen and to manipulate apps. These methods are gesture navigation, which is available on newer phones and tablets, and the traditional navigation icons, found at the bottom of the touchscreen. Between the two, I recommend using the navigation icons until you become familiar with the tasks they perform. Here are the tasks, along with their stock Android icons shown in the margin.

Home: No matter what you're doing on the phone or tablet, use the Home gesture or tap this navigation icon to display the Home screen. Swipe from the bottom of the screen upward toward the center of the screen to perform the Home gesture.

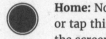

Back: Use the Back gesture or tap this navigation icon to return to a previous page, dismiss an onscreen menu, close a card, and so on. Swipe from the far right side of the touchscreen inward (toward the center of the screen) to perform the Back gesture. You can also swipe in from the left edge of the touchscreen, though swiping in from the right seems more natural.

Recent: Use the Recent gesture or tap this navigation icon to display the Overview, a list of recently opened or currently running apps. Swipe up from the bottom of the screen a short distance and stop, lifting your finger to perform the Recent gesture. See the later section "Switching between running apps" for more information on the Overview.

The icons shown in the margin represent the current, stock Android navigation icons. Table 3-1 lists other varieties, which may be used on your device.

TABLE 3-1   **Navigation Icon Varieties**

Icon	Android 5.0 to 9.0	Earlier Releases	Samsung Var. 1	Samsung Var. 2
Home	○	⌂	⊏⌐	▢
,Back	◁	↩	←	‹
Recent	▢	▭	⇄	‖‖

With gesture navigation active, the traditional navigation icons disappear from the bottom of the touchscreen. To restore them and disable gesture navigation, heed these directions:

1.   **Open the Settings app.**

It's found on the apps drawer. If the Apps Drawer icon isn't visible on the Home screen, swipe from the bottom upward to show the apps drawer.

2. **Choose the System category.**

3. **Choose Gestures.**

   If you don't see this item, your device may not feature gesture navigation.

4. **Choose System Navigation.**

5. **Select 3-Button Navigation.**

On Samsung devices, obey these directions:

1. **Open the Settings app.**

2. **Choose Display.**

3. **Choose Navigation Bar.**

4. **Choose Navigation Buttons.**

   Optionally, you can set the navigation button order on your Samsung Galactic gizmo, though be aware that this book and other documentation assumes the order Recent, Home, and Back.

If you prefer gesture navigation, follow the preceding steps to enable it, but choose Gesture Navigation from Step 5 in the first set of instructions; on Samsung devices, choose Full Screen Gestures in Step 4 in the second set of steps.

>> The gestures for showing the Home screen, viewing the Overview, as well as accessing the apps drawer are all annoying similar. This is one reason I recommend using the traditional navigation icons first, before you try using gesture navigation — if you desire to use gesture navigation at all.

>> The Back navigation icon changes its orientation during some operations, but it's still the same icon, performing the same purpose.

 >> Some apps feature a left-pointing arrow in the upper left corner of the screen to represent Back navigation.

>> Navigation icons disappear during games and when using other full-screen apps. To see the icons again, tap the screen or swipe from the top of the screen downward.

>> Another common gesture or navigation technique is to view the apps drawer, where all your Android apps are listed. See the later section "Finding an app in the apps drawer."

>> Older Samsung devices feature a physical Home button or key, which performs the same duties as the Home navigation icon. The key may double as a fingerprint reader.

Setting the volume

The volume key is located on the edge of your Android. Press the top part of the key to raise the volume. Press the bottom of the key to lower the volume. When the volume key is located on the top edge of an Android tablet, press the left side to increase volume and the right side to decrease volume.

As you press the volume key, a card appears on the touchscreen, shown in Figure 3-2. Continue pressing the volume key, or use your finger to adjust the onscreen slider, to set the volume.

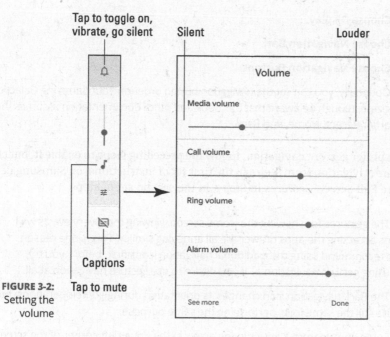

FIGURE 3-2: Setting the volume

 To view additional volume controls, tap the card as illustrated in the figure. On some devices, you tap a chevron (shown in the margin) to view controls for specific noise-generating items on your Android. Though not every volume card looks identical, they all feature slider controls.

>> The volume key controls whatever noise the device is making when you use it: If you're on a call, the volume key sets the call level. When you're listening to music or watching a video, the volume key adjusts those sounds.

>> When the volume is set all the way down, the speaker is muted.

» The volume key works even when the touchscreen is locked. This feature means you don't need to unlock the device if you're playing music and need to adjust the volume.

» Some Androids may enter Vibration mode when the volume is muted. All Android phones have Vibration mode, though not every tablet has this feature.

» Refer to Chapter 21 for more details on volume controls.

"Silence your phone!"

How many times have you heard the admonition "Please silence your cell phone"? The quick way to obey this command with an Android phone is to keep pressing the bottom part of the volume key until the phone vibrates. You're good to go.

» Some phones feature a Mute action on the Device Options card: Press and hold the Power/Lock key and then choose Mute or Vibrate.

» When the phone is silenced or in Vibration mode, an appropriate status icon appears on the status bar. The stock Android status icon is shown in the margin.

» You make the phone noisy again by reversing the directions in this section. Most commonly, press the "louder" end of the volume key to restore the phone's sound.

Changing the orientation

Your Android features a gizmo called an *accelerometer*. It determines in which direction the device is pointed when its orientation has changed from horizontal to vertical — or even upside down. That way, the information displayed on the touchscreen always appears upright, no matter how you hold it.

To demonstrate how the phone or tablet orients itself, rotate the gizmo to the left or right. Most apps, such as the web browser app, change their presentation between horizontal and vertical to match the device's orientation.

» The rotation feature may not work for all apps or even for the Home screen. Specifically, most games present themselves in one orientation only.

» The onscreen keyboard is more tolerable when the device is in its horizontal orientation. Chapter 4 covers using the onscreen keyboard.

» You can lock the orientation if the rotating screen bothers you. See Chapter 21.

» A great app that demonstrates the device's accelerometer is the game Labyrinth. You can purchase it at Google Play or download the free version, Labyrinth Lite. See Chapter 17 for more information about Google Play.

Home Screen Chores

The *Home screen* is where you begin your Android day. It's the location from which you start an app and perform other duties. Knowing how the Home screen works is an important part of understanding your Android.

To view the Home screen at any time, swipe the screen from bottom to top. If your device doesn't use gesture navigation, tap the Home navigation icon, found at the bottom of the touchscreen.

Exploring the Home screen

Typical Android Home screens are illustrated in Figure 3-3. Several fun and interesting doodads appear there. Find these items on your own device's Home screen, and recognize and use their common names:

Status bar: The top of the Home screen shows the status bar. It contains notification icons, status icons, and the current time. If the status bar disappears, a quick swipe from the top of the screen downward redisplays it.

Notifications: These icons come and go, depending on what happens in your digital life. For example, a new notification icon appears whenever you receive a new email message or a pending appointment notice. See the later section "Reviewing notifications."

Device Status: Icons on the right end of the status bar represent the Android's current condition, such as the type of network connection, signal strength, Wi-Fi status, and battery charge, as well as other items.

Launchers: Tap a launcher to run, or "launch," the associated app.

Widgets: Widgets display information or let you control the phone or tablet, manipulate a feature, access an app, or do something purely amusing.

Folders: Multiple launchers can be stored in a folder. Tap the folder to open it and view the launchers inside.

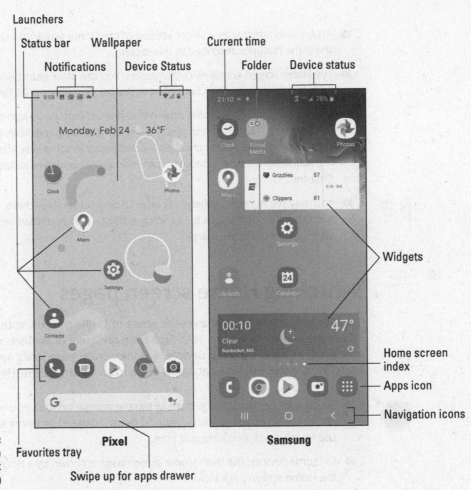

FIGURE 3-3:
The Home screen (phone left, tablet right)

Wallpaper: The Home screen background image is the wallpaper, which can be changed.

Favorites Tray: The bottom of the screen is reserved for popular launchers. The favorites tray shows the same launchers at the bottom of every Home screen page. One of these launchers is the Phone app, which plays a kind of vital role for an Android phone.

Apps icon: Tap this icon to view the apps drawer, a collection of all apps available on your Android. For devices without the Apps icon, swipe up the screen to access the apps drawer. See the later section "Finding an app in the apps drawer."

REMEMBER

Ensure that you recognize the names of the various parts of the Home screen. These terms are used throughout this book and in whatever other scant Android documentation exists.

>> An Android tablet uses a larger version of the Home screen, though it sports the same features described in this section.

>> The Home screen is entirely customizable. You can place launchers, create folders, add widgets, and change the wallpaper. See Chapter 21 for information.

>> Touching a part of the Home screen that doesn't feature an icon or a control does nothing. That is, unless you're using the live wallpaper feature. In this case, touching the screen changes the wallpaper in some way, depending on the wallpaper that's selected. You can read more about live wallpaper in Chapter 21.

>> You may see numbers affixed to certain Home screen launchers. These numbers are notifications for pending actions, such as unread email messages, as shown in the margin.

Switching Home screen pages

The Home screen is actually an entire street of Home screens, with only one Home screen page visible at a time. To switch from one page to another, swipe the Home screen left or right. On some devices, a Home screen page index appears above the favorites tray. You can tap a dot on the index to zoom to a specific Home screen page.

>> When you use the Home gesture or tap the navigation icon, you return to the last Home screen page you viewed. To return to the main Home screen panel, use Home navigation a second time.

>> On some devices, the main Home screen page is shown by a House icon on the Home screen page index.

>> The far left Home screen page might be occupied by a full-screen app, such as the Google app or Google Assistant. On Samsung devices, the Bixby assistant appears on the far left page.

>> The number of available Home screen pages depends on the device. See Chapter 21 for directions on adding or removing Home screen pages.

Reviewing notifications

Notifications appear as icons on the status bar atop the Home screen, as illustrated earlier, in Figure 3-3. To review them, or to pull down the notifications drawer, drag your finger from the top of the screen downward. The notifications drawer is illustrated in Figure 3-4.

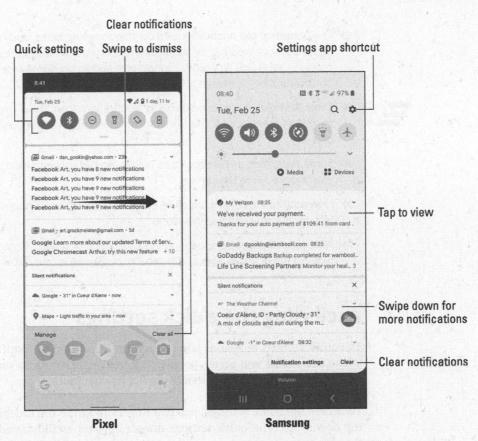

Clear notifications

Quick settings   Swipe to dismiss   Settings app shortcut

Pixel   **Samsung**

Tap to view

Swipe down for
more notifications

Clear notifications

FIGURE 3-4:
The notifications
drawer

Swipe the list of notifications up or down to peruse them. To deal with a specific notification, tap it. What happens next depends on the notification or the app that generated it. Typically, the app runs and shows more details.

To dismiss an individual notification, swipe it left or right. To dismiss all notifications, tap the Clear button or Clear All button dwelling at the end of the list.

To hide the notifications drawer, swipe the screen upward, use the Back gesture or navigation icon, or tap anywhere else on the Home screen.

>> Notifications can stack up if you don't deal with them!

>> When more notifications are present than can appear on the status bar, the More Notifications icon appears, similar to what's shown in the margin.

>> Dismissing a notification doesn't prevent it from appearing again in the future. For example, notifications to update your apps continue to appear, as do calendar reminders.

» The bottom of the notifications list contains ongoing items, such as details about traffic or weather, or status information such as when the device is charging, Wi-Fi and Bluetooth connections, and so on. Some of these notifications cannot be dismissed.

» Older Android devices used the Clear Notifications icon, shown in the margin, to dismiss notifications. This icon dwells at the bottom of the notifications drawer.

» Some apps, such as Facebook and Twitter, don't display notifications unless you're signed in to the service.

» New notifications are heralded by a notification ringtone. Chapter 21 provides information on changing the sound.

» Notifications may also appear on the Android's lock screen. Controlling which types of notifications appear (for security purposes) is covered in Chapter 22.

Accessing the quick settings

The quick settings appear as large buttons or icons atop the notifications drawer. These buttons let you access popular features or turn options on or off, such as Bluetooth, Wi-Fi, Airplane mode, Auto Rotate, and more.

To access the quick settings, use two fingers to swipe the touchscreen from the top downward. The quick settings drawer appears as illustrated in Figure 3-5, though many devices have variations on the quantity and presentation icons. Swipe the quick settings drawer left and right to see additional items.

To use a quick setting, tap its icon. Some icons represent on–off features, such as Flashlight mode and Airplane mode, shown in Figure 3-5. Other buttons feature menus that let you select options, such as Wi-Fi and Bluetooth. Tap the menu to peruse additional options.

To dismiss the quick settings drawer, swipe up the screen, use either the Back or Home navigation gesture, or tap either the Back or Home navigation icon.

TIP

» Tap the Settings icon on the quick settings drawer to quickly open the useful Settings app.

» The Edit (pencil) icon, shown in Figure 3-5, lets you add or remove items from the quick settings drawer.

» The features accessed from the quick settings drawer are covered in detail elsewhere in this book.

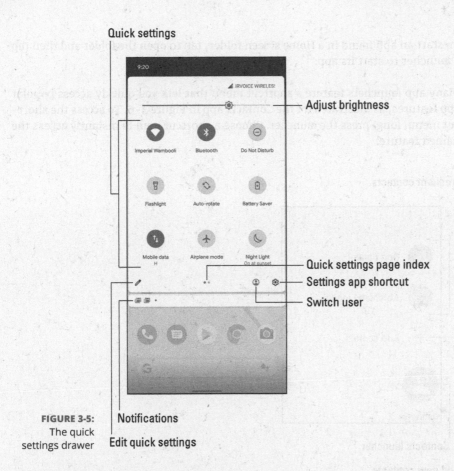

Quick settings

Adjust brightness

Quick settings page index

Settings app shortcut

Switch user

FIGURE 3-5: The quick settings drawer

Notifications

Edit quick settings

The World of Apps

The Android operating system can pack thrill-a-minute excitement, but it's probably not the only reason you purchased the device. No, Android's success lies with its apps. Knowing how to deal with apps is vital to becoming a successful, happy phone or tablet user.

Starting an app

To start an app, tap its launcher icon. The app starts.

Apps are started from the Home screen: Tap a launcher icon to start its associated app. You can also start an app from the apps drawer, as described in the later section "Finding an app in the apps drawer."

To start an app found in a Home screen folder, tap to open the folder and then tap a launcher to start its app.

Many app launchers feature a shortcut menu that lets you quickly access popular app features, as illustrated for the Contacts app in Figure 3-6. To access the shortcut menu, long-press the launcher. Choose a shortcut item to instantly access the named feature.

Frequent contacts

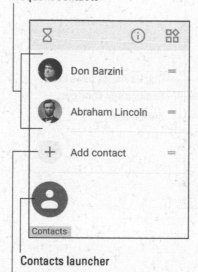

App launcher shortcut menu

Contacts launcher

Add new contacts

Quitting an app

Unlike on a computer, you need not quit apps on your Android. To leave an app, use the Home gesture or tap the Home icon to return to the Home screen. You can also use the Back gesture, or keep tapping the Back navigation icon, to back out of an app. Or you can access the Overview to switch to another running app, as described in the later section "Switching between running apps."

>> Some apps feature either a Quit or Exit command, but for the most part, you don't quit an app like you quit a program on a computer.

>> If necessary, the Android operating system shuts down apps you haven't used in a while. You can halt apps run amok, as described in Chapter 20.

WONDERFUL WIDGETS

Like apps, widgets appear on the Home screen. Some widgets are look-only, but for most of them you tap the widget to use it. What happens next depends on the widget and what it does.

For example, the YouTube widget lets you peruse videos. The Calendar widget shows a preview of your upcoming schedule. A Twitter widget displays recent tweets. Other widgets do interesting things, display useful information, or give you access to the device's settings or features.

New widgets are obtained from Google Play, just like apps. See Chapter 17 for information on Google Play; Chapter 21 covers working with widgets on the Home screen.

Finding an app in the apps drawer

The launchers you see on the Home screen don't represent all apps on the device. To view all installed apps, visit the apps drawer: Swipe the Home screen from the bottom upward. For devices that show the Apps icon on the favorites tray, tap that icon, similar to what's illustrated in the margin.

The apps drawer lists all installed apps on your phone or tablet. You may see a long list, or the apps may be presented on pages you swipe left and right. Atop the list you might find a row of apps you use most frequently.

To launch an app, tap its icon. The app starts, taking over the screen and doing whatever magical thing that app does.

>> See Chapter 17 for information on adding apps to the Home screen.

>> The apps drawer features a search bar, which helps you quickly locate a specific app: Tap the search box and type the app's name. This tool is handy for locating a specific app in a highly populated apps drawer.

>> Like the Home screen, the apps drawer may also feature folders. These folders contain multiple apps, which helps keep things organized. To access apps in a folder, tap the Folder icon.

>> The stock Android apps drawer displays apps alphabetically. Some devices let you change the order and edit the apps drawer. Look for an Edit (pencil) or Action Overflow icon on the apps drawer to edit the pages.

Switching between running apps

The apps you run on your phone or tablet don't quit when you dismiss them from the screen. For the most part, they stay running. To switch between running apps, or to access any app you've recently opened, use the Recent navigation gesture or tap the Recent navigation icon, shown in the margin. You see the Overview, similar to what's shown in Figure 3-7.

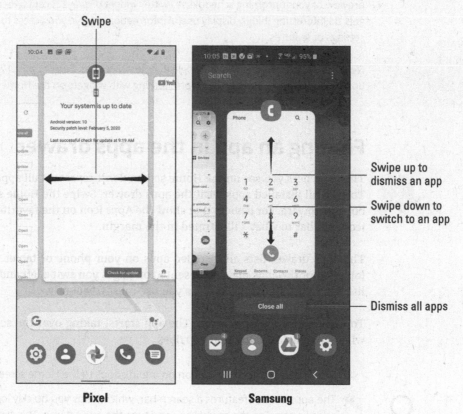

Swipe

Swipe up to dismiss an app

Swipe down to switch to an app

Dismiss all apps

Pixel   **Samsung**

FIGURE 3-7: The Overview shows recently opened apps

Swipe the list left and right to view all the apps, though the presentation differs on some devices. For example, you may see a grid of thumbnails on an Android tablet. Tap an app's card to switch to that app.

To switch to an app, tap its thumbnail or swipe the thumbnail downward. Swipe an app thumbnail upward to dismiss it. Some devices, such the Samsung phone shown on the right in Figure 3-7, feature the Close All button to dismiss all open apps.

To exit from the Overview, use the Back gesture or tap the Back navigation icon.

TIP

» To quickly switch back and forth between two apps, tap the Recent navigation icon twice. This trick works only when you use the navigation icons, not gesture navigation.

» Removing an app from the Overview is as close as you'll get to quitting an app.

» For older Androids that lack the Recent navigation icon, long-press the Home navigation icon to see the Overview.

REMEMBER

» The Android operating system may shut down apps that haven't received attention for a while. Don't be surprised when you can't find a recent app on the Overview. If so, just start it again as you normally would.

Common Android Icons

The Android operating system features a consistent armada of helpful icons. These icons serve common and consistent functions in apps as well as in the Android operating system. Table 3-2 lists the most common of these icons and their functions.

TABLE 3-2   **Common Icons**

Icon	Name	What It Does
⋮	Action Overflow	Displays a list of actions, similar to a menu.
✚	Add	Adds or creates an item. The plus symbol (+) may be used in combination with other symbols, depending on the app.
⌄	Chevron	Points in various directions to expand or collapse a card, menu, or list or another item. This icon might also appear as a solid triangle.
✕	Close	Dismisses a card, clears text from an input field, or removes an item from a list.
🗑	Delete	Removes one or more items from a list or deletes a message.
🎤	Dictation	Activates voice input.

(continued)

TABLE 3-2 *(continued)*

Icon	Name	What It Does
✓	Done	Dismisses the action bar or confirms and saves edits.
✏	Edit	Edits an item, adds text, or fills in fields.
★	Favorite	Flags a favorite item, such as a contact or a web page.
⟳	Refresh	Fetches new information or reloads.
🔍	Search	Searches the screen, the device, or the Internet for a tidbit of information.
⚙	Settings	Adjusts options for an app.
⋘	Share	Shares information via a specific app, such as Gmail or Facebook.
☰	Side Menu	Opens the navigation drawer, which is available in most Android apps. This icon is also called the *hamburger*.

Various sections throughout this book give examples of using these icons. Their images appear in the book's margins where relevant.

TIP

» Some Androids offer a Help app or provide help in the Settings app, which lists all available icons and their functions. This list may include notification and status icons as well.

» Other common symbols are used on icons in various apps. For example, the standard Play and Pause icons are used as well.

» The Share icon, shown in Table 3-2, has an evil twin, shown in the margin. Both icons represent the Share action.

» Some gizmos use text buttons instead of icons. For example, on Samsung devices, the MORE button appears in place of the Action Overflow icon. In fact, you often see text buttons such as SAVE or DONE instead of icons.

» Another variation on the Settings icon is shown in the margin. It serves the same purpose as the Gear icon (refer to Table 3-2), though this older icon is being phased out.

Chapter **4**

Text to Type, Text to Edit

I seriously doubt that anyone would consider using an Android phone to write the Great American Novel. The gizmo lacks a real keyboard! Even so, typing is something you do on a phone or tablet, thanks to something called the onscreen keyboard. You can also dictate to generate text. No matter how it gets in there, your Android is ready to accept, process, and even edit text.

Onscreen Keyboard Mania

The onscreen keyboard reveals itself on the bottom half of the touchscreen whenever text input is required. The stock Android keyboard is called the *Gboard* ("jee-bord"), for Google Keyboard. The phone version of the Gboard is shown in Figure 4-1. The tablet version is wider and has additional keys.

Samsung gizmos use the Samsung Keyboard, illustrated in Figure 4-2. It works like the Gboard, but offers its own Samsung galactic features — primarily, a useful row of number keys, as shown in the figure.

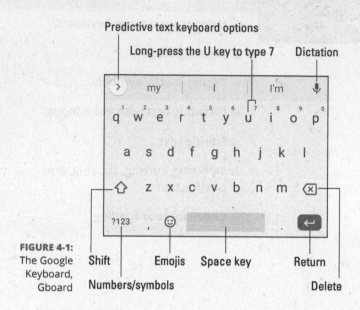

Predictive text keyboard options

Long-press the U key to type 7   Dictation

FIGURE 4-1:
The Google
Keyboard,
Gboard

Shift   Emojis   Space key   Return

Numbers/symbols   Delete

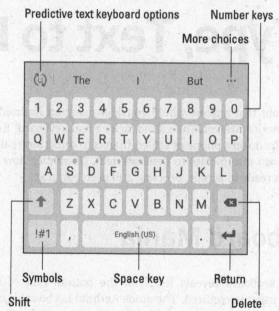

Predictive text keyboard options   Number keys

More choices

FIGURE 4-2:
The Samsung
Keyboard

Symbols   Space key   Return

Shift   Delete

No matter how the keyboard looks, all onscreen keyboards are based on the traditional QWERTY layout: You see keys from A through Z, albeit not in that order. You also see the Shift key for changing the letter case, and the Delete key, which backspaces and erases.

The Return key changes its look and function depending on what you're typing. Your keyboard may show these variations graphically or by labeling the key with text. The stock Android symbols are illustrated in Figure 4-3. Here's what each one does:

Return: Just like the Return or Enter key on a computer keyboard, this key ends a paragraph of text. It's used mostly when filling in long stretches of text or when multiline input is needed.

Search: This key appears when you're searching for something. Tap the key to start the search.

Go: This key directs the app to proceed with a search, accept input, or perform another action.

Next: This key appears when you type information into multiple fields. Tap this key to switch from one field to the next, such as when typing a username and password.

Done: This key appears when you've finished typing text in the final field and you're ready to submit input.

FIGURE 4-3: Return-key variations

Return   Search   Go   Next   Done

The large key at the bottom-center of the onscreen keyboard is the Space key. It's flanked left and right by other keys that may change, depending on the context of what you're typing. For example, a / (slash) or @ key may appear in order to assist in typing a web page or email address. These keys may change, but the basic alphabetic keys remain the same.

>> To display the onscreen keyboard, tap any text field or spot on the screen where typing is permitted.

>> To dismiss the onscreen keyboard, tap the Back navigation icon. It may appear as shown in the margin.

>> Some onscreen keyboard variations feature a multifunction key that performs many tasks, such as summoning the emojis keyboard, dictation, and keyboard settings. Long-press the multifunction key to view its options.

>> For quickly typing in a web page address, the onscreen keyboard may display the .COM key. Tap this key to quickly type those letters. Long-press this key to view other top-level domains, such as .ORG and .NET.

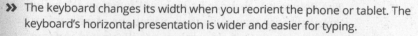

>> The keyboard changes its width when you reorient the phone or tablet. The keyboard's horizontal presentation is wider and easier for typing.

>> If you pine for a real keyboard, one that exists in the fourth dimension, consider getting a Bluetooth keyboard. Such a wireless keyboard also doubles as a docking stand or portfolio cover for an Android tablet. You can read more about Bluetooth in Chapter 18.

TIP

Everybody Was Touchscreen Typing

Typing is a necessary skill, something they now call "keyboarding" in school. That necessity extends to your Android mobile device, though typing on a touchscreen keyboard isn't anyone's favorite activity. That's because, even if you're the world's fastest touch-typist, you can only hunt-and-peck on your phone or tablet. It's a limitation everyone must face. Yes, it's the old hunt-and-peck all over again.

Typing one character at a time

The onscreen keyboard is cinchy to figure out: Tap a letter key to produce the character. As you type, the key you touch is highlighted. The Android may provide a wee bit of feedback in the form of a faint click sound or vibration.

>> A blinking cursor on the touchscreen shows where new text appears, which is how typing text works on a computer.

>> When you make a mistake, tap the Delete key to back up and erase.

>> When you type a password, the character you type appears briefly, but for security reasons, it's then replaced by a black dot.

>> To type in all caps, tap the Shift key twice. The Shift key may appear highlighted, and the Shift symbol may change color, which indicates that Shift Lock is on. Tap the Shift key again to deactivate Shift Lock.

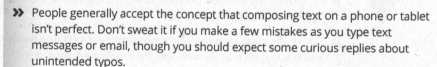

>> People generally accept the concept that composing text on a phone or tablet isn't perfect. Don't sweat it if you make a few mistakes as you type text messages or email, though you should expect some curious replies about unintended typos.

REMEMBER

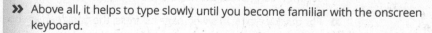

>> Above all, it helps to type slowly until you become familiar with the onscreen keyboard.

TIP

Accessing keyboard variations

You're not limited to typing only the characters shown on the alphabetic keyboard. On the Gboard, tap the ?123 key to access the symbols keyboard. Also available are the emojis and keypad keyboards, as illustrated in Figure 4-4. You can cycle between them.

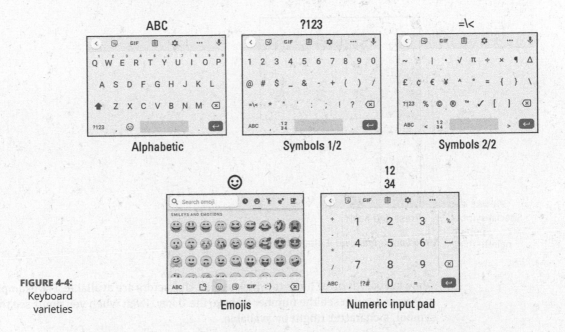

On the symbols keyboard, tap the =\< key to access the second symbols keyboard. The !?# key, found on the numeric input pad keyboard, also accesses the first symbols keyboard (refer to Figure 4-4).

Tap the 1234 key to access the numeric input pad. A similar keyboard is available in the Phone app or Dialer app, though it's called the *dialpad.*

Tap the ☺ key to view the emojis keyboard. This keyboard features several tabs (along the bottom) as well as a scrolling list of categories. Also, use the search bar to find specific emojis by their meaning, such as *celebration* or *angry cat.*

Tap the ABC key to return to the alphabetic keyboard.

On the Samsung Keyboard, tap the !#1 key to access the symbols keyboards. Use the 1/2 and 2/2 keys to page between the two keyboard sets.

Typing accented characters

To access special characters, such as foreign or accented characters, without having to switch keyboard layouts, long-press a key, such as the A key, shown in Figure 4-5. After long-pressing, drag your finger to select the special character. Lift your finger to select the specific accented or special character.

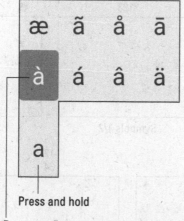

FIGURE 4-5:
Special-symbol
pop-up
palette-thing

Press and hold

Drag your finger over a character to select it

Some keyboards offer hints to which special characters are available. For example, in Figure 4-1 you see the number 7 above the U key. Even when you don't see that symbol, a character might be available.

>> Most keys on the onscreen keyboard feature special characters, though they're not always obvious.

>> If you choose the wrong character, tap the Delete key on the onscreen keyboard to erase the mistyped symbol.

Using predictive text to type quickly

As you type, you see a selection of word suggestions just above the keyboard (refer to Figure 4-1). If not, tap the icon that swaps between keyboard options and the predictive text bar.

To use the onscreen keyboard's predictive text feature, choose a word from the list. Doing so greatly accelerates your typing; the word you tap is inserted into the text.

If the desired word doesn't appear, continue typing: The predictive text feature makes suggestions based on what you've typed so far.

TIP

» If predictive text replaces your correctly typed word with something else, tap the Delete key. The replaced word is restored.

» On some versions of the onscreen keyboard, you can long-press a word to see similar words.

» The predictive text feature is unavailable for typing passwords and filling in forms.

» If the predictive text feature is inactive, see Chapter 21 for information on activating it.

Typing without lifting your finger

If you're really after typing speed, consider using *glide typing*, which allows you to swipe your finger over the onscreen keyboard to type words. It's like mad scribbling but with a positive result.

To use glide typing, drag a finger over letters on the onscreen keyboard. Figure 4-6 illustrates how the word *taco* is typed in this manner.

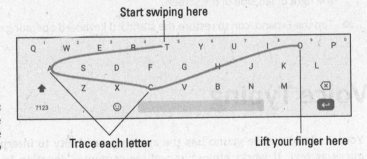

FIGURE 4-6:
Using gesture typing to type *taco*

Start swiping here

Trace each letter

Lift your finger here

Gesture typing is disabled when typing a password or an email address or for other specific typing duties. When it doesn't work, tap one letter at a time.

» The glide typing feature was once called *gesture* typing.

» Refer to Chapter 21 for glide typing settings.

Using One-Handed mode

Despite having both arms free, many Android users desire to type by using the same hand that holds their phone. To accommodate such busy people, activate One-Handed mode, which adjusts the keyboard a smidge to the left or right to assist with one-handed, or "thumb," typing. Follow these steps to activate this feature:

1. Open the Settings app.

2. In the Search box, type one handed mode or as much of that text until you see the One-Handed Mode item.

3. Choose One-Handed Mode from the search results list.

4. On the Preferences screen, Layout area, choose One-Handed Mode.

5. Select Right-Handed Mode to slide the onscreen keyboard a notch to the right, or choose Left-Handed Mode to slide the onscreen keyboard a notch to the left.

For Samsung phones with the One-Handed Mode feature, tap the Settings icon while the onscreen keyboard is visible, choose Style and Layout, Modes, and then One-Handed Keyboard.

>> While One-Handed mode is active, tap the chevron to slide the keyboard to the right or left side of the screen.

>> Tap the Expand icon to restore the standard keyboard operating mode.

Google Voice Typing

Your Android mobile gizmo has the amazing capability to interpret your utterances as text. It works almost as well as computer dictation in science fiction movies, though I can't seem to find the command to locate intelligent life.

>> The dictation feature is available whenever you see the Dictation (microphone) icon. This icon appears on the keyboard as well as in other locations, such as search boxes.

>> If you don't see the Dictation icon, tap the Predictive Text/Keyboard Options icon (refer to Figures 4-1 and 4-2). On older Samsung keyboards, the Microphone icon appears on a multifunction key. Long-press this key to locate the Dictation icon.

Dictating text

Talking to your phone or tablet works quite well, providing that you tap the Dictation icon and you don't mumble.

After you tap the Dictation icon on the Gboard, text appears, saying that the device is "listening," as shown in Figure 4-7, on the left. Samsung gizmos may display a card that covers the onscreen keyboard, as shown on the right in Figure 4-7.

Pixel

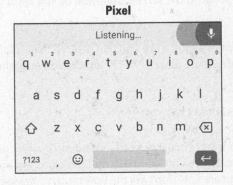

Samsung

Dismiss dictation

FIGURE 4-7:
Google Voice
Typing

To pause, tap the Dictation icon again or tap the text *Tap to Pause*.

On a Samsung phone or tablet, tap the Keyboard icon to dismiss dictation. The Close (X) icon may be used instead on older Samsung devices.

TIP

>> The first time you try voice input, you might see a description displayed. Tap the OK or GOT IT button to continue.

>> Tap misinterpreted words to view a pop-up list of alternatives. Choose an alternative to replace the text.

>> Speak the punctuation in your text. For example, you would say, "I'm sorry comma and it won't happen again" to produce the text *I'm sorry, and it won't happen again* or something close to that.

>> Common punctuation you can dictate includes the *comma, period, exclamation point, question mark, colon,* and *new line.*

>> If keys are visible on the onscreen keyboard, you can type them as you dictate. This feature makes it easier to add punctuation, which is a weak spot in the Android dictation feature.

>> You cannot dictate capital letters. If you're a stickler for such things, you must go back and edit the text.

>> Dictation may not work without an Internet connection.

Uttering s**** words

WARNING

Dictation input has a voice censor. It replaces those naughty words you might utter; the first letter appears on the screen, followed by the appropriate number of asterisks.

For example, if *spatula* were a blue word and you uttered "spatula" when dictating text, the dictation feature would place s****** on the screen rather than the word *spatula*.

Yeah, I know: silly. Or, should I say, "s****"?

>> Your Android knows a lot of naughty words, including George Carlin's infamous "Seven Words You Can Never Say on Television," but apparently the terms *crap* and *damn* are fine. Don't ask me how much time I spent researching this topic.

>> See Chapter 25 if you'd like to disable the dictation censor.

Text Editing

You'll probably do more text editing on your Android than you anticipated. That editing includes the basic stuff, such as spiffing up typos and adding a period here or there as well as complex editing involving cut, copy, and paste. The concepts are the same as you find on a computer, but the process can be daunting without a physical keyboard and a mouse.

Moving the cursor

The first part of editing text is moving the cursor to the right spot. The *cursor* is that blinking, vertical line that marks the location where new text appears, edited text changes, or cut/copied text is pasted.

To set the cursor's location, tap the text. To help your accuracy, a tab appears below the cursor, as shown in the margin. Drag that tab to precisely locate the cursor.

After you move the cursor, you can continue to type, tap the Delete key to back up and erase, or paste text copied from elsewhere.

» You may see the Paste button appear above the cursor tab. Use this button to paste in text, as described in the later section "Cutting, copying, and pasting text."

» Samsung keyboards may feature cursor movement keys. Use these keys to move the cursor in addition to the stab-your-finger-on-the-screen method.

Selecting text

Selecting text on an Android phone or tablet works just like selecting text in a word processor: You mark the start and end of a block. That chunk of text appears highlighted on the screen. How you get there, however, can be a mystery — until now!

To select text, long-press a word. Upon success, you see a chunk of selected text, as shown in Figure 4-8.

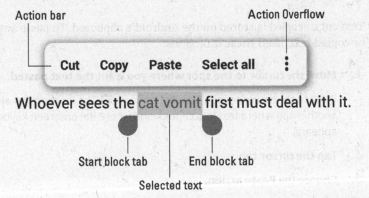

Action bar

Action Overflow

Cut   Copy   Paste   Select all   ⋮

Whoever sees the cat vomit first must deal with it.

Start block tab

End block tab

Selected text

FIGURE 4-8:
Text is selected

Drag the start and end markers around the touchscreen to define the block of selected text. Use the action bar to choose what to do with the text, as shown in Figure 4-8. Tap the Action Overflow to view additional commands.

What can you do with selected text? Just like on a computer, tap the Delete key to remove the block. Type new text to replace. You can also copy, cut, and paste, as covered in the following section.

To cancel text selection, tap elsewhere in the text.

TIP

>> On some devices, the action bar may appear atop the touchscreen. Icons might be used instead of the text buttons illustrated in Figure 4-8.

>> Selecting text on a web page works the same as selecting text in any other app. The difference is that text can only be copied from the web page, not cut or deleted.

>> Seeing the onscreen keyboard is a good indication that you can edit and select text.

>> The Select All action marks all text as a single block, though to see this command, you must select at least some text.

>> With text selected, tap the Shift key on the keyboard to change the text case.

Cutting, copying, and pasting text

Selected text is primed for cutting or copying, which works just like it does in your favorite word processor. After you select the text, choose the proper action: Copy to copy text or Cut to cut the text.

Text cut or copied is stored on the Android's clipboard. To paste any previously cut or copied text, heed these directions:

1. Move the cursor to the spot where you want the text pasted.

Refer to the earlier section "Moving the cursor." The location can also be in another app where text is accepted (and where the onscreen keyboard appears).

2. Tap the cursor tab.

3. Choose the Paste action.

The text appears at the cursor's location or, if any text is selected, the pasted text replaces it.

Some Androids feature a Clipboard app, which lets you peruse, review, and select previously cut or copied text or images. If the action bar shows a Clipboard action, choose it to access the Clipboard app.

Dealing with speling errrs

As you plunk away on the onscreen keyboard, misspelled words are highlighted. A vicious red underline appears beneath the suspect spelling, drawing attention to the problem and reminding you of how poorly you did in elementary school English.

» Words may be autocorrected as you type them. To undo an autocorrection, tap the word again. Choose a replacement word from the predictive text list, or tap the original word to keep it.

» Yes! Your Android has a personal dictionary. See Chapter 25 for details.

2

Stay Connected

IN THIS CHAPTER

» **Calling someone**

» **Phoning in an emergency**

» **Getting a call**

» **Dismissing calls**

» **Using text message rejection**

» **Handling multiple calls**

» **Setting up a conference call**

Chapter **5**

Telephone Stuff

I n 1876, Alexander Graham Bell beat a host of competitors to the patent office and has since been credited with the invention of the telephone. Other great dates in phone history are 1878, when the busy signal was invented; 1896, when the Clayton household added a second line for their teenage daughter; and 1902, when the extension cord was patented to allow for simultaneous talking and pacing.

In the modern world, a phone call is only a minor feature of the device known as an Android phone. Yet the namesake feature offers a host of handy calling tools, all fully patented or in current legal battles, that telephone users from the past century could only dream of.

Reach Out and Touch Someone

Making a phone call is the second most popular way you can use your Android phone to connect with another human. Number one is texting. In fact, phone calls are kind of quaint, but still necessary — sort of like the turn signal on a BMW.

Placing a phone call

To place a call on your phone, heed these steps:

1. **Open the Phone app.**

The Phone app's launcher is found on the Home screen, on the favorites tray. The app's icon looks similar to the one shown in the margin.

2. **If necessary, display the dialpad.**

If you don't see the dialpad, illustrated in Figure 5-1, tap the Dialpad icon, as shown in the margin. Also look for the Keypad tab, popular on Samsung phones.

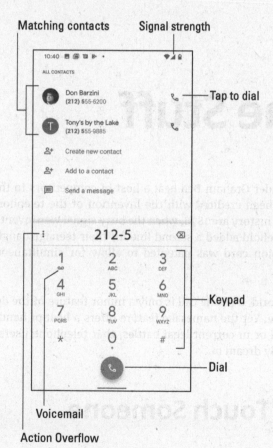

FIGURE 5-1:
The Phone app's
dialpad

3. **Type a phone number.**

You may hear the traditional touch-tone sounds as you punch in the number.

If you make a mistake, tap the Delete icon, labeled in Figure 5-1, to back up and erase.

TIP

The phone displays matching contacts as you type. Choose a contact to instantly input that person's number.

4. **Tap the Dial icon to place the call.**

   While a call is active, the screen changes to show contact information, or a contact image when one is available, similar to Figure 5-2.

Active call notification

Contact image

Don Barzini

00:16 — Call duration

Mute   Keypad   Speaker

Speakerphone

Show dialpad

Add call   Video call   Hold

Hang Up/End Call

FIGURE 5-2:
A successful call

Mute

5. **Place the phone to your ear and wait.**

6. **When the person answers the phone, talk.**

   What you say is up to you, though it's good not to just blurt out unexpected news, like "I'm eloping with your daughter" or "Your lawn is on fire."

   Use the phone's volume key to adjust the volume during the call.

7. **Tap the End Call icon to end the call.**

   The phone disconnects. You hear a soft beep, which is the phone's signal that the call has ended.

You can do other things while you're making a call: Tap the Home navigation icon to run an app, read old email, check an appointment, or do whatever. Activities such as these don't disconnect you, though not all phone features are available during the call.

To return to a call after doing something else, choose the Call in Progress notification icon, similar to the one shown in the margin.

>> For hands-free operation, use earbuds with a microphone doodle, as discussed in Chapter 1. You can also set the phone into Speaker mode: Tap the Speaker icon, shown in Figure 5-2. Then you can hold the phone flat, like it's a pizza.

>> Don't hold the phone right at your ear while the speaker is active.

>> You can connect or remove the earphones at any time during a call.

>> Use a Bluetooth headset to go hands-free. If the Bluetooth icon doesn't appear on the screen, tap the Speaker icon (refer to Figure 5-2) to ensure that the Bluetooth headset is active. See Chapter 18 for information on Bluetooth.

>> Many hearing aids work with Bluetooth and can be paired with your phone, just like a Bluetooth headset.

>> If you're going hands-free, press the phone's Power/Lock key during the call to lock the phone. Locking the phone doesn't disconnect the call, but it does prevent you from accidentally hanging up or muting the call.

>> To mute a call, tap the Mute icon, shown earlier, in Figure 5-2. The Mute status icon, similar to the one shown in the margin, appears atop the touchscreen.

>> You can't accidentally mute or end a call when the phone is placed against your face; the device's proximity sensor prevents that from happening.

>> If you're wading through one of those nasty voicemail systems, tap the Dialpad icon, labeled in Figure 5-2, so that you can "Press 1 for English" when necessary.

>> You hear an audio alert whenever the call is dropped or the other party hangs up. The disconnection can be confirmed by looking at the phone, which shows that the call has ended.

>> You cannot place a phone call when the phone has no service; check the signal strength (refer to Figure 5-1). You cannot place or receive a call when a signal isn't present. Further, the bars may show the Roaming icon when your phone is out of your cellular provider's service area. See Chapter 23 for roaming information.

>> Also see Chapter 23 for details on international calling.

>> Some phones use Wi-Fi instead of the cellular network to place a call. When Wi-Fi is used, you may see the Wi-Fi icon appear in the Phone app. The call works no differently from a cellular call, and if the Wi-Fi signal is dropped, the cellular network picks it up without so much as a pause in communications.

Making an emergency call

If you are unable to use your Android phone but must make an emergency call, tap the EMERGENCY CALL button on the lock screen. Use the dialpad to place your emergency call.

The Emergency Call screen can display useful information — for example, if someone else were to use your phone to place a call. You can add emergency numbers or even medical details, depending on the device.

>> The stock Android emergency-call info app is titled Safety. Open this app and fill in the details for information you want made available in an emergency: Add contact information, fill in medical details like allergies and known conditions, and so on.

>> Samsung devices use the Emergency Contacts group in the Contacts app for the Emergency Call screen. Medical information is pulled in from your details in the Contacts app.

Dialing a contact

To access your phone's address book, start the Phone app and tap the Contacts tab. Browse the list for someone to call; tap their entry and then tap their phone number or their Phone icon to place the call.

>> You can also use the phone's address book app directly to find and phone a contact. See Chapter 7.

>> A special contact category in the phone's address book is Favorites. To quickly access your favorites, tap the Favorites tab in the Phone app. This tab may feature the Favorites (star) icon, shown in the margin.

Using speed dial

To speed-dial a number, long-press one of the digits on the Phone app's dialpad. For example, the speed dial for digit 1 is always set to the carrier's voicemail service, illustrated in Figure 5-1. Long-press that digit to access voicemail, which is covered in Chapter 6.

Some Android phones allow other digits to be assigned speed dial numbers. To confirm that yours does, open the Phone app and with the dialpad visible, look for the Action Overflow icon. Tap it and look for the Speed Dial action. Use the onscreen controls to add contacts or phone numbers to available digits on the dialpad.

Adding pauses when dialing a number

When you tap the Phone icon to dial a number, the number is instantly spewed into the phone system, like water out of a hose. If you need to pause the number as it's dialed, such as to wait for a prompt you know is coming, you need to insert secret pause characters. Two are available:

>> The comma (,) adds a 2-second pause.

>> The semicolon (;) adds a wait prompt.

To insert the pause or wait characters into a phone number, obey these directions:

1. **Type the number to dial.**

2. **At the point that the pause or wait character is needed, tap the Action Overflow icon.**

   The Action Overflow icon is illustrated in Figure 5-1.

3. **Choose the action Add 2-Sec Pause or Add Wait.**

4. **Continue composing the rest of the phone number.**

When the number is dialed and the comma (,) is encountered, the phone pauses two seconds and then dials the rest of the number.

When the semicolon (;) is encountered, the phone prompts you to continue. Tap the YES or OK button to continue dialing the rest of the number.

TIP

>> The comma (,) and semicolon (;) can also be inserted into the phone numbers you assign to contacts in the phone's address book. See Chapter 7.

>> Alas, you cannot program an interactive phone number, such as one that pauses and lets you provide input and then continues to dial. You must perform such a task manually on an Android phone.

It's for You!

Who doesn't enjoy getting a phone call? It's an event! Never mind that it's a tele-marketer or some robot. The point is that someone cares enough to call. Truly, your Android phone's ringing can be good news, bad news, or mediocre news, but it always provides a little drama to spice up an otherwise mundane day.

Receiving a call

Several things can happen when you receive a phone call on your Android phone:

>> The phone sounds a ringtone, signaling an incoming call.

>> The phone vibrates.

>> The touchscreen reveals information about the call, as shown in Figure 5-3.

>> The car in front of you explodes in a loud fireball as your passenger screams something inappropriately funny.

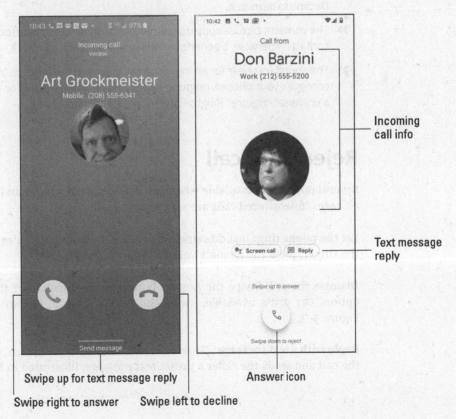

FIGURE 5-3:
You have an
incoming call

Swipe up for text message reply

Swipe right to answer   Swipe left to decline

Incoming
call info

Text message
reply

Answer icon

That last item happens only in Bruce Willis movies. The other three possibilities, or a combination thereof, are signals that you have an incoming call.

To answer the call, swipe the Answer icon as indicated on the touchscreen. If you're using a Bluetooth headset, tap the button or otherwise work the gizmo to use that device for listening and speaking.

When you're done jabbering, tap the End Call icon to hang up: Move the phone away from your face to activate the touchscreen, and then tap the icon. If the other party hangs up first, the call ends automatically.

>> You don't have to work a screen lock to answer a call. The phone remains locked, however, so if you want to do other things while you're on the call, you must work the screen lock.

>> Other options may appear on the Incoming Calls screen, including sending the call immediately to voicemail, responding with a text message, and others. Directions on the touchscreen explain your choices.

>> When the phone is unlocked, incoming calls are heralded by a card that appears atop the screen. Tap the Answer button to receive the call; tap Decline to dismiss it.

>> The contact's picture appears only when you've assigned a picture to the contact. Otherwise, a generic contact image appears.

>> The sound you hear for an incoming call is termed the *ringtone.* You can configure your phone's ringtone depending on who is calling, or you can set a universal ringtone. Ringtones are covered in Chapter 21.

Rejecting a call

Several options are available when you don't want to answer an incoming call. In all cases, unanswered calls are sent to voicemail:

Let the phone ring: Just do something else or pretend that you're dead. To silence the ringer, press the phone's volume key.

Dismiss the call: Swipe the Answer button in the direction of the call-rejection option. Or, if it's available, swipe the Decline button, shown on the right in Figure 5-3.

Reply with a text message: Choose the text message reply option, which dismisses the call and sends the caller a preset text message, illustrated in Figure 5-3.

Perhaps the most useful option is to use the text message reply. Choose a preset reply to communicate to the caller that you're on the other line or in a meeting or will call them back in a jiffy. Alas, not every phone offers the text message reply.

» See Chapter 6 for information on voicemail. Chapter 6 also covers the call log, which shows a list of recent calls incoming, missed, or rejected.

» The method for adding, removing, or editing the call rejection messages differs from phone to phone. Generally, tap the Action Overflow icon while using the Phone app. Choose Settings. Look for a Quick Responses or Quick Decline Messages action.

» See Chapter 8 for more information on text messaging.

Multi-Call Mania

Because you're a human being, your brain limits your ability to hold more than one conversation at a time. Your phone's brain, however, lacks such a limitation. It's entirely possible for an Android phone to handle more than one call at a time.

Putting someone on hold

It's easy to place a call on hold — as long as your cellular provider hasn't disabled that feature. Tap the Hold icon, shown in the margin.

To take the call out of hold, tap the Hold icon again. The icon may change its look — for example, from the Pause symbol to the Play symbol.

TIP

If the Phone app lacks the Hold icon, tap the Mute icon. That way, you can sneeze, scream at the wall, or flush the toilet and the other person will never know.

Receiving a new call when you're on the phone

You're on the phone, chatting it up. Suddenly, someone else calls you. What happens next?

Your phone alerts you to the new call, perhaps by vibrating or making a sound. Look at the touchscreen to see who's calling and determine what to do next. You have three options:

>> **Answer the call.** Slide the Answer icon just as you would answer any incoming call. The current call is placed on hold.

>> **Send the call directly to voicemail.** Dismiss the call as you would any incoming phone call.

>> **Do nothing.** The call eventually goes into voicemail.

When you choose to answer the second call, additional options become available to manage both calls. Use special icons on the Call in Progress screen to perform special, multi-call tricks:

Swap/Switch Calls: To switch between callers, tap the Swap or Switch Calls icon on the touchscreen. You might instead see a card at the bottom of the screen; tap the card to switch to that caller. The current person is placed on hold when you switch calls.

Merge Calls: To combine all calls so that everyone is talking (three people total), tap the Merge Calls icon. This icon may not be available if the merge feature is suppressed by your cellular provider.

End Call: To end a call, tap the End Call icon, just as you normally do. You're switched back to the other caller.

To end the final call, tap the End Call or Hang Up icon, just as you normally would.

>> The number of different calls your phone can handle depends on your carrier. For most subscribers in the United States, your phone can handle only two calls at a time. In that case, another person who calls either hears a busy signal or is sent directly to voicemail.

>> When you end a second call on the Verizon network, both calls may appear to have been disconnected. That's not the case: In a few moments, the call you didn't disconnect "rings" as though the person is calling you back. No one is calling you back, though: You're returning to that ongoing conversation.

Making a conference call

You can call two different people by using your Android phone's merge calls feature. To start, connect with the first person and then add a second call. Soon, everyone is talking. Here are the details:

1. **Phone the first person.**

2. **After the call connects and you complete a few pleasantries, tap the Add Call icon.**

   The Add Call icon may appear as shown in the margin. If not, look for a generic Add (+) icon. After you tap that icon, the first person is placed on hold.

3. **Dial the second person.**

   You can use the dialpad or choose the second person from the phone's address book or the call history.

   Say your pleasantries and inform the party that the call is about to be merged.

4. **Tap the Merge or Merge Calls icon.**

   The two calls are now joined: Everyone you've dialed can talk to and hear everyone else.

5. **Tap the End Call icon to end the conference call.**

   All calls are disconnected.

REMEMBER

When several people are in a room and want to participate in a call, you can always put the phone in Speaker mode: Tap the Speaker icon on the Ongoing Call screen.

Your Android phone may feature the Manage icon while you're on a conference call. Tap this icon to list the various calls, to mute one, or to select a call to disconnect.

Chapter 6

Forward Calls, Missed Calls, and Voicemail

G one are the days when you could say you were "out" and missed a call. That's because your Android phone goes with you everywhere. The excuses for not taking a call are weak and limited. You can blame call forwarding. You can confirm a missed call on the call log. And you can always resort to voice-mail, which is becoming more accepted — especially when the message is sincere.

Forward Calls Elsewhere

Call forwarding is traditionally a trick you used from your old landline phone to a cell phone. It's odd to think of it used another way, but the tool still exists. In fact, voicemail itself is a form of call forwarding in action.

Forwarding phone calls

The Android operating system offers call forwarding options, though your cellular provider might control that feature instead. To determine which is which, follow these steps to configure call forwarding:

1. **Open the Phone app.**

2. **Tap the Action Overflow icon.**

3. **Choose Settings or Call Settings.**

4. **Choose Calls and then Call Forwarding, or just Call Forwarding if it's the only option available.**

   If you don't see any of these similar options, your carrier most likely doesn't allow the phone to manipulate call forwarding settings directly.

5. **Select a call forwarding option.**

   Sometimes only one option is available: a phone number to use for forwarding all incoming calls. You might instead see separate options, such as these:

   - *Always Forward:* All incoming calls are sent to the number you specify; your phone doesn't even ring. This option overrides all other forwarding options.

   - *When Busy:* Calls are forwarded when you're on the phone and choose not to answer. This option normally sends a missed call to voicemail.

   - *When Unanswered:* Missed calls are forwarded. Normally, the call is forwarded to voicemail.

   - *When Unreachable:* Calls are forwarded when the phone is turned off, out of range, or in Airplane mode. As with the two previous settings, this option normally forwards calls to voicemail.

6. **Set the forwarding number or edit an existing number.**

   For example, you can type your home landline number for the Forward When Unreached option so that your cell calls are redirected to your home number when you're out of range.

   To disable the option, tap the Turn Off button.

7. **Tap the Update button to confirm the new forwarding number.**

If your phone lacks call forwarding settings, you must rely upon the other methods to set up and forward your calls. For example, Verizon in the United States uses the call forwarding options described in Table 6-1.

TABLE 6-1 **Verizon Call Forwarding Commands**

To Do This	Input First Number	Input Second Number
Forward unanswered incoming calls	*71	Forwarding number
Forward all incoming calls	*72	Forwarding number
Cancel call forwarding	*73	None

So, to forward all calls to (714) 555-4565, open the Phone app and dial the number ***727145554565**. You hear only a brief tone after dialing, and then the call ends. After that, any call coming into your phone rings at the other number.

REMEMBER

You must disable call forwarding to return to normal cell phone operations: Dial ***73**.

Call forwarding may affect your phone's voicemail service. See the later section "Voicemail" for details.

Blocking calls

To stifle those calls that bug you repeatedly, block the phone number before it rings. Obey these steps in the Phone app:

1. **Tap the Action Overflow icon.**
2. **Choose Settings.**
3. **Choose Blocked Numbers or a similar action.**
4. **Tap the ADD A NUMBER button or just type a number to block.**
5. **Tap the Block button or Add icon to confirm.**

   Repeat Steps 4 and 5 to add more numbers.

An easier way to block calls is to use the call log, or history list, which is covered in the next section. From the list, long-press an entry and choose the Block action.

To remove a number from the Blocked Numbers list, follow Steps 1 through 4 to view blocked numbers. Tap the X or minus (–) icon next to a number, and then tap the Unblock button to confirm.

Who Called Who When?

All phone calls made on your Android phone are noted: to whom, from whom, date, time, duration, and whether the call was incoming, outgoing, missed, or dismissed. I call this feature the *call log*.

In the Phone app, tap the Recents or Call History tab. You see a list of recent calls received, missed, or dismissed, similar to what's shown in Figure 6-1.

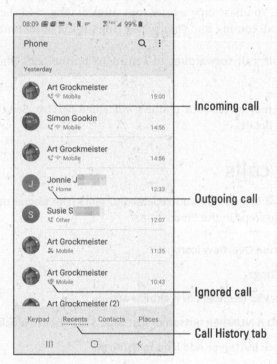

FIGURE 6-1:
The call log

Swipe through the list to examine recent calls. The list is sorted so that the most recent calls appear at the top. Information is associated with each call, such as the date and time, the call duration, and whether the call was incoming, outgoing, missed, or ignored.

To see more details about the call, tap an item in the list. You see the call history specific to that number or contact, options to block the call, or an action to display the contact's information.

>> When you miss a call, the Missed Call notification icon appears atop the touchscreen. This icon, similar to the one in the margin, specifically applies to a call you didn't pick up; it doesn't appear for calls you dismiss or calls missed because the phone was turned off or in Airplane mode.

>> Some Android phones show more details on the Missed Call notification, including icons that let you return the call, text, and so on.

TIP

>> On Samsung phones, you swipe right an item in the call log to return the call; swipe the item to the left to send a text message.

Voicemail

"At the sound of the tone . . ." You know the drill. The once humble tape recorder that connected to a landline, or "answering machine," gained the fancy term *voicemail* back in the 1990s. The service is a collection bin at the bottom of the rejection chute for your phone's incoming messages. Missed calls, dismissed calls, calls received while the phone is offline — they all go to voicemail for later retrieval.

Setting up carrier voicemail

The most basic and least sophisticated form of voicemail is the free voicemail service provided by your cell phone company. This standard feature has few frills and nothing that stands out differently for your nifty Android phone.

One of the first duties you must do on your phone is set up that boring voicemail service. Obey these steps:

1. **Open the Phone app.**

2. **Display the dialpad.**

3. **Long-press the 1 key.**

The 1 key is preset to speed-dial your carrier's voicemail service. It's adorned with the standard Voicemail icon, shown in the margin.

4. **Pull the phone away from your head to activate the speaker and dialpad.**

Tap the Speaker and Dialpad icons so that you can listen to the robot and type options as you configure the carrier's voicemail service.

5. **Heed the directions as dictated.**

Obey the robot to set up the voicemail service.

REMEMBER

Your callers are unable to leave messages until you configure carrier voicemail. Even when you plan on using another voicemail service, such as Google Voice, I recommend that you set up carrier voicemail.

>> Your phone may also feature a Voicemail app, which you can use to collect and review your messages.

TIP

>> The most important step for voicemail setup is to create a customized greeting. If you don't do so, you may not receive voicemail messages, or people may believe that they've dialed the wrong number.

Picking up carrier voicemail messages

 Carrier voicemail collects missed calls as well as calls you thrust into voicemail. The standard Voicemail notification icon appears, looking like the one shown in the margin, whenever a new message is pending. You can choose this notification to dial into your carrier's voicemail system, listen to your calls, and use the phone's dialpad to manage the carrier voicemail system.

Most carrier voicemail systems work the same: You dial in, type your PIN, and then use the dialpad to review and delete messages. Therefore, it's best to look at the phone and display the dialpad and then activate the speaker as you hear the prompts and listen to the messages.

To help you remember the prompts, write them down here:

Press _____ to listen to the first message.

Press _____ to delete the message.

Press _____ to skip a message.

Press _____ to hear the menu options.

Press _____ to hang up.

While you're at it, write your voicemail PIN: _____

Using Google Voice for voicemail

Perhaps the best option I've found for working with voicemail is Google Voice. It's more than just a voicemail system: You can use the service to make phone calls in the United States, place cheap international calls, and perform other amazing feats, though I use it primarily for voicemail.

To configure your Android phone for use with Google Voice, you must do two things:

1. **Create a Google Voice account.**

2. **Obtain the Google Voice app.**

Start your adventure by visiting the Google Voice home page at:

```
https://voice.google.com
```

I recommend using a computer to complete these steps: Follow the directions on the screen. Log in to your Google account, if necessary, and agree to the terms of service.

Click the Settings icon on the web page to link your Android's phone number with the Google Voice service. You must set up a Google Voice number for your account, so choose a number if one isn't already available.

After getting a Google Voice number, visit Google Play to get the Google Voice app. Specific directions for using Google Play are offered in Chapter 17. Install the app and open it to complete configuration.

When you're ready to go, use the Google Voice app to review your voicemail messages. Google Voice transcribes your voicemail messages, turning the audio from the voicemail into a text message you can read. The messages show up eventually in the Google Voice app and in your Gmail inbox, if you've configured that option on the Google Voice website.

>> Even when you choose to use Google Voice, I still recommend setting up and configuring the boring carrier voicemail, as covered earlier in this chapter.

>> Your phone's call forwarding feature disables Google Voice. If you forward calls, you must reset Google Voice after you're done. That's because Google Voice relies upon call forwarding to deal with unanswered or dismissed calls.

WARNING

IN THIS CHAPTER

» **Exploring the address book**

» **Searching and sorting contacts**

» **Creating a new contact**

» **Editing contacts**

» **Putting a picture on a contact**

» **Finding duplicate contacts**

» **Deleting contacts**

Chapter **7**

The Address Book

I remember the day back when I had a dozen or so important phone numbers memorized. Instantly, using only the power of my brain, I could dial either set of grandparents, Dad or Mom at work, my work, my best friend, the movie theater, and others. It was amazing such a thing could be done without any technology.

Thank goodness today we have smartphones to keep all those names, phone numbers, and addresses in one handy place. The app is called Contacts, and it's home to your life's digital address book. Using your brain is optional. Truly, mankind has reached its pinnacle.

The People You Know

The address book app is central to many operations in an Android device. It's used by Gmail, Email, social networking, and (most obviously) the Phone app.

TECHNICAL STUFF

» Your Android's digital address book is probably full of people already; your Gmail contacts are instantly synchronized, as are social networking contacts and any contacts associated with other accounts and apps you've added to the device.

» The address book app might be named People on some devices.

Accessing the address book

To open the Contacts app, hunt for its launcher on the Home screen. It might be in the Google folder. And if it's not available on the Home screen, look for it in the apps drawer.

Figure 7-1 shows how the Contacts app might look, though its appearance differs from device to device. Specifically, some apps list favorites at the top, followed by frequently contacted entries. A full index might also appear on the side of the list.

Favorites

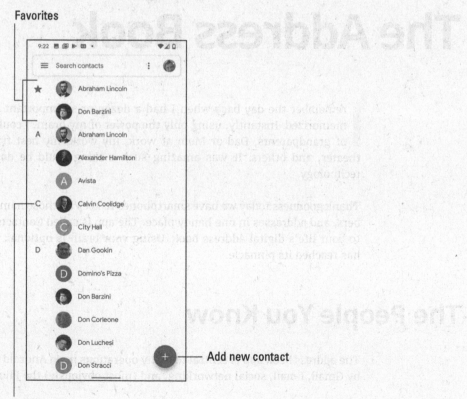

Add new contact

FIGURE 7-1:
The Contacts list   Index

By default, the Contacts app shows all contacts presented alphabetically by first name. Swipe your finger on the touchscreen to scroll the list.

To see more details about a contact, tap the entry. The details screen varies, depending on the Contacts app, but it looks similar to what's shown in Figure 7-2.

FIGURE 7-2:
More details
about a contact

Mug shot

Favorite

Send email

Loan sharking

Get directions

Text message

Edit contact

Locate in the Maps app

Call phone

The number of things you can do with a contact depends on the information shown and the apps installed on your Android. Here are some common activities:

Place a phone call. To call a contact on an Android phone, tap one of the phone entries. This activity works on an Android tablet as well, providing you have a phone dialer app installed, such as the Hangouts Dialer or Skype.

Send a text message. Tap the Text Message icon (refer to Figure 7-2) to open the text messaging app and send the contact a message. See Chapter 8 for information about text messaging.

Send email. Tap the contact's email address to compose an email message. When the contact has more than one email address, you can choose to which one you want to send the message. Chapter 9 covers email.

View a social networking status. Some address book apps display social networking information on the contact's screen, such as a tweet or Facebook status update. See Chapter 11 for more information on social networking.

Locate the contact's address. When the contact's information shows a home or business address, tap that item to summon the Maps app and view the location. Refer to Chapter 12 to see all the fun stuff you can do with Maps.

Some tidbits of information that show up for a contact have no associated actions. For example, the Android doesn't sing "Happy Birthday" whenever you tap a contact's birthday information.

>> You can also access the list of contacts from within the Phone app: Tap the Contacts tab to view the list.

>> Not every contact has a picture, and the picture can come from many sources (Gmail or Facebook, for example). See the later section "Adding a contact picture" for more information.

>> Many Androids feature an account named Me. It shows your personal information as known by the device. The Me account may be in addition to your other accounts shown in the address book.

>> Some cellular providers add accounts to an Android's address book. You may see entries such as BAL, MIN, or Warranty Center. Those aren't real people; they're shortcuts to various services. For example, the BAL contact is used on some Verizon phones to get a text message detailing your current account balance.

>> Also see the later section "Managing contacts" for information on how to deal with duplicate entries for the same person.

Sorting the address book

Your Android gizmo's address book displays contacts in a certain order. By default, that order is alphabetically by first name. You can change this order if the existing arrangement drives you nuts. Follow these steps when using the Contacts app:

1. **Tap the Side Menu icon.**

2. **Choose Settings.**

   In some Contacts apps, tap the Action Overflow icon and then choose Settings. Some Samsung devices use the MORE button instead of the Action Overflow icon.

3. **Choose Sort By.**

4. **Select First Name or Last Name, depending on how you want the contacts sorted.**

5. **Choose Name Format.**

6. **Choose First Name First or Last Name First.**

   This command specifies how the contacts appear in the list: first name first or last name first.

The list of contacts is updated, displayed per your preferences.

Searching contacts

The Contacts app doesn't provide a running total for all your contacts. Either you have very few friends or a lot of people owe you money. When it's the latter, you can choose to endlessly scroll the list of contacts, or you can employ the powerful Search command to quickly find a contact:

1. **Tap the Search text box.**

   The Search icon, shown in the margin, may or may not appear in the Search text box.

2. **Start typing a contact name.**

   As you type, a list of matching contacts appears. The list narrows as you type.

3. **Once you see the matching person, tap that entry.**

To clear a search, tap the X at the right side of the Search text box. To exit the search screen, tap the Back navigation icon.

REMEMBER

No, there's no correlation between the number of contacts you have and how popular you are in real life.

Make New Friends

Having friends is great. Having more friends is better. Keeping all those friends as entries in the Contacts app is best.

>> Contacts are associated with your various online accounts and services. For example, your Google account plays host to all your Gmail contacts as well as to new contacts you create.

>> If you use Yahoo! as your primary email account, create new contacts and associate them with that account. The next section offers details.

Creating a new contact from scratch

Sometimes it's necessary to create a contact when you actually meet another human being in the real world. Or, maybe you finally got around to transferring information from your old datebook. In either instance, you have information to input, and it starts like this:

1. **Tap the Add Contact icon in the Contacts app.**

   The Add button is illustrated in the margin, as well as shown earlier, in Figure 7-1. The icon may appear in a festively colored circle.

2. **Ensure that your Google account is associated with the new contact.**

   You may see your Google (or Gmail) account listed on the Create Contact card. If not, choose that account from a list. Or, if you primarily use another email service, such as Yahoo!, choose that account instead.

TIP

   I recommend choosing your Google account because this account is synchronized with the Internet and any other Android gizmos you may own.

WARNING

   Do not choose the Device or Phone account. When you do, the contact information is saved only on your Android. It won't be synchronized with the Internet or with any other devices.

3. **Fill in the contact's information as best you can.**

   Type text in the various boxes with the information you know. The more information you provide, the better. At minimum, the contact needs a name.

   Tap the chevron to the right of a field to set more details, such as whether a phone number is Mobile, Home, or Work, for example.

REMEMBER

To add a second phone number, email, or location, tap the ADD NEW button, which may look like a large Plus icon.

Always type a phone number with the area code.

4. **Tap the Save button to complete editing and add the new contact.**

The new contact is created. As a bonus, it's also automatically synced with your Google account on the Internet, or with whichever account you chose in Step 2.

Adding a contact from the call log

A quick and easy way to build up the address book on an Android phone is to add people as they call. To do so, check the call log:

1. **Open the Phone app.**

2. **Display the call log.**

Tap the Recents tab. See Chapter 6 for specific directions.

An unknown phone number appears without a contact picture, name, or other details.

3. **Display details about the phone number for an incoming call.**

If the details aren't presented right away, long-press the entry or tap the Details button.

4. **Choose Add Contact or Add to Contacts.**

Two additional options may present themselves: one to update an existing contact and a second to create a new contact.

5. **Continue adding contact details.**

If the contact already exists, such as a new cell number, tap the Add to Existing button and choose the contact from the list.

6. **Save the new contact.**

If you make a mistake and create a new contact for an entry already in the address book, you can merge the contacts later. See the later section "Managing contacts."

TIP

Contacts can also be added or updated from an email message. View the message in the email app and tap the sender's name or address. Choose the option to create a contact or update an existing contact, which echoes the steps outlined in this section.

Manage Your Friends

Sure, some folks just can't leave well enough alone. For example, Tracy may change her phone number. Sandy moves all the time. And Steve finally got rid of his 25-year-old AOL email address. When such things occur, you must undertake the task of address book management.

Making basic changes

To make minor touch-ups on any contact, locate and display the contact's information. Tap the Edit icon, similar to the Edit (pencil) icon shown in the margin. The button might say Edit, or you can tap Action Overflow and choose Edit.

To change or add information, tap a field and then edit or add new text.

Some contact information cannot be edited. For example, fields pulled in from social networking sites can be edited only by that account holder on the social networking site.

When you're finished editing, tap the Done icon or the Save button.

Adding a contact picture

Contact photos are supplied automatically, depending on the contact's email address. For example, your Android may show the contact's photo from their own Gmail or Facebook accounts. If not, you can assign your own picture of the contact, a photo that reminds you of the contact, or something wholly inappropriate.

To use the Android's camera to snap a contact picture, heed these directions:

1. **Edit the contact's information.**

2. **Tap the contact's picture or the Picture Placeholder icon.**

   The placeholder may feature the Camera icon, like the one shown in the margin.

3. **Choose Take Photo or Camera.**

   Some devices may skip this step, automatically displaying the Camera app (or a variation).

4. **Use the device's camera to snap a picture.**

   Chapter 13 covers using the Camera app. Both the front and rear cameras can be used (though not at the same time). Tap the Shutter icon to take the picture.

5. Review the picture.

Nothing is set yet. If you want to try again, tap the Retry icon, similar to what's shown in the margin. Repeat Step 4. This icon might appear as the Minus (–) icon on the Camera app.

6. Tap the Done icon to confirm the new image and prepare for cropping.

Some devices skip this step, automatically setting the image you just took. If so, skip to Step 9.

7. Crop the image.

Adjust the cropping box so that it surrounds only the portion of the image you want to keep. Refer to Chapter 14, which specifically covers how to use the cropping tool.

8. Tap the Done button to crop the image.

9. Tap the Save button to save and update the contact's information.

The contact's image appears onscreen when the person calls, as well as when referenced in other apps, text messaging, Gmail, and so on.

If the contact isn't around, or nothing nearby is worthy of snapping a picture, you can assign one of the device's images to the contact. In Step 3, choose the action Choose Photo, which on Samsung phones is called Gallery. Browse the device's images to pluck out something suitable.

>> To remove an image from a contact, edit the contact and tap their image icon, as described in this section. Choose the action Remove Photo or tap the Minus (–) icon to reset the image.

>> To replace an existing image, choose the action Select New Photo in Step 3. Or, on some devices, you're presented with the Camera app and you can immediately shoot a new image.

>> Some stored images may not work for contact icons. For example, images synchronized with your online photo albums may be unavailable.

Playing favorites

A *favorite* contact is someone you stay in touch with most often. The person doesn't have to be someone you like — just someone you (perhaps unfortunately) contact often, such as your parole officer.

To make a contact a favorite, display the contact's information and tap the Favorite (star) icon by the contact's image, as shown in Figure 7-2. When the star is filled, the contact is one of your favorites and is stored in the Favorites group.

To remove a favorite, tap the contact's star again and it loses its highlight.

>> The Contacts app lists favorites first, atop the list. You may see the Star icon in the index, or the favorites might be shown on their own tab.

>> Removing a favorite doesn't delete the contact, but instead removes it from the Favorites group.

>> By the way, contacts have no idea whether they're among your favorites, so don't believe that you're hurting their feelings by not making them favorites.

Managing contacts

To review your Android's address book for potential duplicate contacts, follow these steps while using the Contacts app.

1. **Tap the Side Menu icon to display the navigation drawer.**

2. **Choose Suggestions.**

   A Description card may appear. If so, tap the Got It button.

3. **Peruse the suggestions.**

   Or, if you see the message "Good work, no new suggestions," you're done. Otherwise, merge duplicate contacts and update details pulled in from multiple sources.

On some Samsung devices, choose Manage Contacts in Step 2. Choose the option Merge Contacts to review any duplicates.

It's up to you whether you merge the contacts shown, and it's not something you must do. For example, different individuals at an organization might have the same main phone number, but different email addresses. In that case, don't merge the contacts.

TIP

Removing a contact

Every so often, consider reviewing your Android's address book. Purge the folks whom you no longer recognize or you've forgotten. It's simple:

1. **Edit the forlorn contact.**

For some versions of the Contacts app, this step isn't necessary. Instead, display the contact's info, and then move on with Step 2.

2. **Tap Action Overflow and choose Delete.**

If you don't see the Delete item, the contact is brought in from another source, such as Facebook. You need to use that app to disassociate the contact.

3. **Tap the Delete button to confirm.**

Poof! They're gone.

 On some devices, you may find the Delete icon (shown in the margin) directly on the contact's Details card. Tap that icon to remove it, and then tap the OK button to remove the contact.

WARNING

>> To purge multiple contacts, long-press the first one in the address book list. This step activates mass-selection mode: Continue tapping unwanted contacts. When you've built the list, tap the Delete icon to remove the batch.

>> Because the Contacts list is synchronized with your Google account, the contact is also removed there — and on other Android devices.

>> Removing a contact doesn't kill the person in real life.

IN THIS CHAPTER

» **Creating a text message**

» **Sending a group message**

» **Getting a text message**

» **Texting pictures, videos, and media items**

» **Managing your text messages**

» **Specifying a text message ringtone**

Chapter **8**

Text Me

Texting is the popular name for a cell phone's capability to send short, typed messages to another cell phone. The process echoes earlier technology, including telegraph and teletype. Curiously, the acronym *LOL* dates to a telegraph message sent in the 1880s:

```
Butch Cassidy robbed the 302 out of Belle Fourche.
It was carrying steer manure. LOL.
```

Despite its seemingly anachronistic nature, texting remains a popular form of communications. Indeed, some people text more than they use their Android to place a call. It's a convenient and popular way to quickly communicate.

TECHNICAL STUFF

» Android tablets do not have the capability to send or receive text messages. Yes, even LTE tablets, though they may have a phone number assigned, cannot do text messaging.

» The nerdy term for text messaging is *SMS,* which stands for Short Message Service. The newer service is called *RCS,* for Rich Communications Service, though it's more commonly called "chat." It supports features such as read receipts, animation stickers, and other fun stuff.

Msg 4U

Text messaging allows you to send short quips of text from one cell phone to another. As long as the other phone is on and receiving a signal, the message is received instantly. That makes texting a quick and worthy form of communication.

WARNING

» Don't text while you're driving.

» Don't text in a movie theater.

» Don't text in any situation where it's distracting.

» Most cell phone plans include unlimited texting; however, some older plans may charge you per text. Texting to international numbers incurs a charge. Check with your cellular provider to be sure.

» If you're over 25, you might want to know that the translation of this section's title is "Message for you."

Opening the texting app

The stock Android text messaging app is called Messages. Your phone may feature a similarly named app. For example, Samsung uses Message+ as the name of its texting app.

Regardless of its name, the text messaging app is found on the Home screen in the favorites tray, usually right next to the Phone app. Tap this launcher to open the text messaging app.

» Many Android phones have multiple text messaging apps in addition to the stock Android text messaging app. See the section "Choosing another texting app," later in this chapter.

» The Facebook Messenger app is used for text chat within Facebook. It is not a text messaging app.

Texting a contact

You must desperately tell your friend Cody that kitty has been rescued from the tree. Here's how to convey your joy in a text message:

1. **Open the phone's address book app.**

Refer to Chapter 7 for details on the address book app, usually named Contacts.

WHETHER TO SEND A TEXT MESSAGE OR AN EMAIL

Sending a text message is similar to sending an email message. Both involve the instant electronic delivery of a message to someone else. And both methods of communication have their pros and cons.

The primary limitation of a text message is that it can be sent only to another cell phone. Email, on the other hand, is available to people who have an email address, which might be in addition to their cell phone.

Text messages are best when pithy: short and to the point. They're informal because the speed of reply is more important than trivia such as proper spelling and grammar. And just like with email, sending a text message doesn't guarantee a reply.

An email message can be longer than a text message. You can receive email on just about any Internet-connected device. Email message attachments (pictures, documents) are handled better and more consistently than text message (MMS) media.

When you're sending to multiple people, I strongly recommend using email, because it's easier to manage. A multi-person message, or "group text," is the bane of many smartphone users.

2. **Select a contact.**

   For example, select Cody.

3. **Tap the Text Messaging icon next to the phone number.**

   The stock Android icon for text messaging is shown in the margin.

   On a Samsung phone, swipe the contact's entry right-to-left.

   Upon success, you see a text message window. Any previous conversation you've had appears on the screen, similar to what's shown in Figure 8-1.

TIP

4. **Tap the text field, labeled *Type an SMS Message*.**

   The field might also read *Type a Message* or something similar.

5. **Type the message.**

6. **Tap the Send icon to send the message.**

SMS

   The Send icon may look like the one shown in the margin.

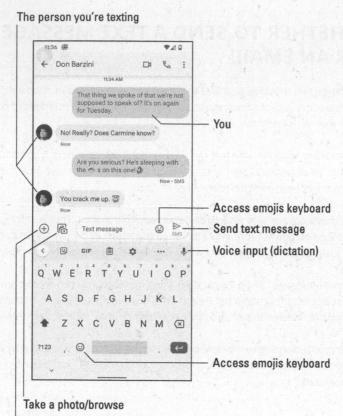

The person you're texting

You

Access emojis keyboard

Send text message

Voice input (dictation)

Access emojis keyboard

FIGURE 8-1:
Sending a text
message

Take a photo/browse

Attachment

The message is delivered (almost) instantly, though getting an instant reply isn't guaranteed.

WARNING

>> You can send text messages only to cell phones. Aunt Opal cannot receive text messages on her landline that she's had since the 1960s.

>> Do not text and drive. Do not text and drive. Do not text and drive.

Composing a new text message

To start a new message in the texting app, whether the person is already in your Android's address book or you know only a cell phone number, follow these steps:

1. View the app's main screen.

Use the Back gesture or tap the Back navigation icon to back out of any current conversation.

2. **Tap the Start Chat icon to start a new conversation.**

   Many texting apps use the Add (Plus) icon or the Edit (pencil) icon, shown on the main screen in the texting app.

3. **Type the phone number.**

   As you type, matching contacts appear. You can also type a contact name, if the person is already in the phone's address book.

4. **Tap the Done key on the onscreen keyboard.**

5. **Type the message.**

6. **Tap the Send icon to send the message.**

Sending a text to multiple contacts

To send the message to multiple contacts, repeat the steps from the preceding section but in Step 3 continue typing phone numbers or contact names. That's what makes the message a group text.

WARNING

When you receive a group text message (one that has several recipients), you can choose whether to reply to everyone. Look for the Reply All button when composing your response. Please use caution when replying to everyone. Many people dislike group text messages because they're persistently tedious and interminable.

Continuing a text message conversation

The text messaging app keeps track of old conversations, and you can pick up where you left off at any time: Open the texting app, peruse the list of existing conversations, and tap one to review what has been said or to begin something new.

Typing emojis, stickers, and fancy things

The current trend in text messaging communications dates to the Egyptians, though people today don't call them "hieroglyphics." No, they're *emojis*, which is from the Japanese words for "picture letter/character." These teensy symbols frequently inhabit text messages.

To type an emoji, tap the happy face symbol, either near the text field where you type the message or on the onscreen keyboard, as illustrated earlier, in Figure 8-1. You can then pluck out an emoji from the many palettes displayed.

In addition to emojis, the palette of icons above the onscreen keyboard offers selections for adding stickers (larger images than emojis), GIF animations, and other whimsical items. Enrage your friends by sending them these items instead of something in plain text.

TIP

>> When you type a word strongly associated with an emoji, like *cake,* the word turns into a button. Tap the button to choose the associated emoji and insert it into your text message.

>> Computer scientists (I kid you not) have created hundreds of emoji symbols. These are common across all cell phones, though the pictures may not look identical.

>> Don't be surprised to see a parade of emojis in a text message. They can express a complete thought.

Receiving a text message

New text messages are heralded by a notification atop the screen, similar to the one shown in the margin. Choose the notification to view the message.

>> If the phone is on, you may even see a card slide in with the message. Tap the card to view the message, or tap the Reply button to compose an instant reply.

>> Some texting apps may provide preset replies you can quickly choose from a new text message notification. For example, "Okay," "Yes," "Not now," and "Who dis?"

Multimedia Messages

The term *texting* sticks around, yet a text message can contain media — usually a photo — though short videos and audio can also be shared with a text message. Such a message ceases to be a mere text message and becomes a *multimedia message.*

>> Multimedia messages are handled by the same app you use for text messaging.

>> Not every cell phone can receive multimedia messages. Rather than receive the media item, the recipient may be directed to a web page where the item can be viewed on the Internet. Or the message may never show up.

>> The official name for a multimedia text message is Multimedia Messaging Service, abbreviated MMS.

Creating a multimedia text message

As with other things on your Android phone, you need to think of sharing when it comes to attaching media to a text message. Obey these steps:

1. **Open the app that contains or shows the item you want to share.**

For example, open the Photos app to view a picture or view a page in the web browser app.

2. **View the item and tap the Share icon.**

3. **Choose the phone's text messaging app from the list of apps.**

4. **Continue sending the text message as described earlier in this chapter.**

It's also possible to attach media to a message from within the text messaging app. To do so, tap the Add icon or Plus icon to the left of the text message box, similar to what's shown in the margin. Choose the media to attach. Optionally, type some text. Tap the Send icon.

In just a few, short, cellular moments, the receiving party will enjoy your multimedia text message.

Receiving a multimedia message

A multimedia attachment comes into your phone just like any other text message. You may see a thumbnail preview of whichever media was sent, such as an image, a still from a video, or the Play icon to listen to audio. To preview the attachment, tap its thumbnail.

TIP

To do more with the multimedia attachment, long-press it and then select an action from the list. For example, to save an image attachment, long-press the image thumbnail and choose Save Picture.

Text Message Management

You don't have to manage your messages. I certainly don't. But the potential exists: If you ever want to destroy evidence of a conversation, or even do something as mild as change the text messaging ringtone, it's possible.

Removing messages

Although I'm a stickler for deleting email after I read it, I don't bother deleting my text message threads. That's probably because I have no pending divorce litigation. Well, even then, I have nothing to hide in my text messaging conversations. If I did, I would follow these steps to delete a conversation:

1. **Open the conversation you want to remove.**

   Choose the conversation from the main screen in your phone's text messaging app.

2. **Tap the Action Overflow and choose Delete.**

3. **Tap the Delete button to confirm.**

   The entire conversation is gone.

 If these steps don't work, an alternative is to open the main screen in the text messaging app and long-press the conversation you want to zap. Tap the Delete button and then tap the Delete or OK button to confirm.

Individual cartoon bubbles can be removed from a conversation: Long-press the bubble and then tap the Trash icon or the Delete button.

Setting the text message ringtone

The sound you hear when a new text message floats in is the text message ringtone. It might be the same sound you hear for all notifications, though on some Android phones it can be changed to something unique.

Follow these steps in the Messages app to set a new text message ringtone:

1. **From the app's main screen, tap Action Overflow.**

2. **Choose Settings.**

3. **Choose Notifications.**

4. **Choose Incoming Messages.**

5. **Choose Sound.**

   This item is located under the Advanced item in the Android Messages app: Tap the chevron to view it.

6. **Select a sound from the list and tap OK.**

On Samsung phones running the Message+ app, follow these steps:

1. **At the main screen, tap the Side Menu icon to view the notifications drawer.**

2. **Choose Customize.**

3. **Choose Notifications.**

4. **Choose Sound.**

5. **Select a sound from the list.**

You might also be able to change the notification ringtone from the Settings app. Refer to Chapter 21.

Choosing another texting app

Your phone might have more than one text messaging app. For example, it may have the manufacturer's silly app plus the stock Android app. You can use either one, but you must tell the phone which you prefer. Obey these directions:

1. **Open the Settings app.**

   The app is in the apps drawer, though a handy shortcut can be found among the quick settings, as covered in Chapter 3.

2. **Choose Apps & Notifications.**

3. **If necessary, tap the chevron by the item titled Advanced.**

4. **Choose Default Apps.**

5. **Choose SMS App.**

6. **Select your preferred text messaging app from the list.**

On Samsung phones, attempt these steps:

1. **Open the Settings app.**

2. **Choose Apps.**

3. **Select the messaging app from the list.**

4. **Choose Messaging App.**

5. **Choose the app.**

   The app is shown along with other messaging apps on the phone.

The new app may copy over all your conversations, which is a plus — and a motivation to switch apps if you find the current choice disappointing.

See Chapter 20 for more details on setting default apps.

IN THIS CHAPTER

» Adding email accounts

» Receiving email

» Reading, replying to, and forwarding email

» Composing a new message

» Dealing with email attachments

» Sharing stuff in an email message

Chapter 9

You've Got Email

The first official telegraph message was, "What hath God wrought?" The first telephone call was supposedly, "Mr. Watson. Come here. I want you." The first email message, sent back in the early 1970s by programmer Ray Tomlinson, was probably something like, "QWERTYUIOP." It's one for the history books.

Today, email has become far more functional and necessary, well beyond Mr. Tomlinson's early tests. Although you could impress your email buddies by sending them "QWERTYUIOP," you're likely to send and reply to more meaningful communications. Your Android is happily up to the task.

Email on Your Android

You can easily handle all email duties on your Android by using the Gmail app. It works natively with Google's Gmail service, and you can add other email accounts as well.

The Gmail app is already configured to handle your Google email, but my guess is that you have other email accounts. Add them to the Gmail app so that you can collect and read all your email in one, handy spot. Obey these directions:

1. **Open the Settings app.**

    It's found in the apps drawer.

2. **Choose Accounts.**

    This item may be titled Users & Accounts.

3. **Tap the Add Account item.**

    In stock Android, the three options for adding email accounts are

    - *Exchange or Microsoft Exchange ActiveSync:* For a corporate email account hosted by an Exchange Server (Outlook mail)

    - *Personal (IMAP):* For web-based email accounts, such as Microsoft Live

    - *Personal (POP3):* For traditional, ISP-email accounts, such as Comcast

    On some Androids you might see only a single option, Email.

4. **Choose the email account type.**

5. **Type your email address and tap the Next button.**

6. **Type the email account password and tap the Next button.**

    In most cases, that's it!

The new email account is synchronized immediately after it's added, and you see the inbox. See the later section "Checking the inbox."

TIP

>> Though you can use the web browser app to visit the Gmail website, or visit any webmail site to check your message, I recommend that you use the Gmail app instead to pick up your Gmail.

>> In addition to synchronizing email, adding the account to your Android might also synchronize other services as well: Calendar appointments, contact names, and other items come into your device along with email messages.

>> Samsung devices come with a separate Email app, which you can configure for handling non-Gmail electronic messaging. I recommend, however, that you use Gmail for all your email needs.

» Specific apps are available for handling certain email services. For example, if you prefer to use Yahoo! Mail, obtain the Yahoo! app from Google Play; see Chapter 17. An AOL Mail app is also available, for those of you still living in the 20th century.

» If your email account isn't recognized, or if some other boo-boo happens, you must manually add the account. Specific and technical details must be provided. To obtain this information, visit your email provider's website for details on adding that service to an Android mobile device.

Message for You, Sir!

New email arrives into your Android automatically, picked up according to the email account's synchronization schedule — typically, 15 minutes, though "push" email may arrive instantly. A notification icon appears, as shown in the margin, which may differ depending on the account type. Choose that notification or start the Gmail map and read the electronic missive.

Checking the inbox

The Gmail app's primary inbox appears when you first open the app, similar to what's shown in Figure 9-1. Messages appear in chronological order, newest at the top. Unread messages are highlighted in bold text.

To view messages from a non-Gmail account, tap the account icon (refer to Figure 9-1) and choose the account. To view all inboxes at once, choose All Inboxes from the navigation drawer.

Reading email

To view a specific email message, tap its entry in the inbox. To read the previous message, swipe the screen from right to left — or to move forward in the list (chronologically), swipe the screen from left to right.

To return to the inbox, tap the left-pointing arrow or chevron at the top-left corner of the screen.

Each message has an associated set of actions.

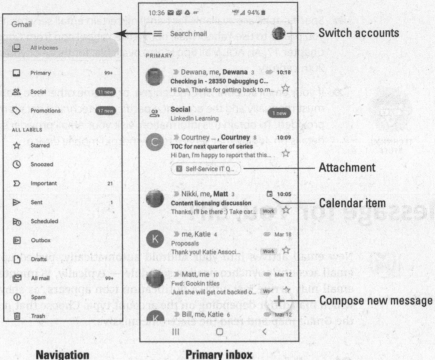

Switch accounts

Attachment

Calendar item

Compose new message

FIGURE 9-1: The Gmail inbox

Navigation drawer

Primary inbox

To work with the message, use the icons that appear above the message. These icons, which may not look exactly like those shown in the margin, cover common email actions:

 Reply: Tap this icon to reply to a message. A new message window appears with the To and Subject fields reflecting the original sender(s) and subject.

 Forward: Tap this icon to send a copy of the message to someone else.

Delete: Tap this icon to delete a message.

 Mark as Unread: Change the message's status so that it shows up as unread in the inbox.

 Other commands are available on the message's Action Overflow menu, such as Reply All, Favorite, Print, and even those actions that would otherwise appear as icons but for space reasons show up on the overflow.

 More icons appear when you turn the device to the horizontal orientation. If the Screen Rotation icon appears, tap it to change the app's orientation.

TIP

Compose a New Email Epistle

I frequently use my Android to check email, but I don't often use it to compose messages. That's because most email messages don't demand an immediate reply. When they do, you'll find that the Gmail app is up to the task.

Crafting a new message

To compose a new email epistle, follow these steps:

1. **Tap the Compose button.**

   This button is also illustrated earlier, in Figure 9-1.

2. **Choose the email account.**

   If necessary, tap the From field to choose an email account. The message is sent from the selected account.

3. **Fill in the fields: To and Subject.**

   To access the Cc and Bcc fields, tap the chevron illustrated in Figure 9-2.

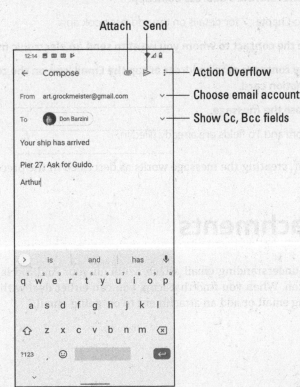

FIGURE 9-2:
Composing a new email dispatch

TIP

You need only type a few letters of the recipient's name. Matching contacts are fetched instantly from the Android's address book. Tap a contact to automatically fill in the To field.

4. **Type the message text in the Compose Email field.**

5. **Tap the Send icon to whisk off the message into the electronic ether.**

To cancel the message, tap Action Overflow and choose Discard. Tap the Discard button to confirm.

If you decide not to send the message, or if you're distracted by some other activity, the message is saved automatically in the Drafts folder. Choose this folder from the navigation drawer to review and revive any drafts for further editing or sending.

Sending email to a contact

A quick and easy way to compose a new message is to find a contact in your Android's address book and then create a message to the contact. Heed these steps:

1. **Open the Android's address book app.**

    Refer to Chapter 7 for details on the address book app.

2. **Locate the contact to whom you want to send an electronic message.**

3. **Tap the contact's email address or tap the Email icon on the contact's Information card.**

4. **Compose the message.**

    The From and To fields are already filled in.

At this point, creating the message works as described in the preceding section.

Message Attachments

The key to understanding email attachments on your Android is to look for the Paperclip icon. When you find that icon, you can either deal with an attachment for incoming email or add an attachment to outgoing email.

Receiving an attachment

Your goal upon receiving an email attachment on an Android is to either view it or save it. The key is to locate the Attachment card in the message, as shown in Figure 9-3.

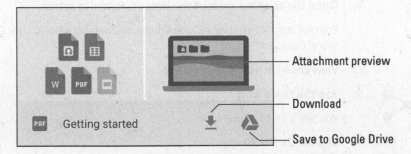

FIGURE 9-3: Attachment methods and madness

— Attachment preview

— Download

— Save to Google Drive

Potential actions you can perform with an attachment include preview, download, and save: Tap the Attachment card to preview; tap the Download icon to save a copy of the attachment to your device; tap the Google Drive icon to save the download to storage there.

As with email attachments received on a computer, you may discover that your Android lacks the app required to deal with the attachment. When an app can't be found, you must either suffer not viewing the attachment or request that the attachment be re-sent in a common file format.

>> Sometimes pictures included in an email message aren't displayed. Tap the Show Pictures button to see the images.

>> By saving the attachment to Google Drive storage, you can access the attachment on a computer or any device from which you can access your Google Drive account.

>> You may see a prompt displayed when several apps can deal with the attachment. Choose one and tap the Just This Once button to view the attachment. Also see Chapter 20 for information on the default app prompt.

TECHNICAL STUFF

>> Attachments are saved in the Downloads folder. See Chapter 19 for details on Android storage, including how to view downloaded files.

Sharing an attachment

To fully appreciate the Android operating system, you must accept that adding a message attachment in email need not start in the Gmail or Email app. No, you start in the app that created the item you want to attach. Heed these steps:

1. **Open the app that created the item you want to attach.**

   Popular apps for sharing include Photos, the web browser app, Maps, Play Store, Drive, and so on.

2. **View the item you want to share.**

3. **Tap the Share icon.**

   You see a list of apps.

4. **Choose the Gmail app.**

5. **Complete the message as described earlier in this chapter.**

   The item you're sharing is automatically attached to the message or included as a link.

When you start a message and then discover that you need to attach something, fret not! Look for and tap the Attachment icon, lurking somewhere on the Compose card, shown in Figure 9-2. (Sometimes the Add or Plus icon is used instead.) Choose the app or category and then select the item to share.

Chapter **10**

Web Browsing

hen Tim Berners-Lee developed the World Wide Web back in 1990, he had no idea that people would one day use it on a mobile device with a tiny screen. Nope, the web was designed to be viewed on a computer. Back then, cell phones had teensy LED screens. Browsing the web on a cell phone would have been like viewing the Great Wall of China through a keyhole.

The good news is that the web has adapted itself to mobile viewing. Whether you have a phone or a tablet, the web presents itself in a comfortable viewing size. You won't miss any information, especially after you've read the tips and suggestions in this chapter.

» Many places you visit on the web can instead be accessed directly and more effectively by using specific apps. Facebook, Gmail, Twitter, YouTube, and other popular web destinations have apps that you may find are already installed on your device or otherwise available for free from Google Play.

» One thing you cannot do with your Android is view Flash animations, games, or videos on the web. The web browser app disables the Flash plug-in, also known as Shockwave. If your favorite website doesn't behave properly on your Android, odds are good that it uses Flash animation. I know of no method to circumvent this limitation.

The Web Browser App

All Androids feature a web browsing app, Google's own Chrome web browser. Your gizmo may feature another web browser app, and it may be given a simple name, such as Web, Browser, or Internet. Each of these apps works in a similar way and offers comparable features.

> » If your Android doesn't have the Chrome app, you can obtain it for free at Google Play. See Chapter 17.

> » A benefit of using Chrome is that your bookmarks, web history, and other features are shared between all your devices on which Chrome is installed. So if you use Chrome as your computer's web browser, it's logical to use Chrome on your Android as well.

Behold the Web

It's difficult these days to find someone who has no experience with the World Wide Web. More common is someone who has used the web on a computer but has yet to sample the Internet waters on a mobile device. If that's you, consider this section your quick mobile web orientation.

Surfing the web on a mobile device

When you first open the Chrome app, you see the last web page you viewed. In Figure 10-1, I was just on Wikipedia, so when I fired up Chrome, it returned to that page on an Android phone; an Android tablet features the same controls, though in different locations on the touchscreen.

TIP

Here are some handy Android web browsing tips:

> » Drag your finger across the touchscreen to pan and scroll the web page. You can pan up, down, left, or right when the page is larger than the device's screen.

> » Pinch the screen to zoom out, or spread two fingers to zoom in.

> » The page you see may be the mobile page, or a customized version of the web page designed for small-screen devices. To see the nonmobile version, tap the Action Overflow icon and choose Request Desktop Site (refer to the right side of Figure 10-1).

» You can orient the Android to read a web page in either portrait or landscape orientation. One view may look better than the other. For example, portrait (vertical) orientation makes long lines of text shorter and easier to read.

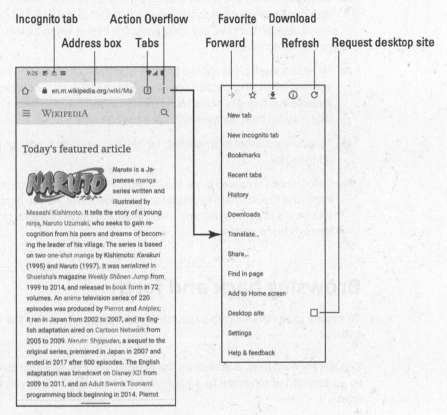

FIGURE 10-1:
The Chrome app beholds Wikipedia's home page

Visiting a web page

To visit a web page, heed these directions in the web browser app:

1. **Tap the address box.**

   Refer to Figure 10-1 for the address box's location. If you don't see the address box, swipe your finger from the top of the app's screen downward.

2. **Use the onscreen keyboard to type the address.**

   You can also type a search word or phrase if you don't know the exact web page address.

3. **Tap the Go button on the onscreen keyboard to visit the specific web page or search the web.**

To "click" links on a page, tap them with your finger. If you have trouble stabbing the correct link, zoom in on the page and try again. You can also long-press the screen to see a magnification window to make tapping links easier.

>> The onscreen keyboard may change some keys to make it easier to type a web page address. Look for the www (World Wide Web) or .com (dot-com) key. If you don't see this key, long-press the Period key to look for a pop-up palette of domains.

>> To reload a web page, tap the Refresh icon (refer to Figure 10-1). If you don't see that icon, tap the Action Overflow icon to look for it. Refreshing updates a website that changes often. Using the command can also reload a web page that may not have completely loaded the first time.

>> To stop a web page from loading, tap the Cancel (X) icon that appears by the address box.

>> To locate text on a web page, tap the Action Overflow and choose Find in Page. Use the onscreen keyboard to type search text. As you type, matching text on the page is highlighted. Use the up and down chevrons to page through found matches.

Browsing back and forth

To return to a previous web page, use the Back gesture or tap the Back navigation icon.

Tap the Forward icon, available on the Action Overflow, as illustrated in Figure 10-1, to go forward or to return to a page you were visiting before you tapped the Back icon.

To check your web browser's history, tap the Action Overflow and choose History. Tap an entry in the list to revisit that site.

TIP

>> You'll notice that the History list is adorned with Delete (trash) icons. See the later section "Clearing your web history" for information on purging items from the History list.

>> If you find yourself frequently clearing the web page history, consider using an incognito tab. See the later section "Going incognito."

Using bookmarks

You might call them bookmarks, but in the mobile world, your Android calls your bookmarks favorites. To mark a web page as a favorite, tap the Favorite (star) icon for that site. Look for the icon on the Action Overflow, as shown in Figure 10-1.

To view bookmarks in the Chrome app, tap the Action Overflow icon and choose Bookmarks. The Bookmarks card is organized by folder, similar to the bookmarks bar on the computer version of Chrome: Tap a folder to browse bookmarks stored in that folder. Tap a bookmark to visit that page.

TIP

>> A great way to find which sites to bookmark is to view the web page history: Tap the Action Overflow and choose History.

>> To quickly visit a bookmarked website, start typing the site's name in the address box. Tap the bookmarked site from the matching list of results displayed below the address box.

>> To edit a bookmark, visit it and tap the Favorite (star) icon again. Use the Edit Bookmark card to change the bookmark's name, organize it into a specific folder, or edit the address.

>> To remove the bookmark, edit the Bookmark (tap the Favorite icon) and tap the Delete icon on the Edit Bookmark card.

REMEMBER

>> Making a favorite web page isn't the same as saving the page. See the later section "Saving a web page."

Managing web pages in multiple tabs

The Chrome app uses a tabbed interface that lets you access more than one web page at a time. On an Android tablet, the tabs appear across the top of the app's screen, similar to the way they appear in Chrome on a computer. On an Android phone, however, the tabs are accessible from the Tabs button, illustrated in Figure 10-1.

Here are some common Chrome tab actions:

To open a blank tab: Tap the Action Overflow and choose New Tab. You can also tap the Add (plus) icon on the Tabs screen, as illustrated in Figure 10-2.

To open a link in a new tab: Long-press the link and choose Open in New Tab.

To open a bookmark in a new tab: Long-press the bookmark and choose Open in New Tab.

To switch tabs: On an Android tablet, tap the tab you want to view. On a phone, tap the Tabs icon. Choose a new tab from the list shown, as illustrated in Figure 10-2.

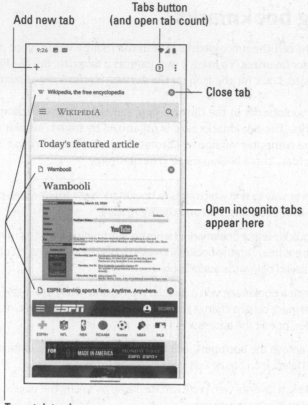

Add new tab

Tabs button
(and open tab count)

Close tab

Open incognito tabs
appear here

FIGURE 10-2:
Switching tabs
on an Android
phone

Tap a tab to view

To close a tab on a phone, tap the Tabs button and tap the Close (X) icon by the tab thumbnail (refer to Figure 10-2). On a tablet, tap a tab's Close (X) icon.

After you close the last tab, you see a blank screen in the Chrome app. Tap the Add (plus) icon to summon a new tab.

Going incognito

TIP

Shhh! For secure browsing, use an incognito tab: Tap the Action Overflow and choose New Incognito Tab. The incognito tab takes over the screen, changing the look of the Chrome app and offering a description page.

When you go incognito, the web browser doesn't track your history, leave cookies, or provide other evidence of which web pages you've visited. For example, if you go shopping in an incognito window, advertiser tracking cookies don't record your actions. That way, you aren't bombarded by targeted advertising later.

>> When an incognito tab is open, the Incognito notification appears on the status bar, like the one shown in the margin.

>> Choose the Incognito notification to close all open incognito tabs.

>> On an Android phone, to switch between incognito and regular tabs, tap the Tabs icon. Swipe the Tabs screen right-to-left to choose an open incognito tab. (Refer to the preceding section.)

>> On an Android tablet, tap the Incognito icon in the top-right corner of the Chrome app's screen to view any open incognito tabs. The icon appears only when an Incognito tab is open.

REMEMBER

>> The incognito tab is about privacy, not security. Going incognito doesn't prevent viruses or thwart sophisticated web snooping software.

Sharing a web page

There it is! That web page you *must* talk about with everyone you know. The gauche way to share the page is to copy and paste it. Because you're reading this book, however, you know better. Heed these steps:

1. **Visit the web page you desire to share.**

2. **Tap the Action Overflow icon and choose Share.**

You see a list of contacts and an array of apps displayed. The variety and number of apps depends on what's installed on the device.

3. **Choose a contact or an app.**

The contact is summoned in the text messaging app. Otherwise, choose an app, such as Gmail, to use the app to share the web page's link.

4. **Do whatever happens next.**

Whatever happens next depends on how you're sharing the link: Write the text, compose the email, write a comment in Facebook, or do whatever. Refer to various chapters in this book for specific directions.

You cannot share a page you're viewing on an incognito tab.

The Art of Downloading

Downloading is a technology term that gets abused often. What it means with regard to an Android and the Chrome app is to transfer information from the Internet into your device. The information transferred is accessed on a web page. It can be a picture, a file, or something else that I can't think of right now.

>> The Download Complete notification appears after your Android has downloaded something. You can choose that notification to view the downloaded item.

>> New apps on your Android are downloaded from the Google Play Store app, not by using the web browser app. See Chapter 17.

TECHNICAL STUFF

>> The opposite of downloading is *uploading*. It's the process of sending information from your gizmo to another source, such as the Internet or orbiting space station.

Grabbing an image from a web page

The simplest thing to download is an image from a web page:

1. **Long-press the image.**

   You see an Action card appear.

2. **Choose Download Image.**

   You may be prompted to allow Chrome to access the device's media. If so, tap the Allow button.

See the later section "Reviewing your downloads," for details on how to access the image.

Downloading a file

The web is full of links that don't open in a web browser window. For example, some links automatically download, such as links to types of files that a web browser is too frightened to display.

To save other types of links that aren't automatically downloaded, long-press the link and choose the Save Link action. If this action doesn't appear, your Android is unable to save the link, because either the file is of an unrecognized type or it presents a security issue.

Saving a web page

To save the entire web page you're viewing, tap the Download icon, shown in the margin and illustrated on the Action Overflow in Figure 10-1.

One reason for downloading an entire page is to read it later, especially when the Internet isn't available. This tip is one of my Android travel suggestions. More travel tips are found in Chapter 23.

Reviewing your downloads

To access any image, file, or web page you've downloaded or saved on your Android, follow these steps in the Chrome web browser app:

1. Tap the Action Overflow.

2. Choose Downloads.

A list of cards appears on the Downloads screen, each one representing something you've downloaded.

3. Tap a card to open and view the item you downloaded.

Photos can also be viewed in the Photos app, which is covered specifically in Chapter 14. In that app, tap the Side Menu icon and choose Device Folders on the navigation drawer. All downloaded images are saved in the Download folder or album.

REMEMBER

>> You can choose the Download notification to quickly review any single downloaded item.

>> If you're quick, you can tap the Open or View button that appears on the toast (pop-up message) immediately after an item is downloaded.

TECHNICAL STUFF

>> Some web pages load dynamic information. If you open a saved web page and find some of the artwork absent or other features disabled, it's that missing dynamic information that makes the page look odd.

Web Browser Controls and Settings

More options and settings and controls exist for web browser apps than for just about any other Android app I've used. Rather than bore you with every dang-doodle detail, I thought I'd present just a few of the options worthy of your attention.

Clearing your web history

When you don't want the entire Internet to know what you're looking at on the web, open an incognito tab, as described in the earlier section "Going incognito." When you forget to do that, follow these steps to purge one or more web pages from the browser history:

1. **Tap the Action Overflow icon and choose History.**

2. **Tap the X icon next to the web page entry you want to remove.**

It's gone.

If you want to remove *all* your web browsing history, after Step 1 choose Clear Browsing Data. You see the Clear Browsing Data screen. The prechecked items are what you need, so tap the Clear Data button to rid your Android of your sordid past.

REMEMBER

You don't need to clean up your web browsing history when you use an incognito tab.

Changing the web's appearance

As I ranted at the start of this chapter, the web on a mobile device never looks as good as the web on a computer. You do have a few options for making it look better.

First and foremost, remember that you can orient the device horizontally and vertically, which rearranges the way a web page is displayed. You can also spread your fingers to zoom in on any web page. When you find yourself doing these things too often, consider resetting the screen text size:

1. **Tap the Action Overflow icon.**

2. **Choose Settings.**

3. **Choose Accessibility.**

This item might be titled Screen and Text in some web browser apps.

4. **Use the Text Scaling slider to adjust the text size.**

The preview text below the slider helps you gauge which size works best.

Setting privacy and security options

The Chrome web browser app presets optimum security settings. The only issue you should consider is how information is retained and automatically recalled. You may want to disable some of those features.

In the Chrome app, tap the Action Overflow icon and choose Settings. Here are the items you should consider adjusting:

Passwords: Ensure that the Save Passwords master control is off. Disable Auto Sign-In.

Payment Methods: Ensure that the master control by the Save and Fill Payment Methods item is disabled (off).

Addresses and More: Disable the master control by the item Save and Fill Addresses.

Privacy: Disable all master controls. Ensure that Do Not Track is on or active.

Site Settings: Review items in the list to see which device features you want accessible to various websites. For example, choose Camera and disable the master control to ensure that access to your Android's camera is blocked from all websites.

With regard to general online security, my advice is always to be smart and think before doing anything questionable on the web. Use common sense. One of the most effective ways that the Bad Guys win is by using human engineering to try to trick you into doing something you normally wouldn't do, such as tap a link to see a cute animation or a racy picture of a celebrity or politician. As long as you use your noggin, you should be safe.

Also see Chapter 22 for information on applying a secure screen lock, which I highly recommend.

IN THIS CHAPTER

» **Exploring Facebook**

» **Sharing pictures on Instagram**

» **Checking in on Twitter**

» **Using Duo for video chat**

» **Making calls with Skype**

Chapter **11**

Digital Social Life

Long ago, social networking eclipsed email as the number-one reason for using the Internet. It has now nearly replaced email, has definitely replaced having a personalized website, and has become an obsession for millions across the globe. Your Android is ready to meet your social networking desires.

TIP

» This chapter covers a handful of popular social networking apps. Others are available, including LinkedIn, MeWe, and more. All apps mentioned in this chapter, if not installed on your Android, can be obtained from the Google Play Store, as covered in Chapter 17.

» Social networking apps generally come with companion widgets that you can affix to the Home screen. Use the widgets to peruse updates and otherwise interact with the service. Refer to Chapter 20 for information on affixing widgets to the Home screen.

» The apps shown in this chapter will change over time. The figures, descriptions, and directions may change subtly.

» It's better to use the social networking app on your Android than the web browser app to access the service.

» Use the Share icon to access your favorite social networking app. It's the quick way to post pictures, share web links, or forward YouTube videos: Tap the Share icon and then choose your favorite social networking app.

Expose Your Life on Facebook

Of all the social networking sites, Facebook is the king. It's the online place to go to catch up with friends, send messages, express your thoughts, share pictures and video, play games, and waste more time than you ever thought you had.

The Facebook app screen is illustrated in Figure 11-1. The News Feed tab is shown, which displays the latest social networking "news" for you to ogle.

News Feed

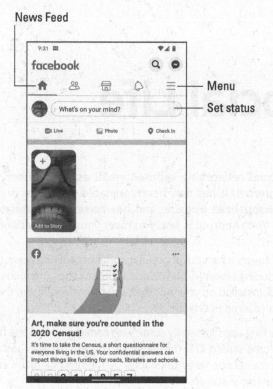

Menu

Set status

FIGURE 11-1:
The Face-
book app

The primary thing you live for on Facebook, besides having more friends than anyone else, is to update your status. Follow these steps in the Facebook app:

1. **Switch to the News Feed.**

Tap the News Feed icon (refer to Figure 11-1).

2. **Tap the text box labeled What's On Your Mind.**

Upon success, you see the Create Post screen, where you can type your musings as well as perform other activities, as illustrated in Figure 11-2.

Choose a sharing audience

Share your status

Status update text

Choose a background

Friends

Share your location

Set the mood

Add a photo

3. **Choose a sharing audience.**

   Tap the Sharing Audience button (refer to Figure 11-2). Choose Public so that everyone can see the message, or Friends so that only people you're friends with can see it.

4. **Type the post.**

5. **Tap the POST button to share your thoughts.**

To cancel the post, use the Back gesture or tap the Back navigation icon. Tap the Discard Post button to confirm.

Other popular Facebook duties include:

Uploading a picture: After starting a new post, tap the Photo/Video icon (refer to Figure 11-2). Choose a photo or video from your phone's storage or tap the Camera icon to take a shot for immediate uploading to Facebook.

Sharing a live video: To broadcast yourself immediately to Facebookland, tap the Go Live button after starting a new post. (The button appears before you start typing, so tap the button first.) The video is presented live to anyone who's on Facebook at the time. It's recorded for playback later.

Several other options are available, including checking in at a given location, tagging friends, asking for recommendations, and more. Icons for these options are presented on the Create Post screen, available before you start typing text.

TIP

» If you've added the Facebook widget to the Home screen, you can use that widget to share a quick post.

» I find it easier to use the Camera app to take a bunch of images or record video and then choose that item later to upload it to Facebook.

» Use the Like, Comment, or Share icons below a News Feed item to like, comment, or share something, respectively. Existing comments appear only when you choose the Comment item.

» The Facebook app generates notifications for news items, mentions, chat, and so on. This notification icon looks similar to the one shown in the margin.

Instagram Me

The social networking service Instagram was purchased by Facebook, so if you have a Facebook account, you also have an Instagram account. It's similar to Facebook, but used primarily to share images such as those pictures you take with your Android mobile device. You can take the picture first or use the Instagram app to launch the Camera app for instant photo gratification.

To share a photo on Instagram, tap the Add Photo icon, as shown in the margin. Choose GALLERY to select an image from the device's storage, PHOTO to take a picture, or VIDEO to shoot video. Continue with the steps presented to share the media.

You need not share a photo or video to use Instagram. It's also entertaining to view what others share, from celebrities to ordinary people who enjoy documenting the most intimate aspects of their lives. Use the Search icon in the app to locate people, places, or topics of interest. Tap the Follow button to continue to receive Instagram updates from the people you deem worthy to follow.

Let's All Tweet

Twitter is a social networking site that lets you share short bursts of text, or *tweets*. You can create your own or just choose to follow others, including news organizations, businesses, governments, celebrities, and robots from alien planets.

Figure 11-3 illustrates the Twitter app's main screen, which shows the current tweet feed. Tap the Twitter Home icon (illustrated in the figure) to read tweets, swiping the screen bottom-up as you go. Tug the list downward to update the tweets: Swipe from just below the status bar to center screen.

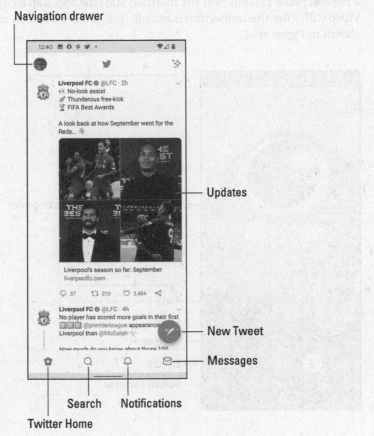

Navigation drawer

Updates

New Tweet

Messages

Search   Notifications

Twitter Home

FIGURE 11-3:
The Twitter app

To tweet, tap the New Tweet icon, shown in Figure 11-3. The "What's happening?" screen appears, where you can compose your musings.

REMEMBER

A tweet has a limited number of characters. An indicator on the New Tweet screen informs you of how many characters remain.

Tap the Tweet button to share your thoughts with the twitterverse.

>> A message posted on Twitter is a *tweet*.

>> To access the Twitter app's navigation drawer, tap your account image in the upper left part of the touchscreen.

Video Calling with Duo

The Duo app provides a way to make video calls with other Android users. If the person's Android has the Duo app (and most do), the connection is made just like a normal phone call but over the Internet. Start the app. Tap a contact and choose Video Call. After the connection is established, you see a screen similar to the one shown in Figure 11-4.

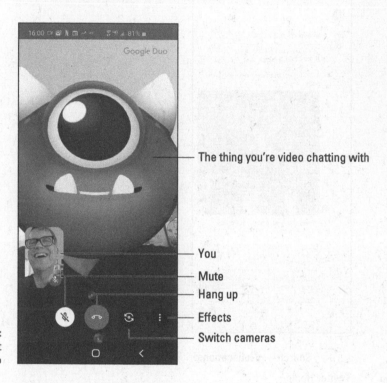

The thing you're video chatting with

You

Mute

Hang up

Effects

Switch cameras

FIGURE 11-4:
Video chat
with Duo

When a Duo video call comes in, swipe to answer per the directions onscreen, just like a regular phone call. In mere moments, you're communicating visually — plus a few visual effects you can add, as shown in Figure 11-4.

Tap the Hang Up icon (refer to Figure 11-4) to end the call.

>> The Phone app may feature the Video Call button. Tap it to use Duo for connecting a video call.

>> You can activate the Effects filter before you make a call: Swipe down the screen and tap the Effects button to view the variety.

Skype the World

Skype is a popular Internet communications tool, allowing you to chat by text, voice, or video with other Skype users. But the big enchilada is Skype's capability to place honest-to-goodness phone calls, including international calls. This feature works on both Android phones and tablets.

TIP

Calls to real phones can be made only when you have Skype Credit on your account. To ensure that you have Skype Credit, tap your account icon atop the main Skype screen. If you see $0.00 for the Skype to Phone item, tap it to either make a one-time Skype Credit purchase or get a subscription. You don't need a lot of Skype Credit to make calls — the rates are quite cheap.

After you've confirmed your Skype Credit, you can use an Android phone or tablet to make a "real" phone call, which is a call to any phone number on the planet (Planet Earth). Heed these steps:

1. **Tap the Calls icon on the Skype app's main screen.**

2. **Tap the Dialpad icon.**

   The Dialpad icon is shown in the margin. After you tap this icon, you see the Skype dial screen.

3. **Use the keypad to punch in the phone number.**

   The +1 prefix is required for dialing to the United States, even when the number is local. Don't erase it!

TIP

   For international dialing, the number begins with a plus sign (+) followed by the country code and then the phone number.

4. **Tap the Phone button at the bottom of the screen to place the call.**

5. **Talk.**

   As you talk, the cost of the call is displayed on the screen. That way, you can keep tabs on the toll.

6. **To end the call, tap the End Call button.**

Lamentably, you can't use Skype to receive a phone call on an Android tablet. The only way to make this happen is to pay for a Skype online number. In that case, you can use Skype to both send and receive regular phone calls.

>> In addition to the per-minute cost, you may be charged a connection fee for making the call.

>> You can check the Skype website at skype.com for a current list of call rates, for both domestic and international calls.

TIP

>> Unless you've paid Skype to let you use a specific number, the phone number shown on the recipient's Caller ID screen is something unexpected — often the text *Unknown*. Because of that, you might want to inform the person ahead of time that you're placing a Skype call. That way, the call won't be skipped because the Caller ID isn't recognized.

TIP

>> If you plan to use Skype a lot, get a good headset.

>> Text, voice, and video chat on Skype over the Internet are free. When you use a Wi-Fi connection, you can chat without consuming your cellular plan's data minutes.

3 Amazing Android Feats

IN THIS CHAPTER

» Exploring your world with Maps

» Choosing a different map type

» Saving a map for later

» Finding your location

» Sharing your location

» Searching for places

» Getting directions and navigation

Chapter 12 There's a Map for That

We were stunned and disoriented. Dr. Cornelius explained it would happen. The room rocked, and gravity tugged left and right instead of down.

Eventually, Ira righted himself; his nausea abated. "They're never going to sell teleportation to the masses with this kind of aftereffect," he grunted.

Phyllis agreed. Holding a hand to her spinning forehead, she asked, "Where are we? And where is a good Hungarian restaurant?"

That's when Dan whipped out his Android. "I'll let you know in just a second," he said proudly, opening the Maps app.

Map 101

To find your location, as well as the location of things near and far, summon the Maps app. Good news: You run no risk of improperly folding the Maps app. Better news: The Maps app charts the entire country, including freeways, highways, roads, streets, avenues, drives, bike paths, addresses, businesses, and various points of interest.

Unfolding the Maps app

To start the Maps app, tap its launcher on the Home screen. You might find the launcher inside a Google folder. And, like all apps, it can be located on the apps drawer.

If you're starting the app for the first time or it has been recently updated, you can read the What's New screen; tap the OK or GOT IT button to continue.

Your Android uses its own GPS radio to communicate with global positioning system (GPS) satellites to hone in on your current location. That location appears on the map, as illustrated in Figure 12-1.

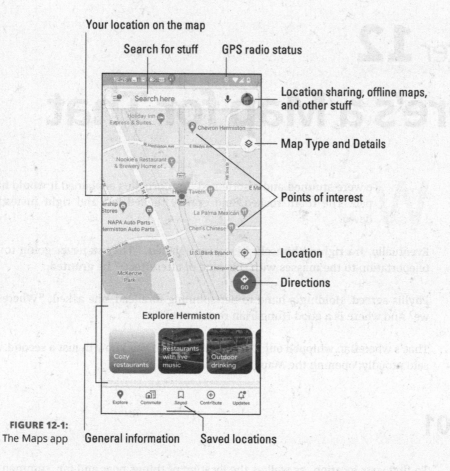

FIGURE 12-1:
The Maps app

Your position appears as a blue dot, illustrated in Figure 12-1. This location is accurate to within a given range, shown by a blue circle around your location. The Android's direction, if detected, is shown by the fuzzy blue triangle that pokes out from under the circle.

Here are some fun things you can do when viewing the map:

Zoom in: To make the map larger (to move it closer), double-tap the screen. You can also spread your fingers on the touchscreen to zoom in.

Zoom out: To make the map smaller (to see more), pinch your fingers on the touchscreen.

Pan and scroll: To see what's to the left or right or at the top or bottom of the map, swipe your finger on the touchscreen. The map scrolls in the direction you swipe.

View your current location: Tap the Location icon, as shown in the margin, to view your location (the blue dot). This feature is handy for those times when you pan and scroll too far away.

Rotate: Using two fingers, rotate the map clockwise or counterclockwise. Tap the Compass Pointer icon, shown in the margin, to reorient the map with north at the top of the screen.

Perspective: Touch the screen with two fingers and swipe up or down to view the map in perspective. You can also tap the Location icon to switch to Perspective view, though that trick works only for your current location. To return to Flat Map view, tap the Compass Pointer icon.

The closer you zoom in on the map, the more detail you see, such as street names, address block numbers, businesses, and other sites — but no tiny people.

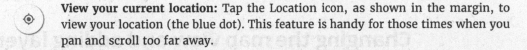

» See the nearby sidebar "Activate location technology!" to confirm that the device's GPS radio presents your location accurately.

» Android tablets are afforded a larger canvas, so the Maps app's features are relocated, thanks to the roomy screen. Despite this difference in presentation, both versions of the app offer the same features.

» When the Location icon is blue, you're viewing your current location on the map. Tap the icon to enter Perspective view. Tap the Perspective icon, shown in the margin, to return to Flat Map view.

» When all you want is a virtual compass, similar to the one you lost as a kid, get a compass app from the Google Play Store. See Chapter 17 for more information about the Google Play Store.

ACTIVATE LOCATION TECHNOLOGY!

The Maps app works best when you activate all the device's location technologies, including both GPS and Wi-Fi radios. To ensure that these technologies are in use, open the Settings app. Choose the Location category and (on non-Samsung devices) tap the Advanced item to ensure that all location services are active.

If you prefer not to allow apps to access your location, deny permission to use the GPS radio to those apps. See Chapter 20 for details on app permissions; Chapter 22 offers information on suppressing location data.

Changing the map view and adding layers

 The standard map view is the street map, shown in Figure 12-1. Two other views are available: Satellite and Terrain. Further, you can add map details to any view. To access these options, tap the Map Type and Details icon, shown in the margin and illustrated in Figure 12-1.

For example, choose Satellite view to observe details on the ground, building locations, and other details normally visible only to aliens planning an invasion. Terrain view is marvelous for bicycling because those streets in Seattle otherwise look pretty flat.

To add a layer to any view, choose the layer from the Map Type and Details palette. For example, the Traffic layer highlights streets green, yellow, and red, depending on the congestion.

To restore the street map, tap the Map Type and Details icon again and choose Default. To remove a layer, such as Traffic, choose it again from the palette.

Saving an offline map

For times when an Internet connection isn't available (which is frequent on a Wi-Fi-only tablet), you can still use the Maps app, though only in a limited capacity. The secret is to save the portion of the map you need to reference. Obey these steps:

1. **View the map chunk you desire to save.**

   Zoom. Pan. Square in the area to save on the screen. It can be as large or as small as you need. Obviously, smaller maps occupy less storage.

2. **Tap your account icon.**

   It's located on the right end of the search box, illustrated in Figure 12-1.

3. **Choose Offline Maps.**

   Any maps you've previously saved appear in the list.

4. **Tap the button labeled Select Your Own Map.**

   Because you've already selected the map in Step 1, you can move on with Step 5.

5. **Tap the DOWNLOAD button.**

   The map's details are downloaded. Eventually, the map appears in the list of offline maps.

To use an offline map, tap your account icon and choose Offline Areas. Choose the offline map to view. The Maps app shows the map's expired data, though if an Internet connection is available, you can tap the UPDATE button to refresh. Otherwise, tap the map's thumbnail to browse the map — but you cannot search or use navigation features while the device is offline.

>> Offline maps remain valid for 30 days. After that time, you must update the map to keep it current. A notification reminds you to update.

>> To remove an offline map, choose it and tap the DELETE button. Tap YES to confirm.

>> If you're out traveling and the Android's Wi-Fi is on, the offline map may display your location. Don't count on this feature to work properly for navigation.

It Knows Where You Are

Many war movies have this cliché scene: Some soldiers are looking at a map. They wonder where they are, when one of them says, "We're not even on the map!" Such things never happen with the Maps app. That's because it always knows where you are.

Well, unless you're on the planet Venus. I've heard that the Maps app won't work there.

Finding a location

The Maps app shows your location as a blue dot on the screen. But where is that? I mean, if you need to contact a tow truck, you can't just say, "I'm the blue dot on the gray slab by the green thing."

Well, you can say that, but it probably won't do any good.

If you desire more information about your location, or any spot on the map, long-press the screen in the Maps app. Up pops a card, like the one shown in Figure 12-2. The card gives your approximate address.

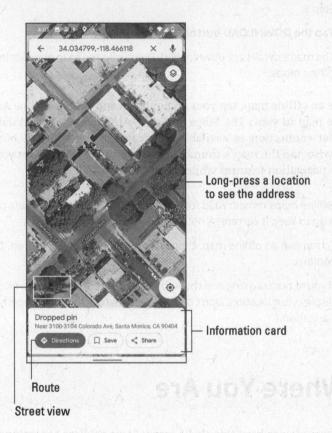

Long-press a location
to see the address

Information card

Route

Street view

On an Android phone, tap the information card to see a screen with more details and additional information. Android tablets show the card on the left side of the screen — no need to tap.

TIP

>> Use the Directions button to get directions to the location. See the later section "Android the Navigator."

>> When you have way too much time on your hands, play with the Street View command. Choosing this option displays the location from a 360-degree perspective. In Street view, you can browse a locale, pan and tilt, or zoom in on details to familiarize yourself with an area, for example — whether you're familiarizing yourself with a location or planning a burglary.

Helping others find your location

TIP

It's possible to use the Maps app to send your current location to a friend. If your pal has a mobile device with smarts like your Android, he can use the coordinates to get directions to your location. Maybe he'll even bring some tacos!

To send your current location, obey these steps:

1. **Tap your account icon on the right end of the Search text box.**

2. **Choose Location Sharing.**

3. **Choose a contact or select an app to share your location.**

For example, tap a contact's thumbnail to compose a text message. Or you can select an app, such as Gmail, to send the location data in an email message.

Any location can be shared by choosing the Share icon from its location card. Follow Step 3 after choosing this icon to select a friend or an app to share the given location.

When the recipient receives the message, he can tap the link to open your location in the Maps app — provided he has an Android device. When the location appears, he can buy this book and follow my advice in the later section "Android the Navigator" for getting to your location. And don't loan anyone this book, either; have them purchase their own copy. Thanks.

Find Things

The Maps app can help you find places in the real world, just like the Google Search app helps you find places on the Internet. Both operations work the same: Open the Maps app and type something to find in the search box. What can you type? Keep reading this section.

Looking for a specific address

To locate an address, type it in the search box. For example:

```
1313 N. Harbor Blvd., Anaheim, CA 92803
```

You may not need to type the entire address: As you tap the keys, suggestions appear onscreen. Choose a matching suggestion to view that location. Otherwise, tap the onscreen keyboard's Search key, and that location appears on the map.

After you find a specific address, the next step is to get directions. See the later section "Android the Navigator."

> You don't need to type the entire address. Oftentimes, all you need is the street number and street name and then either the city name or zip code.

> If you omit the city name or zip code, the Maps app looks for the closest matching address near your current location.

> Tap the X button in the search box to clear the previous search.

Finding a business, restaurant, or point of interest

You may not know an address, but you know when you crave pasta or perhaps the exotic flavors of Manitoba. Maybe you need a hotel or a gas station, or a combination hotel-and-gas-station. To find a business entity or a point of interest, type its name in the search box. For example:

```
Movie theater
```

This search text locates movie theaters on the current Maps screen. Or, to find locations near you, first tap the Location icon (shown in the margin) and then type the search text.

To look for points of interest at a specific location, add the city name, district, or zip code to the search text. For example:

```
Italian food North Park
```

After typing this command and tapping the onscreen keyboard's Search key, you see the assortment of Italian restaurants located in the San Diego metropolitan area, similar to the results shown on the left in Figure 12-3.

Tap a card from the list to view more details, including the exact address, hours of operation, phone number, website, and so on.

> One bonus of searching for a location on an Android phone: On the business's card, tap the Call button. Instantly, your phone dials the location.

> Every pin on the search-results screen represents a matching location. For each pin, a card is available, as shown in Figure 12-3.

> Spread your fingers on the touchscreen to zoom in on the map.

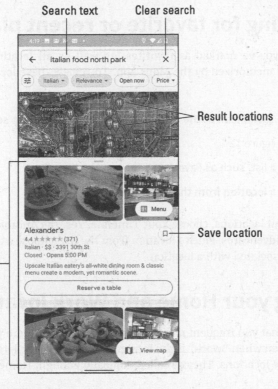

Search text   Clear search

← italian food north park   ✕

Italian ▾   Relevance ▾   Open now   Price ▾

Result locations

Menu

Alexander's   Save location
4.4 ★★★★★ (371)
Italian · $$ · 3391 30th St
Closed · Opens 5:00 PM

Upscale Italian eatery's all-white dining room & classic
menu create a modern, yet romantic scene.

Reserve a table

View map

FIGURE 12-3:
Finding good
pasta near
San Diego   Result card

Marking a favorite place

For locations you visit frequently, consider adding them to your favorite-places list. To do so, follow these steps:

1. **Tap the Save button on a location's card.**

   A card appears, showing location lists available to you. The three preset lists are Favorites, Starred Places, and Want to Go.

2. **Choose a list, such as Favorites.**

   The location is saved.

No difference exists between Favorite, Want to Go, and Starred locations. All are saved, just in different lists. See the next section.

Searching for favorite or recent places

Places that you've marked as favorites, as well as all locations you've visited recently, are memorized by the Maps app. To review these locations, heed these steps:

1. **Tap the Saved icon at the bottom center of the Maps app screen.**

   Refer to Figure 12-1.

2. **Choose a list, such as Favorites.**

3. **Choose a location from the list.**

To view recent locations, choose Your Timeline. Yes, the Android has kept track of your recent adventures. Pluck a location from the list, choose a category, or examine a card associated with a location.

Setting your Home and Work locations

Two places that you frequent most in the real world are where you live and where you work, even when "work" is the local pub. The Maps app lets you create shortcuts for these locations. They're called, logically enough, Home and Work.

To set the Home and Work locations, follow these steps in the Maps app:

1. **Tap your account icon on the right end of the Search text box.**

2. **Choose Settings.**

3. **Choose Edit Home or Work.**

4. **Tap the Home item to enter your home address.**

5. **Tap the Work item to set your work address.**

   If the Home or Work items are already set, tap the Action Overflow and choose the Edit item to change the location.

You can use the Home and Work shortcuts when searching for a location or getting directions. For example, type **Home** into the search box to instantly see where you live, or whichever place you call home. To get directions from your current location to work, type **Work** as the destination. Keep reading in the next section.

Android the Navigator

The real point of having a map and finding a location is to get somewhere else. In the old days, you'd use your eyeballs to plot your route or rely upon directions from an acquaintance or friendly local, or you'd struggle with a folding map you bought at a gas station.

Things are better now. With your Android mobile gizmo, you tap the Directions button and you're on your way. In case you need specifics, here are the steps involved:

1. **Tap the Directions button on a location's card.**

   A card appears, providing spaces to enter the start and destination locations. Your current location is chosen as the default starting point. The destination is set based on the card (or another location) you chose.

2. **Set a starting point.**

   You can type another location or use the Home or Work shortcuts, as described in the preceding section.

   TIP

   If the starting point and destination are reversed, tap the Swap Endpoints icon, illustrated in Figure 12-4.

3. **Choose a mode of transportation.**

   The available options vary, depending on what's available. In Figure 12-4, the items are (from left to right) Car, Public Transportation, On Foot, Ride Services, and Bicycle.

4. **If necessary, tap the alternative route.**

   Alternative routes appear in gray (refer to Figure 12-4). You might choose that route because it's faster, avoids slow traffic, skirts toll roads, and so on. You can also drag the route lines on the map to set your own path.

5. **Tap the Steps button to view a turn-by-turn description of your journey.**

6. **Tap the Start button to begin navigation.**

   The Android narrates your journey, which can be really annoying when you take the bus.

While the Android is navigating, the Navigation notification appears on the status bar, as shown in the margin.

WARNING

The Navigation is important to note because turn-by-turn navigation consumes a lot of battery power, especially when the device's screen is on and the voice is narrating. Ensure that you connect your phone to a power source when navigating. Car adapters are available at any electronics or phone store.

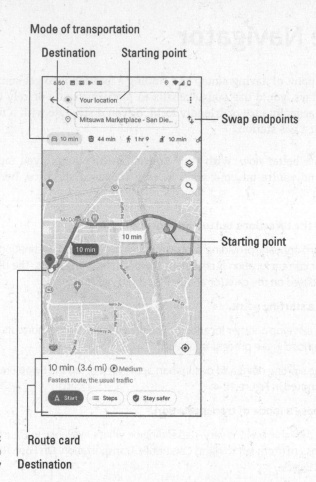

Mode of transportation

Destination   Starting point

Your location

Mitsuwa Marketplace - San Die...   — Swap endpoints

🚗 10 min   🚆 44 min   🚶 1 hr 9   🚴 10 min

Starting point

10 min (3.6 mi) ⓟ Medium
Fastest route, the usual traffic

Start   Steps   Stay safer

Route card

Destination

REMEMBER

>> The map shows your route, highlighted as a blue line on the screen. Detailed directions also appear. Traffic jams show up as red, with slow traffic as yellow.

>> If you tire of hearing the voice, tap the Speaker icon on the navigation screen. Choose Mute or the option to announce alerts-only.

>> If you encounter any issues navigating, tap the Add Report icon, shown in the margin. Choose the type of report to add, such as a traffic incident, detour, speed trap, and so on. Your fellow Android travelers will thank you.

>> To exit from Navigation mode, tap the Close icon on the screen.

>> The Start button appears as Preview whenever you get directions not involving your current location.

>> The Android stays in Navigation mode until you exit. The navigation notification can be seen atop the touchscreen while you're in Navigation mode.

Chapter **13**

Everyone Say "Cheese!"

I have no idea why people say "Cheese" when they get their pictures taken. Supposedly, it's to make them smile. Yet even in other countries, where the native word for *cheese* can't possibly influence the face's smile muscles, they say their word for *cheese* whenever a picture is taken. Apparently, it's a tradition that's present everywhere.

Alexander Graham Bell never thought anyone would utter "cheese" around his invention. That's because the notion of integrating the phone with a camera didn't occur until just before his death. Folks had to wait decades for a phone to take a picture. You don't have to wait at all.

The Android's Camera

A camera snob gladly tells you, "No true camera has a ringtone." You know what? He's correct: Phones and tablets don't make the best cameras. Regardless, the mobile device has completely replaced cameras for all but professionals and serious amateur photographers.

Mobile device cameras have improved over the years, and some take pretty good pictures. That's great. The problem, however, is that not every Android has the same type of camera. Worse: Each manufacturer has its own Camera app.

This section covers the current incantation of the Google Camera app. Your device's Camera app may differ, but basic items are covered in this section.

>> All Androids feature front and rear cameras, though some low-end models may lack one or the other.

>> Both cameras can take still shots and record video.

>> The front camera isn't as powerful as the rear camera. Therefore, the rear camera is considered the primary camera.

TIP

>> If your pictures or videos appear blurry, ensure that the camera lens on the back of the device isn't dirty. Or you may have neglected to remove the plastic cover from the rear camera when you first set up your Android.

>> Only the rear camera features an LED flash, which can be used for both still shots and video. Some tablets lack the LED flash.

>> The Camera app sets the camera's resolution as well as the zoom and whether the flash activates. It's also used to switch between front and rear cameras.

REMEMBER

>> You can take as many pictures or record as much video as you like, as long as the device doesn't run out of space.

Using a mobile camera

To snap a photo or record video, use your Android's Camera app. Its launcher is found on the Home screen, usually in the favorites tray. A lock screen launcher might also be available.

Here are some general tips and suggestions for using the Camera app:

>> The Camera app's basic shooting modes are Still Shot and Video. Additional modes include Panorama, Photo Sphere, and others. Some manufacturers include a host of different shooting modes.

TIP

>> I strongly recommend that you record video in horizontal orientation only. This presentation appears more natural, though most people hold their phones in a vertical orientation.

>> The device's touchscreen serves as the viewfinder; what you see on the screen is exactly what appears in the final photo or video.

- » Like many apps, the Camera app takes over the entire touchscreen. To summon the notifications or navigation icons (Back, Home, Recent), tap the screen or swipe top-to-bottom.

- » Tap the screen to focus on a specific object. You see a focus ring or square that confirms how the camera lens is focusing. Not every device's camera hardware can focus; the front-facing camera features a fixed focus.

- » Spread your fingers on the screen to zoom in.

- » Pinch your fingers on the screen to zoom out.

- » Some Androids let you use the volume key to zoom in or out, though, more commonly, pressing the volume key snaps a still shot — even while recording video.

REMEMBER

- » Hold the Android steady! I recommend using two hands for taking a still shot *and* shooting video.

TECHNICAL STUFF

- » All Androids store pictures and videos in the DCIM/Camera folder. Still images are saved in the JPEG or PNG file format; video is stored in the MPEG-4 format. If your Android offers removable storage, the Camera app automatically saves images and videos to that media, though you might be able to control this feature.

Capturing a still shot

Taking a still image requires only two steps. First, ensure that the Camera app is in Single Shot mode. Second, tap the Shutter icon to snap the photo.

In Still Shot mode, you see the Shutter button appear, as shown for the Google Camera app in Figure 13-1. (Your device's Camera app will look different.) If you don't see the Shutter button, choose the option to enter Still Shot mode, which is titled Camera in the figure. On Samsung devices, Single Shot mode may be titled Photo.

Frame the image. Pinch or spread your fingers on the touchscreen to zoom out or in, respectively. Tap the Shutter icon to snap the photo. You may hear a shutter noise or see a screen effect. The picture is saved and appears as a thumbnail preview in the Camera app, illustrated as "Previous shot" in Figure 13-1.

REMEMBER

- » Items illustrated in Figure 13-1 are available on all Android camera apps. They may not appear in the same location or use the same icon.

- » Set the resolution before you shoot. See the later section "Setting resolution and quality."

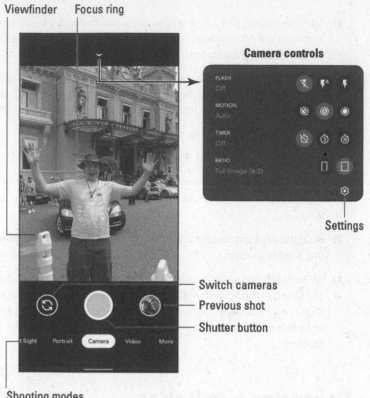

Viewfinder Focus ring

Camera controls

FLASH
Off

MOTION
Auto

TIMER
Off

RATIO
Full image (4:3)

Settings

Switch cameras

Previous shot

Shutter button

t Sight   Portrait   **Camera**   Video   More

FIGURE 13-1:
Still Shot
shooting mode

Shooting modes

>> To review the image, tap the Thumbnail icon. You can swipe through the various shots you've taken. Tap the Back navigation icon to return to the Camera app.

>> If you don't like a photo you just took, tap the Thumbnail icon to view the image. Tap the Delete (trash) icon to remove it.

Recording video

To record video, switch the Camera app to Video mode. For the Google Camera app, choose (or swipe to) the Video shooting mode icon, illustrated in Figure 13-1. To start recording, tap the Record icon, shown in the margin. The elapsed time, and maybe even storage consumed, appears on the touchscreen as video is being recorded.

While recording, the Record icon changes to the Stop icon. You may also see the Pause icon, which temporarily halts recording. Otherwise, tap the Stop icon to end the recording.

REMEMBER

» Video quality is set before you shoot. See the later section "Setting resolution and quality."

» Hold the Android horizontally when you record video. Keep your hands steady. Do not zoom in and out!

Exploring other shooting modes

Beyond still shots and video, all Camera apps offer additional shooting modes. The variety depends on the app, though common modes include Panorama and Photo Sphere.

To select another shooting mode in the Google Camera app, choose the mode from the scrolling list at the bottom of the screen, as illustrated in Figure 13-1. Choose the More item to view additional shooting modes, including Slow Motion, Time Lapse, and Playground. For each mode, a description may appear onscreen to explain what it does and how to shoot in the chosen mode.

The Google Camera app automatically exits a special shooting mode, returning to Still Shot or Video mode. Other Camera apps, however, may require that you reselect the shooting mode.

Camera Settings and Options

The variety of Camera app controls can be overwhelming, especially when a manufacturer gussies up the app with multiple shooting modes. Among the many choices, a few settings and options are common and necessary to properly use the Android's camera.

Switching cameras

You can do more with the device's front-facing camera than take those infamous selfie shots. Exactly what more you can do, I can't think of right now, but the point is how to switch between front and rear cameras while using the Camera app.

The Switch Cameras icon is usually found right on the main Camera app screen, as illustrated in Figure 13-1. Variations of these icons appear in Figure 13-2. If you don't see such an icon on your gizmo's Camera app screen, tap the Action Overflow or Settings icon to look for the Switch Cameras icon or action.

FIGURE 13-2:
Switch Camera icons

Tap the same icon again to switch back to the rear camera. The icon may change its appearance, but you should find it in the same location on the Camera app's screen.

Setting the flash

All Android Camera apps feature three flash settings, Auto, On, and Off, as illustrated in Table 13-1. The current setting may appear on the screen, or, as shown in Figure 13-1, you may have to access settings or some other control to view the current setting.

TABLE 13-1 **Flash Settings**

Setting	Icon	When the Flash Activates
Auto		During low-light situations but not when it's bright out
On		Always
Off		Never, even in low-light situations

If only one setting icon appears, tap it to cycle through and set the camera's flash setting.

>> Not all Android tablets feature a flash on the rear camera, so the flash setting is unavailable on these devices.

>> No Android — phone or tablet — features a flash for the front camera, which is a good thing.

TIP

» A good time to turn on the flash is when taking pictures of people or objects in front of something bright, such as Aunt Ellen showing off her prized peach cobbler in front of a burning munitions factory.

» For shooting video, the flash setting activates the device's LED, turning it on. This setting is made similarly to setting the flash, though the options are only On and Off. It must be set before you shoot video, and yes, it devours a lot of battery power.

Using the self-timer

One common feature found on just about every Camera app is the self-timer. Though it's normally disabled, you can enable this feature to delay taking a still image for a given number of seconds after you tap the Single Shot shutter icon. Supposedly, that gives you enough time to run in front of the device so that you, too, can be in the photo.

To activate the self-timer feature, tap its icon. In the Google Camera app, tap the chevron atop the screen to view the camera controls, as illustrated in Figure 13-1. The TIMER option shows three settings: no delay, a 3-second delay, or a 10-second delay. Tap an icon to choose the self-timer mode.

After you set the timer, tap the Still Shot shutter icon. Then dash out in front of the Android so that it can take your photo.

Oh: You probably want to prop up the phone or tablet on something stable, or even get a mobile device tripod mount. The self-timer is pretty useless without one.

REMEMBER

Turn off the self-timer when you want to return to standard Still Shot mode or when you're exhausted from running around.

Setting resolution and quality

You don't always have to set the highest resolution or top quality for images and videos. Especially when you're shooting for the web or uploading pictures to Facebook, top quality is a waste of storage space and upload time because the image is shown on a relatively low-resolution computer monitor or mobile device screen.

As you may suspect, setting the image resolution or video quality is done differently by the various Camera apps. No matter what, you must set the new still-shot resolution or video quality *before* you shoot.

In the Google Camera app, follow these steps to access still-shot resolution and video quality settings:

1. **Tap the chevron to display the Camera app's controls.**

Refer to Figure 13-1, though on some Camera apps, the Settings icon (see Step 2) is visible on the main screen.

2. **Tap the Settings icon.**

Look for the categories named Photo and Video.

3. **Choose the Photo (or still shot) or Video item to choose a resolution.**

After choosing the proper shooting mode, you may be presented with a slate of options for both the front and rear cameras. Some Camera apps, however, may list fewer options or simply aspect ratios (width-by-height) without listing megapixels or resolution.

>> The *aspect ratio* expresses the relationship between an image's horizontal and vertical dimensions. The 4:3 aspect ratio is 4 units wide by 3 units tall. The typical widescreen computer monitor has an aspect ratio of 16:9.

>> A picture's *resolution* describes how many *pixels,* or dots, are in the image. The more dots, the better the image looks when enlarged.

>> The video quality settings HD and SD refer to High Definition and Standard Definition, respectively. Qualities shown with a "p" value indicate vertical resolution, with higher values for higher quality.

>> The resolution and video quality choices are more limited on the front-facing camera because it's not as sophisticated as the rear camera.

>> Choose lower picture resolution or video quality for recordings you want to share on social media or send as an email or text message attachment.

TECHNICAL STUFF

>> *Megapixel* is a measurement of the amount of information stored in an image. One megapixel is approximately 1 million pixels, or individual dots that comprise an image. It's often abbreviated MP.

Checking the location tag feature

The Camera app not only takes pictures but also keeps track of where you're located when you take the picture — if you've activated this option. The feature is called *save location*, *location tag*, *geotag*, or *GPS-tag*.

To confirm the location tag setting in the Google Camera app, follow these steps:

1. **Tap the chevron to show the camera controls.**

   If the Settings Icon is visible on the main Camera app screen, choose it and skip to Step 3.

2. **Choose Settings.**

3. **Enable or disable the Save Location or Location Tags feature.**

   The master control by the Save Location item is either on or off, reflecting the location tag setting.

The new setting affects only pictures taken from this point forward; deactivating the location tag feature doesn't remove that information from photos you've already taken.

» The location tab information is stored in the picture itself. This means that other devices, apps, and computer programs can read the GPS information to determine where the image was taken.

» See Chapter 14 for information on reviewing a photograph's location.

Chapter **14**

Your Digital Photo Album

Those photos you snap on your Android must go somewhere. The nerds know about folders and files, so they're happy. But how can mere mortal users access their wealth of images and videos? The answer is to open the digital photo album app. It lets you review, manage, edit, and share your visual treasures.

The Photos App

The stock Android app for viewing pictures and videos is called Photos. It's the natural companion to the Camera app, covered in Chapter 13. To start the app, tap its launcher, which may be lurking on the Home screen in the Google folder or, like all apps, found on the apps drawer.

» Not only does the Photos app let you look at pictures and watch videos, but you can also manage that media, edit, and share your visual creations online.

>> The traditional Android photo-management/album app is Gallery. You may still find the Gallery app on your device, though this chapter is specific to the Photos app.

Viewing pics and vids

The Photos app organizes your photos and videos in multiple and confusing ways. The app's main screen, shown in the center of Figure 14-1, lists items by date. Tap the Photos icon at the bottom of the screen to ensure that this view is active.

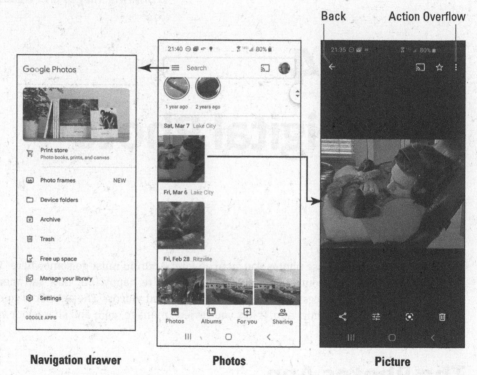

FIGURE 14-1:
Image
organization in
the Photos app

Navigation drawer　　　**Photos**　　　**Picture**

To see any photo albums, tap the Albums icon at the bottom of the screen. Albums are closely associated with your online photos accessed from your Google account, covered elsewhere in this chapter, so these could be albums created on another device that uses your same Google account.

To view an image, tap its thumbnail. You see the image appear full-screen, as shown on the right in Figure 14-1. Swipe the screen left or right to browse your images.

Video thumbnails feature the Play icon, shown in the margin. Tap that icon to view the video. As the video is playing, tap the screen again to view onscreen controls.

>> While you're viewing an image or a video full-screen, the navigation icons may disappear. Tap the screen to view them.

>> Use the Back navigation icon to return to an album after viewing an image or a video. This icon appears in the upper left corner of the screen when viewing a photo, as illustrated in Figure 14-1. (Alas, getting the Back gesture to work in the Photos app is problematic.)

Creating an album

If you prefer to organize your images by album instead of by date, follow these steps in the Photos app:

1. **View an image that you want to add to an album.**

   Ensure that the image is shown full-screen, as shown on the far right in Figure 14-1.

2. **Tap Action Overflow.**

3. **Choose Add to Album.**

4. **Choose an existing album from the list or tap New Album.**

   If you choose an existing album, the image is added to it. Otherwise, continue with Step 5.

5. **Type a name for the album.**

6. **Tap the Done icon to create the album and add the first image.**

7. **Use the Back gesture or tap the Back navigation icon to return to your photo library.**

To add more images to the album, repeat these steps, but choose the specific album in Step 4.

TIP

To add a swath of images to an album, long-press the first one. Continue tapping images to build up a group. Tap the Add (plus) icon, and choose the album from the list.

REMEMBER

To switch between Album and Photos mode, tap the proper icon at the bottom of the Photos app's main screen, as shown in the center in Figure 14-1.

Starting a slideshow

The Photos app can display a slideshow of your images, but without the darkened room and sheet hanging over the mantle. To view a slideshow, follow these steps:

1. **View an image full-screen.**

2. **Tap the Action Overflow icon.**

3. **Choose Slideshow from the scrolling list atop the picture's detail screen.**

   Images from that particular album or date appear one after the other on the screen.

Use the Back gesture or tap the Back navigation icon to exit the slideshow.

 Slideshows don't have to remain on your Android. If a nearby HDMI TV or monitor features a Chromecast dongle, tap the Chromecast icon, as shown in the margin. Choose a specific Chromecast gizmo from the list to view the slideshow on a larger screen. See Chapter 19 for more details on using Chromecast to stream media.

Finding a picture's location

In addition to snapping a picture, your Android's camera records the specific spot on Planet Earth where the photo was taken. This feature, often called a location tag, is covered in Chapter 13. To exploit its efforts and view the map information, view an image in the Photos app and then tap the Action Overflow to view image details. The screen that appears lists details about the image, a date/time stamp, and a map thumbnail showing the location.

Refer to Chapter 13 for directions on disabling the location tag feature.

Edit and Manage Images

The best tool for image editing is a computer amply equipped with photo editing software, such as Photoshop or a similar program that's also referred to as "Photoshop" because the term is pretty much generic. Regardless, you can use the Photos app to perform some minor image surgery.

Editing an image

To enter Image Editing mode in the Photos app, view the image you want to modify and tap the Controls icon, shown in the margin. (This icon is actually the old Settings icon from the 1954 version of the Android operating system, Apple Pie.) If you don't see the editing icon, tap the screen and it shows up.

Editing tools are presented in three categories, shown at the bottom of the screen and illustrated in Figure 14-2: preset effects, image settings, crop/rotate, draw, and extensions.

>> The Preset Effects item presents a scrolling palette (swipe left to right) of options, each of which adjusts the image's tonal qualities.

>> The Image Settings control lets you adjust specific aspects of an image: light, color, and blur. A chevron by the Light and Color items provides more detailed image control.

Cancel edits   Save changes

Action Overflow

Image preview

Extensions

FIGURE 14-2:
Image editing in
the Photos app

Image Settings   Draw/Scribble

Preset Effects   Crop/Rotate

>> The crop and rotate functions are covered in the later sections "Cropping an image" and "Rotating a picture."

>> The draw option lets you scribble on the image using different pen styles and colors.

>> The final item, Extensions, may show one item, Crop, which lets you snip the image in a nonrectilinear fashion.

Tap the Save or Save Copy button when you're done editing. This action replaces the image with your edited copy.

 Tap the Close button to discard your edits. Tap the Discard button to confirm.

Un-editing an image

TIP

The changes you make are directly applied to the image; an original copy isn't retained. To remove any previously applied edits, crops, or rotation effects, view the image in the Photos app and follow these steps:

1. **Tap the Edit icon to edit the image.**
2. **Tap the Action Overflow.**
3. **Choose Undo Edits.**
4. **Tap the Save button.**

The original image is restored.

Cropping an image

To *crop* an image is to snip away parts you don't want or need, similar to taking a pair of scissors to a photograph of you and your old girlfriend, though the process is far less cathartic. To crop an image, obey these steps:

1. **View the image in the Photos app.**
2. **Tap the Edit icon.**
3. **Tap the Crop / Rotate icon.**

   The icon is shown in the margin. The screen changes as illustrated in Figure 14-3. The tools that are presented crop and rotate the image.

Cropping corners

Cropping rectangle

Set rotation angle

Set aspect ratio   90° Tool

FIGURE 14-3:
Rotating and
cropping an
image

4. **Drag any of the four corners to crop the image.**

   As you drag, portions of the image are removed.

TIP

   You can also drag the image within the cropping rectangle to modify the crop action.

5. **Tap the Done button.**

   The image is cropped. You can continue to edit, or tap the Save button to make the changes permanent.

   If you're unhappy with the changes after tapping the Done button, tap the Action Overflow and choose Undo Edits.

TIP

Use the Aspect Ratio icon (refer to Figure 14-3) to adjust the cropping box for the image to a new presentation, such as square, or widescreen.

Rotating a picture

Showing someone else an image on a mobile device can be frustrating, especially when the image is a vertical picture that refuses to fill the screen when the Android is in vertical orientation. To fix this issue, rotate the image in the Photos app. Follow these steps:

1. **Display the cockeyed image.**

2. **Tap the Edit icon.**

3. **Choose the Crop / Rotate tool.**

4. **Tap the 90° icon to rotate the image in 90-degree increments, or drag the rotation angle slider to set a specific angle.**

   Refer to Figure 14-3 for the location of these controls on the editing screen.

5. **Tap the Done button to save the changes.**

   You can continue editing.

6. **Tap the Save button to make the changes permanent.**

Rotating an image to a specific angle also crops the image. This step is necessary to maintain the image's aspect ratio.

Deleting images and videos

It's entirely possible, and often desirable, to remove unwanted, embarrassing, or questionably legal images and videos from the Photos app.

To banish something to the bit dumpster, tap the Delete (trash) icon on the screen when viewing an image or a video. Tap the Move to Trash button to confirm.

>> If you don't see the Delete icon, the item cannot be deleted. It's most likely a copy pulled in from a web photo-sharing service or a social networking site.

>> To view the Trash album, tap the Side Menu icon and choose Trash from the navigation drawer.

>> Items held in the Trash album are automatically deleted after 60 days. To hasten their departure, long-press items in the Trash album and then tap the Delete icon atop the screen.

Set Your Pictures and Videos Free

Keeping your precious moments and memories in your phone or tablet is an elegant solution to the problem of lugging around photo albums. But when you want to show your pictures to the widest possible audience, you need a bigger stage. That stage is the Internet, and you have many ways to send and save your pictures.

Visiting Google Photos online

The Photos app is linked with your Android account, and your device's photos have a home on the Internet, called Google Photos. To visit that site on a computer, go to photos.google.com and sign in to your Google account.

Your Android automatically synchronizes your photos and videos with Google Photos, so don't be surprised when you see them online. The process is called *image backup*, and you can check its status by following these steps:

1. **In the Photos app, tap the Side Menu icon.**

2. **On the navigation drawer, choose Settings.**

3. **Choose Back Up & Sync.**

4. **Check the master control by the Back Up & Sync item.**

   If the master control is off, turn it on to enable photo backup.

Disabling this setting doesn't affect any images already backed up to Google Photos, though any new images you snap or videos you record are no longer shared online and you won't be able to access those images from other Android devices.

Posting a video to YouTube

The best way to share a video is to upload it to YouTube. As a Google account holder, you also have a YouTube channel. It's like Channel 6 on the TV when you grew up, but far fewer people watch it. That's because you've not yet populated your channel with exciting videos. Start now:

1. **Ensure that the Wi-Fi connection is activated.**

   The best way to upload a video is to turn on the Wi-Fi connection, which (unlike the mobile cellular network) doesn't incur data surcharges.

2. **Open the Photos app.**

3. **View the video you want to upload.**

   You do not need to play the video; just have it on the screen.

4. **Tap the Share icon.**

   If you don't see the Share icon, tap the screen and it shows up.

5. **Choose YouTube from the list of sharing apps.**

   The Add Details card appears. You may first see a tutorial on trimming the video, which is the next step.

6. **Trim the video, if necessary, resetting the starting and ending points.**

   If you opt to trim, drag the starting and ending points for the video left or right. As you drag, the video is scrubbed, allowing you to preview the start and end points.

7. **Type the video's title.**

8. **Set other options.**

   Type a description, set the privacy level, add descriptive tags, and so on.

9. **Tap the UPLOAD button.**

   You return to the Photos app, and the video is uploaded. It continues to upload even if the screen locks itself out of boredom or you do other things on the Android.

When the upload has completed, a YouTube notification appears. After the video has finished processing on the Internet and is available for viewing, you receive a Gmail message, announcing your video's publication.

To view your video, open the YouTube app. See Chapter 16 for details.

Sharing images with other apps

Just about every app wants to get in on the sharing bit, especially when it comes to pictures and videos. The key is to view an item full-screen in the Photos app and then tap the Share icon, as shown in the margin. Choose an app to share the image or video, and that item is instantly sent to that app.

What happens next?

That depends on the app. For Facebook, Twitter, and other social networking apps, the item is attached to a new post. For Gmail, the item becomes an attachment. Other apps treat images and videos in a similar manner, somehow incorporating the item(s) into whatever wonderful thing that app does. The key is to look for that Share icon.

IN THIS CHAPTER

» **Finding music on your Android**

» **Enjoying a tune**

» **Managing the song queue**

» **Adding music to the library**

» **Organizing your tunes into a playlist**

» **Listening to Internet radio**

Chapter **15**

Music, Music, Music

Your Android's amazing arsenal of features includes the capability to play music. I'm not referring to the sounds made by the touch-tone dialing on an Android phone, either. Playing music is why your phone or tablet is an all-in-one device. It's the reason you don't need to lug around that Edison wax cylinder phonograph everywhere you go.

The Hits Just Keep on Comin'

Your Android mobile gizmo is ready to entertain you with music whenever you want to hear it. Plug in some headphones, summon the music-playing app, and choose tunes to match your mood.

The stock Android music-playing app is called Play Music. It might be in addition to other musical apps on your device. For now, the topic is Play Music.

>> As with other Google services, music on your Android that's available through the Play Music app is also available online at play.google.com/music.

>> See the later section "Music from the Stream" for details on streaming music apps.

Browsing your music library

The music stored on your Android, or available through your Google account in the cloud, is referred to as your *music library*. To view its collection of tunes, heed these directions:

1. **Open the Play Music app.**

2. **Tap the Side Menu icon to display the navigation drawer.**

   The Side Menu icon is found in the upper left corner of the screen, similar to the one shown in the margin. If you see a left-pointing arrow instead, tap that arrow until the Side Menu icon appears.

3. **Choose Music Library.**

Figure 15-1 shows the Play Music app with the Music Library screen selected. Your music is organized by categories, shown as tabs on the screen. Tap a tab to switch categories, or swipe the screen left or right to browse your music library.

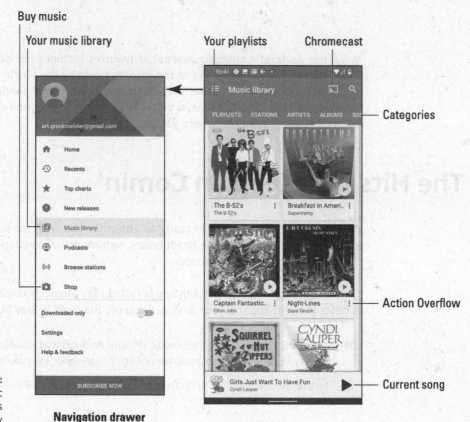

Buy music

Your music library

Your playlists

Chromecast

Categories

Action Overflow

Current song

FIGURE 15-1: The Play Music app, Albums category

Navigation drawer

The categories make your music easier to find, because you don't always remember song, artist, or album names. The Genres category is for those times when you're in the mood for a certain type of music but don't know, or don't mind, who recorded it.

>> Is your music library empty or pathetically small? Get some music! See the later section "Add Some Music to Your Life."

>> Songs and albums feature the Action Overflow icon, shown in the margin. Use that icon to view actions associated with the album or artist.

>> Two types of album artwork are used by the Play Music app. For purchased music, or music recognized by the app, original album artwork appears. Otherwise, the app shows a generic album cover.

>> When the Play Music app doesn't recognize an artist, it uses the title Unknown Artist. This happens with music you copy manually to your device, but it can also apply to audio recordings you make.

Playing a tune

When you've found the proper tune to enhance your mood, play it! Tap a song to play that song. Tap an album to view songs in the album, or tap the album's large Play button, shown in the margin, to listen to the entire album.

While a song plays, controls appear at the bottom of the screen, as shown at the bottom of Figure 15-1. Tap that strip to view the song full-screen, as shown in Figure 15-2.

After the song is over, the next song in the list plays. The order depends on how you start the song. For example, if you start a song from Album view, all songs in that album play in the order listed.

The next song doesn't play when you have the Shuffle button activated (refer to Figure 15-2). In that case, the Play Music app randomly chooses another song from the same list. Who knows which one is next?

The next song also might not play when you have the Repeat option on: The three repeat settings, along with the shuffle settings, are illustrated in Table 15-1. To change settings, tap the Shuffle button or Repeat icon.

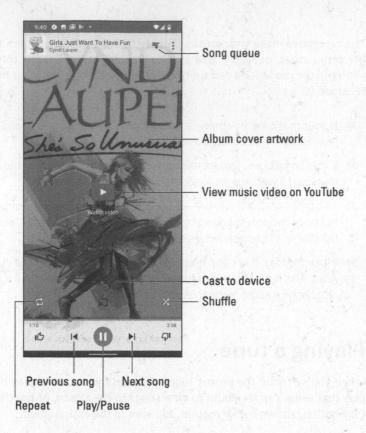

— Song queue

— Album cover artwork

— View music video on YouTube

— Cast to device

— Shuffle

| | 1:10 | | | | 3:58 | |

Previous song   Next song

Repeat   Play/Pause

TABLE 15-1

Shuffle and Repeat Icons

Icon	Setting	What Happens When You Touch the Icon
	Shuffle Is Off	Songs play one after the other.
	Shuffle Is On	Songs are played in random order.
	Repeat Is Off	Songs don't repeat.
	Repeat Current Song	The same song plays over and over.
	Repeat All Songs	All songs in the list play over and over.

While the song plays, you're free to do anything else on your Android. In fact, the song continues to play even when the device is locked. Choose the Play Music notification, shown in the margin, to return to the Play Music app, or you can use the controls on the notification drawer or on the lock screen to pause the song or skip to the next or previous tune.

To stop the song from playing, tap the Pause icon, labeled in Figure 15-2.

REMEMBER

» Use the device's volume key to set the volume. This key works whether the device is locked or unlocked.

» Music controls appear on the lock screen as a notification. Use the controls to play, pause, or skip the song. This feature is available only when lock screen notifications are displayed. See Chapter 22.

» On an Android phone, an incoming call stops the music. You hear the ringtone and can answer the call. After the call ends, you must restart the song: Visit the Play Music app and tap the Play icon.

» The music does not stop playing for an incoming call when it's being streamed to another device. Streaming or casting music is a great way to share it with friends or during a party. Refer to Chapter 19 for details about casting.

» Music on your Android is streamed from the cloud. That means music won't play when an Internet connection is unavailable. Unless:

» You can download music to play it without an Internet connection. Directions are offered in Chapter 17.

» Use the Play Music app's Search command to locate tunes in your music library. Tap the Search icon, illustrated in the margin. Type a song name, artist, or album, and then tap the Search icon on the onscreen keyboard. Choose the song you want to hear from the list that's displayed.

» When a song is playing or paused, its album artwork might appear as the lock screen wallpaper. Don't let this change alarm you.

Queuing up the next song

It's fun to randomly listen to your music library, plucking out tunes like a mad DJ. Oftentimes, however, you don't have the patience to wait for the current song to finish before choosing the next tune. The solution is to add songs to the queue. Follow these steps:

1. Browse your music library for the next song (or album) you want to play.

2. Tap the song's Action Overflow.

3. **Choose Add to Queue.**

The Play Music app adds the song to the list of tunes to play next.

Songs are added to the queue in the order you tap them. That is, unless you choose instead the Play Next command in Step 3, in which case the tune is inserted at the top of the queue.

 To review the queue, tap the Song Queue icon, shown in the margin as well as in Figure 15-2. Songs in the queue play in order, from the top down. To change the order, drag a song card up or down. To remove a song from the queue, swipe its card left or right.

 If you like your queue, consider making a playlist of those same songs. See the section "Saving the song queue as a playlist," later in this chapter.

TIP

Add Some Music to Your Life

To pack your Android full of those songs you adore, you have two options:

» Buy lots of music from the Google Play Store, which is what Google stockholders want you to do.

» Borrow music from your computer, which Google stockholders also want you to do, just not as enthusiastically as the first option.

Buying music

To buy a song or an album, tap the Side Menu icon to display the navigation drawer and then choose the Shop item (refer to Figure 15-1). You're immediately thrust into the Google Play Store, where you can browse music, listen to samples, and purchase tunes until your bank account is dry. Though it's not the same experience as spending a gentle summer evening in a Tower Records store during your youth, it's the "Googly" way to build your Android's music library.

» Refer to Chapter 17 for more information on Google Play, including how to purchase an item. As this book goes to press, you cannot use the Play Store app directly to buy music; you must access the musical portion of the store from the Play Music app.

>> Music you purchase from Google Play is available to all your Android devices or any computer that can access the play.google.com/music page on the Internet.

Getting music into the Google cloud

Realizing that you probably don't want to buy yet another copy of the Beatles' *White Album*, you can take songs from your computer and transfer them to your Google Play Music library on the Internet. Here's how that procedure works:

1. **Open the computer's web browser and visit** music.google.com.

2. **If necessary, sign-in to your Google/Gmail account.**

You see a copy of your Play Music library, including your playlists and any recent songs. You can even listen to your music right there on the computer, but no: You have music to upload.

3. **On the web page, click the Side Menu button.**

It's located in the upper left corner of the window.

4. **From the list of commands, choose Upload Music.**

5. **Drag music into the web browser window.**

Drag from a folder directly or, better, open a music-playing program such as Windows Media Player and drag directly from there into the browser window.

Google may prompt you to configure your PC, so work through those gyrations described on the web page. Follow the steps presented on the web page to continue uploading music.

>> You can repeat these steps to upload tens of thousands of songs. Yes, this task takes time, but think of all the money you're not spending twice.

>> The songs you upload are available to your Android, just like any other songs in your music library.

Synchronizing music directly

Some Androids may let you copy music directly from the computer. The trick is to convince the computer's music jukebox program that the Android is a portable MP3 player — which it is, of course. Then you transfer or "sync" the music, adding a copy of the computer's music to the Android.

The process works like this:

1. **Connect the Android to your PC.**

   See Chapter 19 for details on making the connection. Choose the File Transfer option to connect.

2. **On the PC, choose Windows Media Player from the AutoPlay notification or dialog box.**

   If the AutoPlay dialog box doesn't appear, start the Windows Media Player program: Press the Windows key on the PC's keyboard and type **windows media player**. Choose that program from the list of search results.

3. **Choose your Android from the Sync List, as illustrated in Figure 15-3.**

   Click the Next Device link until you see your gizmo, such as the Samsung phone shown in Figure 15-3.

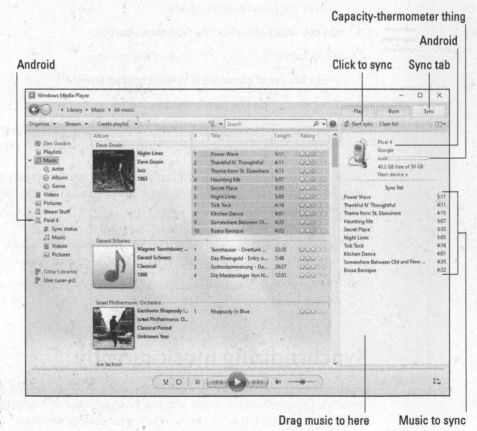

FIGURE 15-3: Windows Media Player meets Android phone

4. **Drag music to the Sync area.**

Drag an individual song or an entire album.

5. **Click the Start Sync button to transfer the music from the PC to your Android.**

The Start Sync button may be located atop the list, as shown in Figure 15-3, or at the bottom.

When you're done, close Windows Media Player and disconnect the Android.

This technique may not work for all devices. In some cases, the manufacturer may configure the device to ignore the Windows Media Player music file format. Therefore, I recommend trying to sync a few tunes to start and then confirm that they appear in the Play Music app.

>> You cannot use iTunes to synchronize music with Android devices. Duh.

WARNING

>> Your Android can store only so much music! Don't be overzealous when copying your tunes. In Windows Media Player (refer to Figure 15-3), a capacity-thermometer thing shows you how much storage space is used and how much is available on your Android. Pay heed to the indicator!

Organize Your Music

The Play Music app categorizes your music by album, artist, song, and so forth, but unless you have only one album and enjoy all the songs on it, this organization probably won't do. To better manage your music, you can create playlists. That way, you can hear the music you want to hear, in the order you want, for whatever mood hits you.

Reviewing your playlists

To view available playlists, choose the PLAYLISTS category on the Music Library screen in the Play Music app (refer to Figure 15-1). Playlists are displayed in two categories: Auto Playlists, generated by the Play Music app, and All Playlists, which contains playlists you created.

To see which songs are in a playlist, tap the playlist's card. To play the songs in the playlist, tap the first song in the list.

TIP

>> The Auto playlists include Thumbs Up, which lists songs you've liked by tapping the Thumbs Up icon; Last Added, which includes songs recently purchased or added; and Free and Purchased, which includes just about everything.

>> Use the playlist feature to organize music that isn't otherwise organized in the Play Music app. For example, if you're like me, you probably have a lot of songs labeled *Unknown*. A quick way to remedy this situation is to name a playlist after the artist and then add those "unknown" songs to the playlist.

Building a playlist

To create a new playlist, follow these steps:

1. **Locate some music you want to add to a playlist.**

Ensure that you're viewing a song or an album; otherwise, the Action Overflow icon and Add to Playlist action don't show up.

2. **Tap the Action Overflow icon by the album or song.**

3. **Choose Add to Playlist.**

4. **Tap NEW PLAYLIST.**

5. **Type a name for the playlist.**

Make the name short and descriptive. *Elvis*. That's a playlist.

6. **Tap the CREATE PLAYLIST button.**

The song or album is added to the new playlist.

To add songs to an existing playlist, choose the playlist in Step 4.

>> You can have tons of playlists and stick as many songs into them as you like. Adding songs to a playlist doesn't noticeably affect the device's storage capacity.

>> To remove a song from a playlist, open the playlist and tap the Action Overflow by the song, and then choose Remove from Playlist.

>> Removing a song from a playlist doesn't delete the song from the music library; see the later section "Removing unwanted music."

>> Songs in a playlist can be rearranged: While viewing the playlist, use the tab on the far left end of a song's card to drag it up or down in the list.

>> To delete a playlist, tap the Action Overflow icon in the Playlist icon's lower right corner. Choose Delete and tap OK to confirm.

Saving the song queue as a playlist

If you've created a song queue and it's a memorable one, consider saving that queue as a playlist that you can listen to over and over. Obey these directions:

1. **Tap the Song Queue icon to view the song queue.**

   Refer to the earlier section "Queuing up the next song" for details on the song queue.

2. **Tap the Action Overflow icon next to the Song Queue icon.**

3. **Choose Save Queue.**

4. **Tap the NEW PLAYLIST button.**

   Or you can add the songs to an existing playlist: Select the playlist from the Add to Playlist card.

5. **Fill in the New Playlist card with a name and description.**

6. **Tap the CREATE PLAYLIST button.**

The songs in the current queue now either dwell in their own playlist or have been added to an existing playlist.

Removing unwanted music

To remove a song or an album, tap its Action Overflow icon. Choose the Delete action. Tap the OK button to remove the song. Bye-bye, music.

TIP

I don't recommend removing music. The music on your Android is actually stored in the cloud, on Google's Play Music service. Therefore, removing the music doesn't affect the device's storage. So, unless you totally despise the song or artist, removing the music has no effect.

>> Music can be stored locally by downloading it to the phone or tablet, as described in the earlier section "Synchronizing music directly." Again, if you remove such music, it's gone for good.

>> You can also download music to the device for listening when an Internet connection isn't available. See Chapter 17.

Music from the Stream

Though they're not broadcast radio stations, some sources on the Internet — *Internet radio* sites — play music. These Internet radio apps are available from Google Play. Some free services that I can recommend are

>> Pandora Radio

>> Spotify

>> TuneIn Radio

These as well as other, similar apps are available for free. Paid versions might also be found on Google Play. The paid versions generally provide unlimited music with no advertising.

>> Google offers an unlimited music listening service. You can tap the item SUBSCRIBE NOW on the navigation drawer to sign up or just succumb to the overabundance of random "subscribe" prompts that appear as you use the app.

>> It's best to listen to Internet radio when your phone or tablet is connected to the Internet via a Wi-Fi connection.

WARNING

>> Be wary of music subscription services offered through your Android's manufacturer or cellular provider. Their services aren't as long-lasting and well-supported as the others mentioned in this section.

TECHNICAL STUFF

>> Music provided over the Internet is referred to as *streaming*. That's because the music arrives on your Android as a continuous download from the source. Unlike music you download and save, streaming music is played as it comes in and isn't stored long-term.

Chapter **16**

Various and Sundry Apps

Your Android has its limitations. For example, you cannot use an Android phone as a yoga block. An Android tablet makes a poor kitchen cutting board. And despite efforts by European physicists, an Android mobile device simply cannot compete with the Large Hadron Collider. Still, for more everyday purposes, I believe you'll find your device more than up to the task.

Clock

Your Android's chronometric app is appropriately named Clock. It features a timer, a stopwatch, an alarm, and world clock functions. Of these activities, setting an alarm is quite useful: In that mode, your gizmo becomes a nightstand companion — and, potentially, your early morning nemesis.

To set an alarm in the Clock app, follow these steps:

1. **Tap the Alarm icon or tab on the Clock app's screen.**

    The four tabs in the stock Android Clock app are Alarms, Clock (for the world clock), Timer, and Stopwatch.

2. **Tap the Add icon.**

   A card appears, which you use to set the alarm time, days, name, and so on.

3. **Fill in details about the alarm.**

   Set the alarm's time. Determine whether it repeats daily or only on certain days. Choose a ringtone. Ponder over any other settings, as shown on the card. The alarm name appears when the alarm triggers.

4. **Set the alarm.**

   Slide the alarm card's master control to the On position to ensure that the alarm signals at the appropriate time and schedule.

You can confirm that an alarm is set when you see the Alarm Set status icon atop the touchscreen, as shown in the margin.

When the alarm triggers, slide the Dismiss icon or press the volume key. Some alarms may feature the Snooze icon. Tap it to be annoyed again after a few minutes.

REMEMBER

>> Alarms must be set to activate.

>> The Clock app is frequently customized by various device manufacturers, though the general operation works as described in this section.

>> Unsetting an alarm doesn't delete the alarm. To remove an alarm, tap the alarm to select it and then tap the Delete (trash) icon.

>> The alarm doesn't work when you turn off the Android. The alarm may not sound when Do Not Disturb mode is active. The alarm does trigger when the touchscreen is locked.

>> So tell me: Do alarms go off, or do they go on?

Calculator

The Calculator is perhaps the oldest of all traditional cell phone apps. It's probably also the least confusing and frustrating app to use.

The stock Android Calculator app appears in Figure 16-1. The version you see on your device may look different, though the basic operation remains the same.

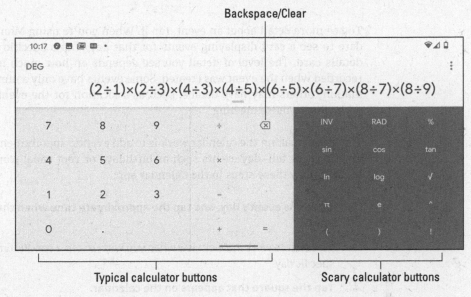

FIGURE 16-1:
The
Calculator app

Typical calculator buttons   Scary calculator buttons

Tap various buttons on the Calculator app screen to input your equations. Parentheses buttons can help you determine which part of a long equation gets calculated first.

>> Also, consider changing the device's orientation to see more or fewer buttons; the image in Figure 16-1 uses horizontal orientation, which shows the calculator's more terrifying buttons.

>> The Calculator app may not rotate automatically. If not, look for a rotation button when reorienting your Android.

>> Long-press the calculator's text (or results) to copy the results. This trick may not work in every Calculator app.

TIP

Calendar

To check your schedule and browse events, open the Calendar app. You see upcoming dates shown in one of several views: Month, Week, and Day views are most common, along with Schedule view, which simply lists upcoming events. Tap the Side Menu icon to view the navigation drawer, from which you can change the current view.

To browse events in the Calendar app, swipe the screen left or right. If you need to return to today's date, tap the Go to Today icon, shown in the margin.

To see more detail about an event, tap it. When you're using Month view, tap the date to see a card displaying events for that day. Tap a specific event to see its details card. The level of detail you see depends on how much information was recorded when the event was created. Some events have only a minimum of information; others may have details, such as a location for the event, the time, and with whom you're meeting.

The key to making the calendar work is to add events: appointments, things to do, meetings, or full-day events such as birthdays or root canal work. To create an event, follow these steps in the Calendar app:

1. Go to the event's day, and tap the approximate time when the event starts.

It's easier to work in Week view when you want to tap a specific time on a specific day.

2. Tap the square that appears on the calendar.

When you tap a specific time, a square appears. This is secretly a new event button.

3. Add information about the event.

REMEMBER

The more information you supply, the more detailed the event and the more you can do with it on your Android and with Google Calendar on the Internet. Here are some of the many items you can set when creating an event:

- *Title:* The name of the event, person you're meeting, or destination.

- *Calendar Category:* Choose a specific calendar to help organize and color-code your events.

- *Time/Duration:* If you followed Step 1 in this section, you don't have to set a starting time. Otherwise, specify the time the event starts and stops, or choose to set an all-day event such as a birthday or your mother-in-law's visit that was supposed to last for an hour.

- *Location:* Type the location just as though you're searching for a location in the Maps app.

- *Repeat:* Use the Repeat setting to configure events on a recurring schedule.

- *Notification/Reminder:* Set an email, text message, or Calendar notification to signal an upcoming event.

4. Tap the Save button to create the new event.

The new event appears on the calendar, reminding you that you need to do something on such-and-such a day with what's-his-face.

When an event's date-and-time arrives, the Event Reminder notification appears, as shown in the margin. You might also receive a Gmail notification or text message, depending on how you chose to be reminded when the event was created. If your Android is handy, the event reminder appears on the lock screen.

>> The Calendar app works with your Google account to keep track of your schedule and appointments. You can visit Google Calendar on the web at

`calendar.google.com`

 >> Before you throw away your datebook, copy into the Calendar app some future appointments and info, such as birthdays and anniversaries.

>> Schedule view might be called Agenda or Tasks in some versions of the Calendar app.

>> Birthdays and a few other events on the calendar may be pulled in from the Android's address book or from social networking apps. That probably explains why some events are listed twice — they're pulled in from two sources.

>> When the event's location is listed, you can tap that item to open the Maps app. See where the event is being held and get directions, as covered in Chapter 12.

>> The Calendar widget also provides a useful way to see upcoming events directly on the Home screen. See Chapter 20 for information on applying widgets to the Home screen.

 >> Tap an existing event to modify it. Tap the Edit icon (shown in the margin) to make any changes.

 >> For events that repeat twice a week or twice a month, create two repeating events. For example, when you have meetings on the first and third Mondays, you create two separate events: one for the first Monday and another for the third. Then have each event repeat monthly.

>> To remove an event, tap the event to bring up its card. Look for the DELETE button or icon. If you don't find it, tap the Action Overflow icon on the card and choose Delete. Tap OK to confirm. For a repeating event, choose whether to delete only the current event or all future events.

>> Setting an event's time zone is necessary only when the event takes place in another time zone or spans time zones, such as an airline flight. In that case, the Calendar app automatically adjusts the starting and stopping times for events, depending on where you are.

 >> If you forget to set the time zone and you end up hopping around the world, your events are set according to the time zone in which they were created, not the local time.

TECHNICAL STUFF

» Avoid using the Phone and Device categories for your events. Events in those categories appear on your Android, but aren't shared with your Google account.

» Calendar categories are handy because they let you organize and color-code your events. They can be confusing because Google calls them *calendars.* I think of them more as *categories:* I have different calendars (categories) for my personal and work schedules, government duties, clubs, and so on.

» New calendar categories are created on the web at calendar.google.com. You cannot create them from within the Calendar app.

eBook Reader

To sate your electronic-book-reading desires, your Android comes with Google's eBook reader app, Play Books. It offers you access to your eBook library, plus the multitudinous tomes available from the Google Play Store; see Chapter 17.

Open the Play Books app. You might find it in the Google folder on the Home screen, or it might be in its own Play folder. The app is also located on the apps drawer. And if it's not installed on your device, you can obtain it from the Play Store app.

The first screen you see might instead be Google Play, trying to sell you books. If so, tap the Library button, shown in the margin and at the bottom center of the Play Books app screen, to view your digital bookshelf.

Swipe the screen to browse and scroll through the library.

Tap a book's cover to open it. If you've opened the book previously, you return to the page you last read. Otherwise, you see the book's first page.

Figure 16-2 illustrates the basic book-reading operation in the Play Books app. You swipe the screen right-to-left to turn pages. You can also tap either the far left or right side of the screen to turn pages. If you don't see this view, tap the touchscreen; normally, the text is displayed in a larger format than is shown in the figure.

TIP

The Play Books app works in both vertical and horizontal orientations. To lock the screen orientation, tap the Action Overflow and choose Settings, and then choose the Auto-Rotate Screen item. Select how you want the screen to present itself while you use the Play Books app.

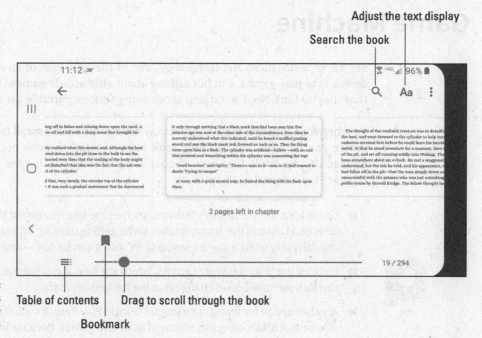

Adjust the text display

Search the book

FIGURE 16-2:
eBook controls
in the Play
Books app

Table of contents

Bookmark

Drag to scroll through the book

>> Books in your Play Books library are stored on the Internet and available to read only when an Internet connection is active. It's possible to keep a book on your Android by downloading it to the device.

>> To remove a book from the library, tap the Action Overflow icon on the book's cover and then choose the Delete from Library command. Tap the DELETE button to confirm.

>> Tap the *Aa* icon to display a menu of options for adjusting the text on the screen and the brightness.

>> eBooks lack indexes. That's because the text layout on digital pages changes based on the book's presentation. Therefore, use the Search icon to look for items in the text.

>> A copy of your eBook library is available on the Play Books website:

```
play.google.com/books
```

>> Refer to Chapter 17 for information on obtaining books from Google Play.

>> If you have a Kindle device, you can obtain the Amazon Kindle app for your Android. Use the app to access books you've purchased for the Kindle or as a supplement to Google Play Books.

Game Machine

For all its seriousness and technology, one of the best uses of an Android mobile device is to play games. I'm not talking about silly arcade games (though I admit that they're fun). No, I'm talking about some serious portable gaming.

To whet your appetite, your Android may have come with a small taste of what the device can do regarding gaming; look for preinstalled game apps on the apps drawer. If you don't find any, choose from among the hordes available from Google Play, covered in Chapter 17.

TIP

>> Game apps use the device's features, such as the touchscreen or the accelerometer, to control the action. It takes some getting used to, especially if you regularly play using a game console or PC, but it can be fun — and addicting.

>> Look for the "lite" versions of games, which are free. If you like the game, you can fork over the pocket change that the full version costs.

>> Another option for trying out games is Google Play Pass. It's a subscription service that offers access to zillions of apps and games. Because you pay for the subscription, the apps are blissfully free of in-game advertising and other annoyances. Visit this website for details:

```
play.google.com/about/play-pass
```

Voice Recorder

Though it can't record conversations on the phone, Google's Recorder app adds another interesting dimension to your Android's capabilities. Use the app to record your voice or any sound, but with your voice the app also transcribes your utterances into text. You can even use your voice to search for items, which is technology Mr. Spock could only dream about.

The Recorder app may not be available on your Android. If not, look for the Voice Recorder app from Google LLC. Some devices may feature another, similar app, such as the Samsung Voice Recorder.

Your Pal, Google

Your Android isn't out to control your life, but it's willing to help. Don't freak out! The device harbors no insidious intelligence, and the Robot Uprising is still years away. What I'm referring to is Google Assistant. It's an upgrade from the old Google Now app, which offers 2-way conversation and helpful information as you go about your daily routine.

The Google Assistant app is titled *Google.* You might also see a Google widget affixed to the Home screen. Tap that widget, open the Google app, or utter "Okay, Google" or "Hey, Google" to access Google Assistant.

The gesture to quickly access your Google assistant is to swipe upward from the lower left or lower right corner of the screen. On some devices, the Google Assistant app dwells on the far-left Home screen page.

When Google Assistant is active, your job is to speak simple search terms. For example, you can utter, "When is the next Billie Eilish album coming out?" or any of these common phrases:

>> Will it rain tomorrow?

>> What time is it in Oslo?

>> Set an alarm for 90 minutes from now.

>> How many euros equal $25?

>> Take a picture.

>> What are the directions to Epcot?

>> Where is the nearest Canadian restaurant?

>> What's the score of the Lakers–Celtics game?

>> What is the answer to life, the universe, and everything?

You can use Google Assistant to search the Internet, just as you would use Google's main web page. In fact, don't even bother going to the web page on your Android; just say, "Okay, Google!"

Samsung galactic gizmos feature Google Assistant in addition to their own Bixby helper-thing. Bixby occupies the far-left Home screen page, and it can also be activated by pressing the Bixby button on newer Samsung devices.

Video Entertainment

Your Android has plenty of options available for your video entertainment. The default apps are YouTube, for general video fun and amazement, and Play Movies & TV, for buying and renting movies and TV shows. And when you tire of these options, you can explore other apps at the Play Store, such as Netflix, Hulu, and HBO Now, or give up on Hollywood and use the Camera app to make your own videos.

YouTube: It's the Internet phenomenon that proves that real life is indeed too boring and random for television. Or is it the other way around? Regardless, you can view the latest videos on YouTube — or contribute your own — by using the YouTube app.

Play Movies & TV: Use the Play Movies & TV app to watch videos you've rented or purchased from Google Play. Open the app and choose the video from the main screen. Items you've purchased show up in the app's library. See Chapter 17.

REMEMBER

>> Because you have a Google account, you also have a YouTube account. I recommend that you sign in to your YouTube account when using YouTube on your Android: Tap the Action Overflow icon and choose Sign In.

>> Use the YouTube app to view YouTube videos, rather than use the web browser app to visit the YouTube website.

>> Orient the device horizontally to view a video in a larger size. Or, better:

>> Tap the Chromecast icon to stream the video to a large-screen HDTV or monitor. See Chapter 19.

>> Any videos you've purchased from Google Play are available on the Internet for anytime viewing. Visit

`play.google.com/movies`

IN THIS CHAPTER

» **Obtaining Android stuff**

» **Downloading an app and more**

» **Dealing with bad apps**

» **Building a wish list**

» **Sending an app suggestion to a friend**

» **Keeping media on the device**

Chapter **17**

Google Play Shopping

The place to find more apps, books, music, and video for your Android mobile gizmo is a digital marketplace called Google Play. The good news is that most of the stuff available is free. Better news is that the non-free stuff is cheap. For little or no cost, you can add new apps and media to expand your Android's capabilities. Alas, I've still not located a Mow the Lawn or Do the Dishes app.

Welcome to the Store

It reads like the name of a kid's clothing store, but Google Play is where you obtain new apps, books, movies, music, and other goodies for your beloved Android gizmo. Google Play is the name of the store. And to keep you confused, the app is named Play Store.

TIP

>> You obtain goodies from Google Play over an Internet connection. Therefore:

>> I recommend that you connect your device to a Wi-Fi network when you shop at Google Play. Wi-Fi not only gives you speed but also helps avoid data surcharges. See Chapter 18 for details.

>> Though you can buy music in the Play Store app, the only way to get there is from the Play Music app. Refer to Chapter 15.

>> The Play Store app is frequently updated, so its look may change from what you see in this chapter. Some devices may display additional items or reorder the categories, though the default Play Store app is shown in this chapter.

Browsing Google Play

To access Google Play, open the Play Store app. You may find the Launcher icon on the Home screen; otherwise, it's located on the apps drawer.

After opening the Play Store app, you see the main screen. The store has categories, or I suppose "departments," shown across the bottom of the screen: Games, Apps, Movies & TV, and Books. In Figure 17-1, the Apps department is shown. In the figure, the category Top Free is shown, which is reflected by the apps listed, each of which is popular and free.

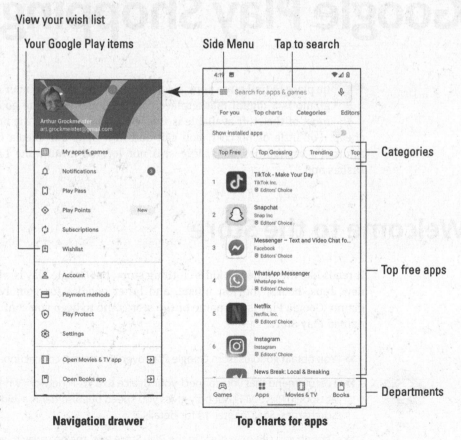

View your wish list

Your Google Play items

Side Menu   Tap to search

Categories

Top free apps

Departments

FIGURE 17-1:
The Google Play
(Play Store) app

Navigation drawer

Top charts for apps

After you browse to a specific item, further categories help you browse. These categories include top sellers, new items, free items, and so on. Eventually, you see a list of suggestions, as shown on the left in Figure 17-2. Swipe the suggestions up and down to peruse the lot.

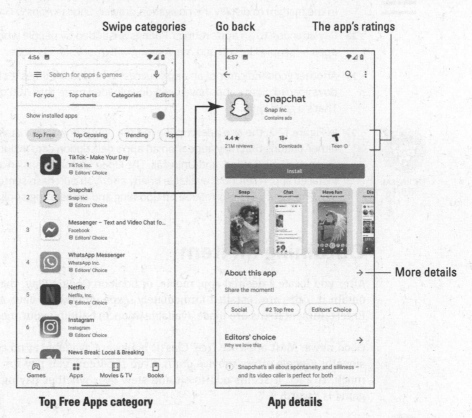

Swipe categories   Go back   The app's ratings

More details

FIGURE 17-2:
App details   **Top Free Apps category**   **App details**

To see more information about an item, tap its card. You see a more detailed description, screen shots, or perhaps a video preview, as shown on the right in Figure 17-2.

>> The first time you enter the Play Store app, or after the app is updated, you must accept the terms of service. To do so, tap the Accept button. This process repeats whenever the app is updated.

>> You can be assured that all apps available on Google Play are compatible with your phone or tablet. You cannot download or buy an incompatible app.

>> Check the Play Store app frequently to bargain-hunt. Many eBook bestsellers offer a button to read a free sample. Likewise, music on Google Play has buttons to let you hear a small sampling.

TIP

>> When you have an idea of what you want, tap the Search icon at the top of the Play Store screen. Type all or part of the item's title, such as an app name or book author or perhaps a description.

>> To view apps you've installed on your Android, tap the Side Menu icon (shown in the margin) to display the navigation drawer. Choose Apps & Games.

>> Pay attention to an app's ratings. Ratings are added by people who use the apps — people like you and me. A rating with more stars is better.

>> Another good indicator of an app's success is how many times it's been downloaded. Some apps have been downloaded more than 100 million times. That's a good sign.

TECHNICAL STUFF

>> In Figure 17-2, the app's description (on the right) shows the Install button. Other buttons that may appear on an app's description card include Open, Update, Refund, and Uninstall. The Open button opens an already installed app. A refund is available briefly after you purchase something. See Chapter 20 for information on updating and uninstalling apps.

Obtaining an item

After you locate a desired app, movie, or book on Google Play, the next step is to obtain it. Apps are installed immediately, expanding what your Android can do. Entertainment items are made available at once, building your media library.

Good news: Most apps are free. Classic books are available at no cost. And, occasionally, Google offers movies *gratis.* Even the items you pay for don't cost that much. In fact, it seems odd to sit and stew over whether paying 99 cents for a game is "worth it."

TIP

I recommend that you download a free app or book first, to familiarize yourself with the process. Then try downloading a paid item.

Free or not, the process of obtaining something from Google Play works pretty much the same whether it's an app, movie, book, or music. Follow these steps:

1. **If possible, activate the Wi-Fi connection to avoid incurring data overages.**

See Chapter 18 for information on connecting your Android device to a Wi-Fi network.

2. **Open the Play Store app.**

3. **Find the item you want and open its description.**

All items in the Play Store app feature a description screen. It looks similar to the app description screen shown on the right in Figure 17-2.

4. **Tap the button to obtain the item.**

A free app features the Install button. A free book features the eBook Free button. For a free movie or TV show or music, look for the Add to Library button. You might also see a Free Sample or Free Trial button for some items. In that case, tap the button to sample the media.

Paid items feature a button that shows the price. For movies and TV shows, you may see the Rent From button or Buy From button. See the later section "Renting or purchasing videos."

5. **For a paid item, tap the BUY button.**

If the item is free, skip to Step 9. Otherwise, a card appears, listing your preferred payment method, such as the example shown on the left in Figure 17-3. In the figure, the app *Minecraft* is listed for $6.99. The chosen payment method is an existing Google Play balance of $25.00.

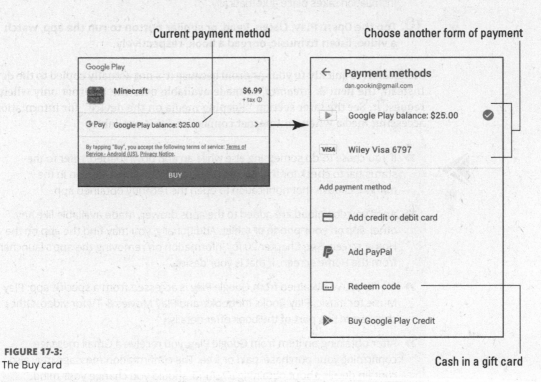

Current payment method

Choose another form of payment

Cash in a gift card

FIGURE 17-3:
The Buy card

6. **To change the method of payment, tap the payment item.**

Other payment options are listed on the right in Figure 17-3. Choose one, and then continue by tapping the BUY button back on the payment card (on the left in Figure 17-3).

7. **Type your Google password.**

For security, you're prompted to type your Google password to verify your account. You may also be asked to confirm your credit or debit card's CVC security code.

8. **Tap the VERIFY button.**

WARNING

I strongly recommend that you *do not* choose the option to avoid password authentication in the future. You want to be prompted every time for your password.

9. **Wait for the item to download or to become available.**

Media items are available instantly. Apps are downloaded and installed, which may take some time. The Downloading notification appears as the app is transferred. Feel free to do something else while the app downloads. Installation takes place automatically.

10. **Tap the Open, Play, Listen, Read, or similar button to run the app, watch a video, listen to music, or read a book, respectively.**

Media arrives quickly to your Android because it's not actually copied to the device. Instead, the item is *streamed*, or made available over the Internet only when you request it. See the later section "Keeping media on the device" for information on accessing media when an Internet connection isn't available.

>> If you chose to do something else while an app downloaded, refer to the status bar to check for the Google Play Store notification, shown in the margin. Choose that notification to open the recently obtained app.

>> Apps you download are added to the apps drawer, made available like any other app on your phone or tablet. Additionally, you may find the app on the Home screen. See Chapter 20 for information on removing the app's launcher from the Home screen, if that is your desire.

>> Media you've obtained from Google Play is accessed from a specific app: Play Music for music, Play Books for books, and Play Movies & TV for video. Other chapters in this part of the book offer details.

>> After obtaining an item from Google Play, you receive a Gmail message confirming your purchase, paid or free. The confirmation message may also contain details about obtaining a refund, should you change your mind.

NEVER BUY ANYTHING TWICE

Any apps or media you obtain from Google Play are available to all your Android devices as well as from your Google account on the Internet. These items include apps, books, music, videos, and anything else.

For example, those apps you've paid for on the phone are also available on the tablet: Open the Play Store and install the paid apps. You don't have to buy it twice. The same goes for purchased music, books, and videos. These media are available in the Play Music, Play Books, and Play Movies & TV apps on all your Android devices.

To review your purchased apps, display the Play Store app's navigation drawer (refer to the left side of Figure 17-1). Choose My Apps & Games. Tap the Library tab to review apps, both paid and free, that you've previously obtained on your current device as well as on other Android gizmos. You can reinstall any item on the list without paying for it a second time.

Avoiding Android viruses

It's important to be concerned about malware and Android viruses, and Google understands your apprehension. Apps available from Google Play have been verified by Google. Regular scans are conducted of apps installed on your device. To wit:

1. In the Play Store app, tap the Sidebar button to view the navigation drawer.

The navigation drawer is shown on the left in Figure 17-1.

2. Choose My Apps & Games.

On the Updates tab, illustrated in Figure 17-4, you see the Play Protect message, indicating that no problems were found and that apps were last scanned at the given time.

3. Choose the Play Protect item.

Any problems are presented.

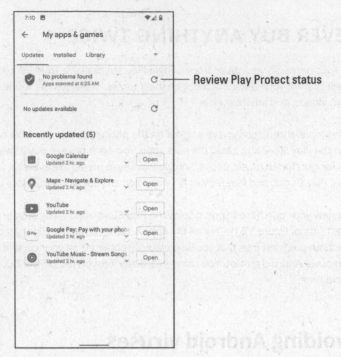

Review Play Protect status

FIGURE 17-4:
Google Play
Protect guards
against malicious
apps

If Play Protect isn't active, tap the Settings icon and ensure that the master controls are all set to the On position.

>> If you remain concerned, consider adding a security app. Many are available, including the popular Lookout Security.

>> One key to determining whether an app is malicious is to look at its access card: Open the app's description in the Play Store app and see which permissions it's requesting. For example, if a simple grocery list app wants to access the address book, it's suspect.

>> Avoid using any Android app store other than Google Play. The Samsung Galaxy Store is legitimate. I would, however, avoid other app stores or apps that require you to modify your device's settings before they can be installed.

WARNING

>> Avoid "hacker" apps, porn apps, and apps that use social engineering to make you do things that you wouldn't otherwise do, such as visit an unknown website to see racy pictures of politicians or celebrities.

>> In the history of the Android operating system, only a handful of malicious apps have been distributed, and most of them were found only on devices used in Asia. Google routinely removes malicious apps from its inventory. It can also remotely uninstall malicious apps, so you're safe.

Renting or purchasing videos

When it comes to movies and TV shows available from Google Play, you have two options: rent or purchase.

When you desire to rent a video, the rental is available to view for the next 30 days. Once you start watching, however, you have 48 hours to finish — you can also watch the video over and over again during that period.

Purchasing a video is more expensive than renting it, but you can view the movie or TV show at any time, on any Android device, or screencast it to a large-screen HDTV or monitor. You can also download the movie so that you can watch it even when an Internet connection isn't available, as described in the later section "Keeping media on the device."

One choice you must make when buying a movie is whether to purchase the SD or HD version. The SD version is cheaper and occupies less storage space (if you choose to download the movie). The HD version is more expensive, but it plays at high definition only on certain output devices. Obviously, when watching only on an Android phone, the SD option is preferred.

>> See Chapter 16 for information on the Play Movies app.

>> Also see Chapter 19 for information on casting videos from your Android to a large-screen device, such as an HDTV.

Google Play Tricks

Like most people, you probably don't want to become a Google Play expert. You just want to get the app you want or music you desire and get on with your life. Yet more exists to the Play Store app than just obtaining new stuff.

Granting permissions

Many apps desire to access different parts of your Android, from software items such as your contacts list to hardware items like the microphone or camera. To see which items an app wants to grab, view its permissions screen. Heed these directions:

1. **Display the app's description card.**

Tap the app as it's listed in the Play Store. An example of a description card is shown earlier, in Figure 17-2, on the right.

2. **Choose the item About This App.**

3. **Swipe down the Details screen and choose the item labeled App Permissions, See More.**

4. **Review the items the app requests access to.**

In addition to disclosing which parts of your Android the app lusts after, when you first run the app you're bombarded with permissions cards. At this time, you can prompt to allow or deny the app access. Be aware, however, that some apps don't work properly when denied access to some of your Android's features. For example, that Camera app should access the phone's camera.

See Chapter 20 for more information about reviewing app permissions.

Using the wish list

While you dither over getting a paid app, music, book, or any other purchase at Google Play, consider adding it to your wish list: When viewing the app's description card (refer to Figure 17-2, right side), tap the Action Overflow and choose Add to Wish List.

To review your wish list, tap the Side Menu icon in the Play Store app (refer to Figure 17-1, left side). Choose the Wish List item from the navigation drawer. You see all the items you've flagged. When you're ready to buy, choose one and dither again.

Sharing a Google Play item

Sometimes you love your Google Play purchase so much that you just can't contain your glee. When that happens, consider sharing the item. Obey these steps:

1. **Browse or search for the app, music, book, or other item you want to share in the Play Store app.**

2. **When you find the item, tap it to view its description screen.**

3. **Tap the Action Overflow and choose Share.**

   You see a card listing contacts as well as various apps.

4. **Choose a contact or an app.**

   For example, choose Gmail to send a Google Play link in an email message.

5. **Use the chosen app to share the link.**

What happens next depends on which sharing method you've chosen. When you choose a contact, you may continue a text message or another type of communication.

The result of following these steps is that your friend receives a link. That person can tap the link on his Android device and be whisked instantly to the Google Play Store, where the item can be obtained.

Keeping media on the device

Books, music, movies, and TV shows you obtain from Google Play aren't copied to your Android. Instead, they're stored on the Internet. When you access the media, it's streamed into your device as needed. This setup works well, and it keeps your phone or tablet from running out of storage space, but the media is accessible only when an Internet connection is available.

When you plan on being away from an Internet connection, such as when you're flying across the country and are too cheap to pay for inflight Wi-Fi, you can download Play Store music, eBook, and movie purchases and save them on your device.

Keeping media on your device applies only to items in your library. From the bottom of the Play Movies or Play Books app, choose Library. In the Play Music app, choose Music Library from the navigation drawer.

 To keep an item on the device's storage, look for the Download icon, shown in the margin. Tap that icon and the item is fetched from the Internet and stored on your Android.

 Items downloaded to your Android's storage feature the On Device icon, similar to the one shown in the margin. The icon's color differs between Play Music, Play Books, and Play Movies & TV apps.

 Keeping media — specifically, movies — on your Android consumes a lot of storage space. That's okay for short trips and such, but for the long term, consider purging some of your downloaded media: Tap the On Device icon. Tap the Remove button to confirm.

WARNING

Removing a downloaded item from your Android doesn't delete it from your account or prevent you from accessing it when an Internet connection becomes available. You can download the movie, music, or book again and again without penalty or wrath.

Buying something remotely

Google Play is available as a website, accessible from a computer or laptop. The address is play.google.com/store.

This Google Play website features the same apps, videos, music, and books that are found in the Play Store app on your mobile device. Further, the website offers Android hardware for sale, including more phones and tablets, one for each limb.

A nifty trick you can pull on the Google Play website is to remotely install apps on your Android device: Visit the website and click the Sign In button if you haven't yet signed in. Use your Google account, the same one you use on your Android.

To remotely install an app from the Google Play website, click the INSTALL button. Then choose a device from the card that's presented. Only compatible gizmos appear in the list, so you can't remote-install the wrong app. Eventually, the app is transferred to the device, made available the next time you use your phone or tablet.

Don't worry! No one else can use the remote-install feature. Only when you use your Google (or Gmail) account to sign in is this service available.

4

Nuts and Bolts

IN THIS CHAPTER

» **Using the mobile-data network**

» **Enabling Wi-Fi**

» **Accessing a Wi-Fi network**

» **Finding hidden networks**

» **Sharing the mobile-data network**

» **Pairing with a Bluetooth peripheral**

» **Transferring information with NFC**

Chapter **18**

It's a Wireless Life

Portable implies that something can be moved, but not how far or how easily. The first commercially successful portable computer, the Osborne 1, weighted a hair under 25 pounds. The suitcase-size beast required a power cord to operate, so it wasn't exactly wireless. This technology from the early 1980s is handily eclipsed by your Android device, many times over.

All Android phones and tablets are portable. Further, these devices are truly wireless, more so if you can charge the thing wirelessly. Even when you need that wire to charge the battery, after the process is complete, you can tote your Android anywhere and use it wire-free. You can access the mobile network, a Wi-Fi network, and wireless peripherals. It's a wireless life that Osborne users never imagined.

Android Wireless Networking

Your phone or tablet demands an Internet connection. To sate this desire, the device communicates with the information superhighway in a wireless way. Given how wireless networking has proliferated around the globe, finding an available connection is no longer a big deal. No, the issue is how to coax the Android into making this connection happen.

Using the mobile-data network

All Android phones and LTE tablets use the mobile–data network to connect to the Internet. For this service, you pay a handsome fee every month. (Phone users pay an additional fee for the telephone service.) The fee grants your Android wireless Internet access anywhere the signal is available.

Several types of mobile–data network service are available:

5G: The fifth-generation wide-area data network is rolling out as this book goes to press. It offers high-speed Internet and avoids the slowdowns that occur when too many mobile users try to access the 4G network.

4G LTE: The fourth generation of wide-area data networks is the most widespread network. Some providers may refer to this type of network as HSPA. The LTE stands for Long-Term Evolution, which means it's good for the long haul, though the appearance of the 5G network kinda dispels this promise.

3G: The third-generation mobile-data network is available in locations that don't offer 4G LTE service or where the signal is unavailable.

1X: The original mobile-data network had no name, but is now called 1X. This service might be available when the faster services have been obliterated by some moron with a backhoe.

Your phone or LTE tablet always uses the best network available. So, when the 5G network is down, 4G is used. When the 4G LTE network is out of reach, the 3G network is chosen. When none of the faster networks is up, 1X networking is accessed in an act of last–ditch desperation.

>> Your phone or LTE tablet shows a special icon that indicates the currently connected mobile-data network type.

>> The H+ status icon represents the HSPA mobile-data network, which is equivalent to 4G LTE.

>> The Signal Strength icon represents the mobile-data network connection, though on some phones it refers only to the telephone service.

>> You can still place calls on an Android phone when the mobile-data network is unavailable.

TIP

>> When both a mobile-data network and Wi-Fi are available, your Android uses Wi-Fi for all Internet access. To avoid data surcharges, I recommend connecting to and using a Wi-Fi network wherever possible.

>> Non-LTE Android tablets use only the Wi-Fi connection for Internet access.

>> Your mobile-data network subscription has its limits — usually, a certain quantity of data you can use monthly for a flat fee. When you exceed that quantity, the costs can become prohibitive.

>> See Chapter 23 for information on how to avoid cellular data surcharges.

Understanding Wi-Fi

The mobile-data connection is nice, and it's available pretty much all over, but it costs you money every month. A better option for Internet access is Wi-Fi, the same wireless networking standard that computers use.

To make the Wi-Fi connection work requires two steps. First, you must activate the device's Wi-Fi radio. Second, connect to a specific wireless network. The next two sections cover these steps in detail.

Wi-Fi stands for *wireless fidelity*. It's brought to you by the numbers 802.11 and various letter suffixes too many to mention.

Activating Wi-Fi

Follow these steps to activate your Android's Wi-Fi radio:

1. **Open the Settings app.**

2. **Choose Network & Internet.**

   On Samsung devices, choose Connections for this step; older Androids, choose Wi-Fi.

3. **Ensure that the Wi-Fi master control is set to the On position.**

   To further access Wi-Fi settings, tap the Wi-Fi item.

To deactivate the Wi-Fi radio, which also disconnects the device from the Wi-Fi network, set the master control to the Off position.

>> Use the Wi-Fi quick setting to instantly activate or deactivate the Wi-Fi connection. See Chapter 3 for information on accessing the quick settings.

>> It's okay to keep the Wi-Fi radio on all the time. It's not a major drain on the battery.

>> Using Wi-Fi to connect to the Internet doesn't incur data usage charges — unless you're accessing a metered network. See the later section "Setting up a metered Wi-Fi connection."

Connecting to a Wi-Fi network

After you've activated the Wi-Fi radio, your Android automatically connects to any known Wi-Fi network, one that you've accessed before where the password is still valid. If not, you can hunt down an available network. Follow these steps:

1. Visit the Wi-Fi screen in the Settings app.

Refer to the preceding section for details.

2. Select a wireless network from the list.

Available Wi-Fi networks appear on the screen, similar to what's shown in Figure 18-1. When no wireless networks are listed, you're out of luck regarding wireless access from your current location.

3. If prompted, type the network password.

Tap the Show Password check box so that you can see what you're typing; some of those network passwords can be long.

TIP

Available Wi-Fi networks

Signal strength   Wi-Fi Master Control

Scan QR code

Wi-Fi network connection card

FIGURE 18-1:
Hunting down a wireless network

Add hidden network

Password-protected network

If the network features a QR code, tap the QR Code icon, shown in the margin and illustrated in Figure 18-1, to instantly input the password. Skip to Step 5.

4. **Tap the Connect button.**

   The network is connected immediately. If not, try the password again.

5. **If prompted to remember the network, do so.**

   Some Androids may ask whether you want to automatically reconnect to the same Wi-Fi network in the future.

While your Android is connected to a wireless network, the Wi-Fi Connected status icon appears atop the touchscreen, looking like the one shown in the margin. This icon indicates that the Wi-Fi radio is on and the device is connected and communicating with a Wi-Fi network.

>> Some public networks require that you sign in to their web pages after connecting. The sign-in page may appear automatically. If not, open the web browser app and visit any page to be redirected to the sign-in page. Heed the directions there to gain network access.

>> See the later section "Managing connections" for more information on dealing with an automatic connection where the password has changed.

WARNING

>> A wireless network without a password is considered unsecure. The absence of security makes it easier for the Bad Guys to do bad-guy things on the network. My advice is to use the connection but avoid sending sensitive information over an unsecure public network.

>> The Wi-Fi connection works best when you plan to be in a specific location for an extended time. That's because the Wi-Fi signal goes only so far. If you wander too far away, the signal — and your connection — are lost.

>> To deliberately disconnect from a Wi-Fi network, turn off the device's Wi-Fi radio, as covered in the preceding section.

Connecting to a hidden Wi-Fi network

Some wireless networks don't broadcast their names, which adds security but also makes it more difficult to connect. In such cases, follow these steps to make the Wi-Fi network connection:

1. **Visit the Wi-Fi screen.**

   Refer to the earlier section "Activating Wi-Fi."

2. Tap the Add Network button.

The button is found at the bottom of the list of available networks (refer to Figure 18-1). It may also appear with the Add icon, shown in the margin.

3. Type the network name or SSID.

4. Choose the security setting.

How do you know which item to choose? Ask the person who gave you the network name. Otherwise, WPA/WPA2 is the most common option.

5. Tap the Save button or Connect button.

6. If prompted, type the network password.

As with other Wi-Fi networks, after the connection is made, your Android memorizes the connection. You must toil through these steps only once.

SSID stands for Service Set Identifier. Any further information on this acronym would needlessly lower your blood pressure, so I'll leave it at that.

Setting up a metered Wi-Fi connection

Not every Wi-Fi network provides free, unlimited service. For example, a metered connection implies that the provider charges you per minute or per megabyte for Internet access. To avoid surcharges, you can configure the connection as metered. Follow these steps:

1. Connect to the network as you normally would.

Directions are found earlier in this chapter.

2. Visit the Wi-Fi screen in the Settings app.

Refer to the earlier section "Activating Wi-Fi" for directions.

3. Choose the connected network, or tap the Settings icon by the network name, if available.

Look for a Network Usage item. If you can't find it, choose Advanced and look for an item titled Metered Network.

If your Android has already detected the connection as metered, you're good to go. Otherwise, continue:

4. Choose Network Usage or Metered Network.

5. Choose Treat As Metered.

When a Wi-Fi connection is set as metered, your phone or tablet monitors and restricts data access. You are warned when a large download or upload is attempted.

Managing connections

It's not necessary to review the list of memorized Wi-Fi networks — unless you need to change a network's password. In that case, you must direct the phone or tablet to forget the network so that you can reestablish the connection and set the new password.

To review the list of memorized networks, visit the Wi-Fi screen in the Settings app and choose Saved Networks. On Samsung devices, follow these steps:

1. **Open the Settings app.**

2. **Choose Connections.**

3. **Choose Wi-Fi.**

4. **Tap Action Overflow and choose Advanced.**

5. **Choose Manage Networks.**

    You see the list of saved Wi-Fi networks.

To forget a network, tap its entry. On the network's card, tap the Forget button or Trash icon. The network is removed from the list. To input the new password, access the network again, as described earlier in this chapter. Set the new password, and you're good.

REMEMBER

Forgetting a network doesn't prevent you from connecting to that same network again. It means only that the connection isn't established automatically.

Connection Sharing

Your Android phone or LTE tablet need not jealously guard its mobile-data connection. It's possible to share that Internet access in one of two ways. The first is to create a mobile *hotspot*, which allows any Wi-Fi–enabled gizmo to access the Internet via your device. The second is a direct connection between your Android and another device via a process called *tethering*.

Creating a mobile hotspot

To share your gizmo's mobile data connection with other Wi-Fi devices in the vicinity, heed these steps:

1. Turn off the Wi-Fi radio.

Why create a Wi-Fi hotspot when one is already available?

Directions for disabling the Wi-Fi radio are found earlier in this chapter; see the earlier section "Activating Wi-Fi."

2. Connect your Android to a power source.

The mobile hotspot feature draws a lot of power.

3. Choose Hotspot & Tethering.

This item might be titled Mobile Hotspot and Tethering.

4. Choose Wi-Fi Hotspot or Mobile Hotspot.

5. Fill in the details, the network name, and password.

You can keep the default settings, which are unique to your device. For example, you can replace the preset password with something less onerous to type.

6. Set the master control to the On position.

Your device may check with the cellular provider's mothership to affirm that your mobile-data subscription plan features the mobile hotspot feature. If so, the Wi-Fi hotspot is up and running right away.

Once it's active, the Wi-Fi hotspot is accessed like any other network and by any device with a Wi-Fi radio.

To disable the mobile hotspot, repeat the steps in this section, and disable the hotspot after Step 4.

TIP

>> Some devices feature a Mobile Hotspot app. If so, use it instead of following the steps in this section.

>> If your phone or LTE tablet is unable to create a mobile hotspot, check with your cellular provider about upgrading your plan to offer that feature. Or, instead, use the tethering feature covered in the next section.

>> While the mobile hotspot is active, the Hotspot Active status icon appears, similar to the one shown in the margin.

>> The range for the mobile hotspot is about 30 feet. Items such as walls and cement trucks can interfere with the signal, rendering it much shorter.

>> When you use the mobile hotspot, data usage fees apply. When a crowd of people are using your hotspot, a lot of data is consumed rather quickly.

>> Don't forget to turn off the mobile hotspot when you're done using it.

Tethering the Internet connection

A more intimate way to share an Android's mobile data connection is to connect the device directly to a computer and activate the tethering feature. Follow these steps:

1. **Use the USB cable to connect the phone or LTE tablet to a computer or laptop.**

   I've had the best success with this operation when the computer is a PC running Windows.

2. **Open the Settings app.**

3. **Choose Network & Internet or, on Samsung devices, choose Connections.**

4. **Choose Hotspot & Tethering.**

   This item is titled Mobile Hotspot and Tethering on Samsung galactic gizmos.

5. **Set the master control by the USB Tethering option to the On position.**

The computer or laptop should instantly recognize the Android as a "modem" with Internet access. Further configuration may be required, which depends on the computer using the tethered connection. For example, you may have to accept the installation of new software in Windows.

To end the connection, repeat the steps in this section but disable tethering in Step 5. Then you can disconnect the USB cable.

>> While tethering is active, the Tethering status icon may appear, similar to what's shown in the margin.

>> Sharing the mobile-data connection incurs data usage charges against your cellular data plan. Mind your data usage when you're sharing a connection.

REMEMBER

The Bluetooth Connection

Bluetooth has nothing to do with the color blue or dental hygiene. No, it's a protocol for wirelessly connecting peripherals. Your Android happens to have a Bluetooth wireless radio in its belly, so it can pal around with Bluetooth devices such as keyboards, headphones, and even your car.

Understanding Bluetooth

To make Bluetooth work, you need a Bluetooth peripheral, such as a wireless ear-piece or keyboard. The goal is to connect, or *pair*, the peripheral with your phone or tablet. The operation works like this:

1. Turn on the Android's Bluetooth wireless radio.

The radio must be on for both your Android and the Bluetooth gizmo.

2. Make the peripheral discoverable.

The peripheral must announce that it's available and willing to date other electronics in the vicinity.

3. On your phone or tablet, choose the peripheral from the list of Bluetooth devices.

4. If required, confirm the connection.

For example, you may be asked to input or confirm a code. You might need to press a button on peripherals that have buttons.

5. Use the Bluetooth peripheral.

You can use the Bluetooth peripheral as much as you like. Turn off the Android. Turn off the peripheral. When you turn both on again, they're automatically reconnected.

 Bluetooth devices are branded with the Bluetooth logo, shown in the margin. It's your assurance that the gizmo works with other Bluetooth devices. Just because a device is wireless doesn't mean it's using the Bluetooth standard.

Activating Bluetooth

You must turn on the Android's Bluetooth radio before you can enjoy using any Bluetoothy peripherals. The cinchy way to do so is to pull down the quick settings drawer and tap the Bluetooth icon: To pull down the quick settings drawer, use two fingers to swipe down from the tippy-top of the touchscreen.

 When Bluetooth is on, the Bluetooth status icon appears, shown in the margin.

To turn off Bluetooth, use the quick settings drawer's Bluetooth button again.

 Bluetooth activation can also be made from the Settings app. All things Bluetooth are found in the Connected Devices category. On Samsung devices, open the Connections category and choose Bluetooth.

TIP

Pairing with a Bluetooth peripheral

To make the Bluetooth connection between your Android and another gizmo, such as a Bluetooth headset, follow these steps:

1. **Ensure that the Bluetooth radio is on.**

Refer to the preceding section.

2. **Make the Bluetooth peripheral discoverable.**

Turn on the gizmo and ensure that its Bluetooth radio is on. Keep in mind that some Bluetooth peripherals have separate power and Bluetooth switches. If so, press the Bluetooth button or take whatever action is necessary to make the peripheral discoverable.

3. **On the Android, open the Settings app.**

4. **Choose Connected Devices or, on a Samsung device, choose Connections and then Bluetooth.**

The screen shows already paired and available peripherals, similar to what's shown in Figure 18-2. If it doesn't, choose the Pair New Device item or tap the Scan button.

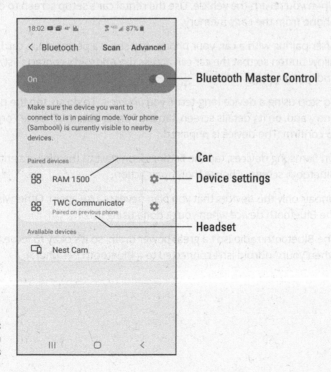

Bluetooth Master Control

Car

Device settings

Headset

FIGURE 18-2:
Finding Bluetooth gizmos

5. **Choose the Bluetooth peripheral from the list.**

6. **If necessary, type the device's passcode or otherwise acknowledge the connection.**

   For example, with a Bluetooth keyboard, you may see on the touchscreen a prompt showing a series of numbers. Type those numbers on the keyboard, and then press the Enter or Return key. That action completes the pairing.

After the device is paired, you can begin using it.

REMEMBER

>> Bluetooth peripherals stay paired whether you turn off the Android, turn off the device, or disable the Bluetooth radio. The connection is reestablished automatically when you turn things on again.

>> Yes, your car can be a Bluetooth peripheral, if it has a Bluetooth radio installed. This connection is how you can use an Android phone hands-free while driving. Pairing the phone with your car works differently for each vehicle, though the general steps proceed as outlined in this chapter. Do be aware that the car won't pair while it's in gear; stop the car to begin the pairing process.

>> When pairing your phone with a rental car, remember to unpair the phone when you return the vehicle. Use the rental car's setup screen to delete your phone from the car's memory.

>> After pairing with a car, your phone may show a permissions card. Tap the Allow button so that the car can access the Android's contacts list, call history, and text message details.

>> To stop using a device long-term, you *unpair* it. To do so, tap the peripheral's entry and, on its details screen, tap the Forget button. Choose Forget Device to confirm. The device is unpaired.

>> On Samsung devices, tap the Settings icon next to the device's entry on the Bluetooth screen. Choose the Unpair action.

>> Unpair only the devices that you plan never to use again. Otherwise, turn off the Bluetooth device when you're done using it.

>> The Bluetooth radio isn't a great power drain, so it's okay to leave it on even when your Android isn't connected to a Bluetooth peripheral.

NFC Is Near to Me

A handful of Android devices feature an NFC radio, where NFC stands for *near field communications* and radio is a type of vegetable. NFC allows your Android to communicate wirelessly with other NFC devices. That connection is used for the quick transfer of information. The technology is called Android Beam.

To play with the Android Beam feature, ensure that the NFC radio has been activated. Follow these steps:

1. **Open the Settings app.**

2. **Choose Connected Devices.**

   On Samsung devices, choose Connections.

3. **Choose Connection Preferences.**

4. **Ensure that the NFC item's master control is set to On.**

   This item might be titled NFC and Payment.

To make the Android Beam feature work, touch your Android to another NFC device, usually back-to-back. As long as both devices have an NFC radio and the Android Beam feature is active, they can share information.

On the sending device, tap the text *Tap to Beam*.

On the receiving device, choose the option to accept the item.

>> Generally speaking, if an app features the Share icon, you can use Android Beam to share an item between two NFC gizmos. These items include contacts, YouTube video links, web page links, photos, and so on.

>> The NFC feature allows you to use NFC tags, which can wirelessly direct the Android to perform a variety of interesting tasks.

>> NFC is also what allows you to use your phone to pay for groceries. The NFC radio works with the payment app to suck money directly from your bank account.

>> This feature was once known as Android Beam, but too many people were confused because they thought "Android Beam" was a robot-manufactured whiskey.

TECHNICAL STUFF

>> NFC is not the same as the Nearby Devices feature found on some Samsung galactic gizmos. The Nearby Devices feature is used for sharing media over a network.

Chapter **19**

Connect, Share, and Store

As a technology gizmo, your Android just can't break free from the old file/folder paradigm that saddles computers. True, your phone or tablet is mobile and wireless, and it does more things and goes more places than any desktop or laptop. But at its core, the thing is a computing device. Somewhere in its bosom likes a storage system with a clutch of files organized into folders. You may wish to access these items, perform a file transfer, or just nerd out and commit the sin of practicing file management on a mobile device.

The USB Connection

Any file transfer starts with a connection. You can use Bluetooth or cloud storage to wirelessly move files between devices, but the most direct way to connect an Android phone or tablet to a computer is to use a wire — specifically, the wire swaddled in the core of a USB cable. Conveniently, such a cable came with the device. It has purposes beyond giving the battery a charge.

Configuring the USB connection

The USB connection is configured automatically whenever you connect your Android to a computer. Everything might work peachy. When it doesn't, you must manually configure the USB connection. Follow these steps:

1. **Swipe down the notifications drawer.**

2. **Choose the USB notification.**

The USB notification might appear at the bottom of the list, down where Android shows system activities. Figure 19-1 illustrates how the notification might appear. Some devices may show two notifications: one for charging the device and another for transferring files.

You might have to tap the USB connection notification twice before you see the connection details, shown on the right in Figure 19-1.

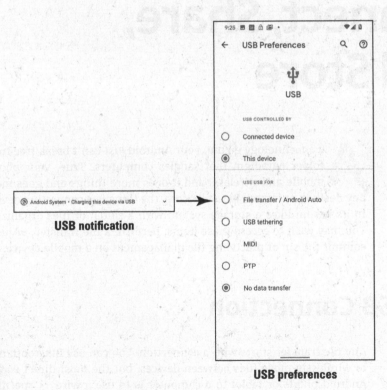

FIGURE 19-1:
USB connection
configuration
details

USB notification

USB preferences

3. **Select a connection option.**

The USB connection card lists several options for configuring the USB connection:

File Transfer / Android Auto: This connection is ideal for transferring files. The computer views the Android as a thumb drive or similar storage device. Other titles for this setting are Transfer Files, Transfer Media Files, MTP, and CTP.

USB Tethering: When chosen, this option shares the Android's mobile-data connection with the computer. Refer to Chapter 18.

MIDI: Choose this mode to use the Android as a keyboard or similar device for musical input.

PTP: In this mode, which might also be labeled Transfer Image, the computer sees the Android as a digital camera, which is ideal for importing photos and videos.

No Data Transfer: The device is charged; no data transfer takes place unless you select another option.

4. If prompted, tap the Save button to save the configuration.

At some point in the process, you may see a permissions card asking for access to the device's storage. If so, tap the Allow button. The top option shown in Figure 19-1 determines whether the connected device controls the USB connection. My advice is to choose This Device to ensure that your Android is in charge.

After configuring the connection, you may see a notification on the computer, prompting you to do something with the Android. Your choices are based on which option you choose in Step 3.

TIP

›› The USB connection always charges your Android when connected to a computer, though it's more efficient to use a direct power source, like a wall socket.

›› If the computer fails to recognize the Android, select another USB connection option.

›› Often, the connection fails because of the Android's security level. If so, unlock the device and then try the connection again.

›› Your Android may not charge its battery when you connect the USB cable to a computer. To ensure that it charges, connect the device to a USB port on the computer's console as opposed to connecting to an external USB hub.

›› If your Android has a microSD card, its storage is also mounted to the computer, in addition to internal storage.

>> For data transfer to take place at top speeds over the USB 3.0 cable, you must connect the Android's USB 3.0 cable to the USB 3.0 port on a computer. These ports are color-coded blue.

>> Most Android mobile devices lack the capability to use the USB connection to add peripherals to the device, such as a mouse or thumb drive. Some devices may come with a multimedia dock that offers this connectivity.

>> PTP stands for Picture Transfer Protocol. This setting misleads the computer into thinking that the phone or tablet is a digital camera, which it is.

TECHNICAL STUFF

Connecting to a PC

Once the USB connection is made between an Android and a PC, a number of things happen. Don't let the flurry of activity frighten you.

You may see drivers install, which is normal Windows behavior when a new USB gizmo is connected.

You may also see a notification, such as the Windows 10 notification, shown in Figure 19-2. Click or tap that notification to see how to deal with the new connection.

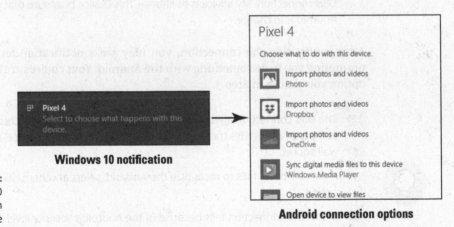

Windows 10 notification

Pixel 4

Choose what to do with this device.

Import photos and videos
Photos

Import photos and videos
Dropbox

Import photos and videos
OneDrive

Sync digital media files to this device
Windows Media Player

Open device to view files

Android connection options

FIGURE 19-2:
Windows 10 connection choice

For example, choose Open Device to View Files (near the bottom in Figure 19-2), and a File Explorer window opens, listing files and folders on the Android. Or you can choose Import Photos and Videos (Photos) to quickly copy over pictures and videos.

>> The choice you make from the list of items is retained by Windows 10. The next time you connect your Android, that option is chosen automatically.

>> Other versions of Windows also display a list of actions, though they appear in an AutoPlay dialog box. As with Windows 10, if you select a specific item, that choice is always selected for you when the Android is connected.

Connecting to a Mac

You need special software to deal with the Android-to-Macintosh connection. For some reason, the Mac doesn't natively recognize Android devices. Weird, huh? It's like Apple wants you to buy some other type of mobile gizmo. I just don't get it.

To help deal with the USB connection on a Mac, obtain the Android File Transfer program. On your Mac, download that program from this website:

    android.com/filetransfer

Install the software. Run it. From that point on, whenever you connect your Android to the Mac, you see a special window appear, similar to the one shown in Figure 19-3. It lists the device's folders and files. Use that window for file management, as covered later in this chapter.

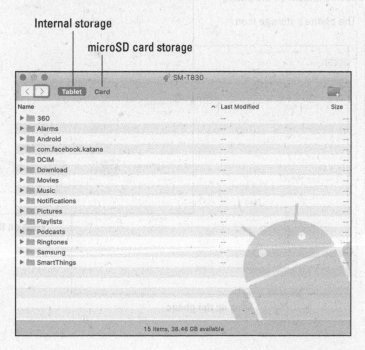

Internal storage

microSD card storage

FIGURE 19-3: The Android File Transfer program

If the phone or tablet has a microSD card inserted, you see two buttons in the Android File Transfer program window: Tablet (or Phone) and Card, as shown earlier, in Figure 19-3. Click one or the other to see files and folders in that storage location.

If the Android File Transfer program doesn't start, choose the USB notification and ensure that the File Transfer option is selected. Refer to the earlier section "Configuring the USB connection."

Using the USB cable to transfer files

After making the USB connection between your Android and a computer, you can transfer files back-and-forth. This is the traditional method of file exchange, though further, and mostly wireless, methods are offered in the later section "Files Back-and-Forth."

To best move files between the two devices, ensure that folder windows for both the Android and the computer are open. Figure 19-4 illustrates such an arrangement.

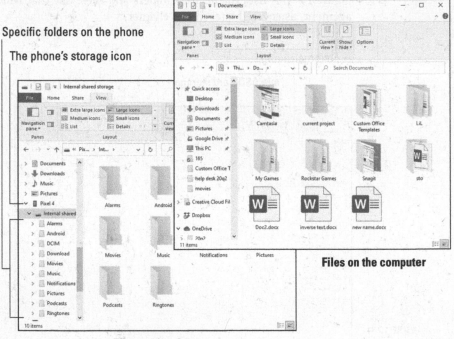

Specific folders on the phone

The phone's storage icon

Files on the computer

FIGURE 19-4: Copying files to an Android phone or tablet

Files on the phone

Drag file icons between the two windows to copy. And keep in mind that if your Android has a microSD card installed, it shows two folder windows on the desktop: one for internal storage and a second for the microSD card (removable) storage.

Here are some suggestions for transferring files:

>> Unless you know specifically where to save a file on the Android, copy the file to the Download folder.

>> Pictures and videos on the Android are stored in the DCIM/Camera folder.

>> Use the MTP configuration to import photos and videos over a USB cable. That way, photos and videos are copied from the Android into the proper folder or program on the PC.

>> If you're transferring music, use the Windows Media Player program, as described in Chapter 15.

When you're done copying files, close both windows and detach the Android, as described in the next section.

Getting a file into your Android is no guarantee that you can do productive things with it. Specifically, don't expect to be able to access an eBook file you've copied from your PC to your mobile device. You must use a specific app to read an eBook on an Android.

A good understanding of basic file operations is necessary for successful file transfers between a computer and your gizmo. Knowing basic procedures such as copy, move, rename, and delete is an important part of the process. Understand how a folder works. The good news is that you don't need to manually calculate a 64-bit cyclical redundancy check on the data, nor do you need to know what a parity bit is.

Disconnecting from a computer

The process is cinchy: When you're done transferring files, music, or other media between a computer and your Android, close all programs and folders you have opened on the computer — specifically, those you've used to work with the device's storage. Then you can disconnect the USB cable. That's it.

>> It's a Bad Idea to unplug the Android while you're transferring information or while a folder window is open on your computer. Doing so can harm the device's storage, rendering unreadable some of the information that's kept there. To be safe, close those programs and folder windows you've opened before disconnecting.

>> Unlike other external storage on the Macintosh, you don't need to eject the Android's storage when you're done accessing it. Quit the Android File Transfer program on the Mac, and then unplug the phone or tablet — or vice versa. The Mac doesn't get angry, either way.

Files Back-and-Forth

The USB connection provides only one way to transfer files between your Android and another device. Files can also flee to and fro on cloud storage, via the microSD card, to a printer, and to a screencasting gizmo. Set your files free!

Sharing files on the cloud

The wireless way to swap files between your Android and just about any other device is to use cloud storage. That's just fancy talk for storing files on the Internet.

Google's cloud storage is called Google Drive. Like other Googley services, it's tied to your Google account. You have access to the storage on your Android or any other device that has Internet access: Sign in to your Google account — *boom!* — you see your files. (The boom is an exclamation; nothing actually explodes.)

On your Android, use the Drive app to browse and manage your Google Drive files. On the Internet, you access your Google Drive at drive.google.com. From that site, you can also obtain the Google Drive program for your computer, which I recommend installing.

To move an item from your Android to your computer via Google Drive, follow these steps:

1. **Locate the item you want to save or copy to your Google Drive storage.**

It can be a picture, movie, web page, YouTube video, or just about anything.

2. **Tap the Share icon.**

If you don't see the Share icon, the item you're viewing cannot be copied to Google Drive.

3. **Choose Save to Drive.**

You may instead see the Google Drive icon, shown in the margin. Tap it.

If you've not yet used Google Drive, you see a permissions card. Tap the Allow button.

4. **Fill in the Save to Drive card.**

The card already lists the item's filename or title, though you can change it to be shorter or more descriptive. Also, because I'm organized, I tap the Folder action bar to choose a specific Google Drive folder on which to save the item. If you're unsure which folder is best, just use the main My Drive folder for now.

5. **Tap the Save button.**

The item is saved or copied to your Google Drive storage. In mere Internet moments, it's available to your computer or any other device where you can access your Google Drive storage.

>> To send a file from a computer to your Android, use Google Drive on your computer: Copy the file to the Google Drive folder. When you next access the Drive app, open the proper folder to find the file.

>> If you frequently share items to Google Drive, a shortcut appears on the Share card. Tap that item to instantly share a picture, music, or whatever to the same folder you've previously used when sharing to Google Drive.

>> Other cloud storage apps include the popular Dropbox, Microsoft's OneDrive, the Amazon Cloud, and more. Each of these works similarly to Google Drive; just choose the proper app in Step 3.

>> Cloud storage apps are free. You're provided with a modest amount of online storage at no charge. For a monthly subscription, you can obtain more storage.

Using the media card to transfer files

Welcome to the 1980s! Back before computers had networking capabilities, and long before Wi-Fi, files moved from one computer to another on removable storage media. The vehicle of choice was the floppy diskette. The power came from your feet. The method was called *sneakernet.* Everyone hated it.

If your Android features removable storage, you can use it to transfer files — just like those proto-geeks from the last century: Remove the microSD card from the phone or tablet and insert it into a computer. From that point, the computer can read the files just as they can be read from any media card.

>> Don't worry about moving or saving stuff to the microSD card. If your Android has a card installed, it's the default location for photos and other media.

>> You can also use a file management app to move files to a microSD card while you use your Android.

>> To read the microSD media on your computer, you need a microSD card adapter. This hardware comes with the microSD card, so don't lose it!

>> See the later section "Removable Storage" for all things microSD.

Adding a print service

Another form of file transfer is printing: The output device is a printer, not storage on another computer. Your Android deftly handles the printer task. Just ensure two things:

>> A printer is available to the same wireless network that the Android uses. It doesn't need to be a wireless printer — just available to the network.

>> The proper print service software is installed.

Printing is covered in the next section. Before you can print, however, your Android must have a print service installed. It probably does, but follow these steps to confirm:

1. Open the Settings app.

2. Choose Connected Devices.

On Samsung galactic gizmos, choose Connections.

3. Choose Connection Preferences.

Samsung devices label this item More Connection Settings.

4. Choose Printing.

You see a list of print services, one of which, hopefully, matches the printer models on the Wi-Fi network — for example, the HP print service, which lets you print to any networked HP printer.

5. If a print service is listed as Off, choose it and switch its master control to the On position.

You're done. Otherwise, if you don't see a print service for the network printer, continue with Step 6.

6. Choose Add Service or Download Plug-In.

The Play Store app opens, listing available printing services.

7. Select and install a print service.

For example, if you use Canon printers, choose and install the Canon print service. Refer to Chapter 17 for details on installing apps. You do not need to open the service after it's installed.

After the service is installed, or if you confirm that the service is available, you can print from your Android. Keep reading in the next section.

Printing

As long as your Android is connected to a Wi-Fi network with an available printer and that printer's printing service is installed, printing works like this:

1. **View the material you want to print.**

You can print a web page, photo, map, or any number of items.

2a. **Tap the Action Overflow and choose the Print action, or:**

2b. **Tap the Share icon, or choose the Share action from the Action Overflow, and then choose Print.**

It's crazy, but both methods (Steps 2a and 2b) are used in different apps. Sometimes the Print action is on an Action Overflow; at other times, you must choose Share and then tap the Print icon.

If you can't find a Print action or icon on a Share menu, your Android lacks this feature or the item cannot be printed.

Sometimes the Print action might be the name of the installed print service. If so, choose it to print.

3. **Select a printer.**

The current printer is shown on the action bar, as shown in Figure 19-5. To view additional printers, tap the action bar.

4. **To change any print settings, tap the Show More Details chevron.**

The items presented let you set which pages you want to print, change the number of copies, and make other common printer settings.

5. **Tap the Print icon or button.**

The item prints.

Not every app supports printing. The only way to know is to look for the Print action or icon. If you can't find it, you can't print.

Streaming media

When you desire to watch movies, look at your photos, or listen to music on a large-format screen, it's time to screencast: This technology takes the media (video or music) presented on your Android and sends it to an HDTV, a monitor, or another compatible device.

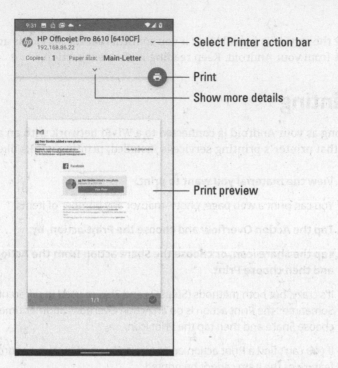

Select Printer action bar

Print

Show more details

Print preview

FIGURE 19-5:
Android printing

You need several items prepared in order for streaming, or *screencasting*, to work properly:

>> An HDTV or a monitor with HDMI input

>> A screencasting dongle, such as Chromecast, attached to one of the HDMI ports

>> Access to the same Wi-Fi network for both the HDTV or monitor and your Android phone or tablet

After the Chromecast dongle is installed and configured on the HDTV, follow these steps to stream media:

1. Open the app that plays the media you want to watch or listen to.

Compatible apps include Play Music, Play Movies & TV, YouTube, Netflix, and so on.

2. Tune the HDTV or monitor to the proper HDMI input.

For example, if a Chromecast dongle is installed on HDMI Input 4, switch the TV to that input. The casting dongle must be awake and active.

3. **Tap the Chromecast icon.**

The icon appears similar to the one shown in the margin. If you don't see this icon, either the Chromecast dongle isn't awake, the media cannot be cast to another device, the network is offline, or your Android's Wi-Fi radio is inactive.

4. **Choose the TV or monitor's Chromecast from the list.**

5. **Play the media.**

The media appears or is heard from the other device.

You can still use your Android while it's casting. The app on the screen may offer you controls, such as Play and Pause, or it might display additional information about the media.

To stop streaming, tap the Chromecast icon and then tap the Stop Casting or Disconnect button.

Removable Storage

A handful of Android devices offer removable storage in the form of a microSD card. This storage is in addition to internal storage that comes with every phone and tablet. The microSD card provides your device with more storage, plus the capability to manually transfer storage between devices.

>> Just because your Android provides a microSD slot doesn't mean that the device comes with a microSD card. It's something you must purchase separately.

>> Your Android works with or without a microSD card installed.

>> Storage capacity for microSD cards is measured in gigabytes (GB). Common capacities are 8GB, 16GB, 32GB, and higher. The maximum size allowed depends on the phone or tablet's design. The side of the box, or scant printed material that came with the Android, lists compatible capacities.

>> Though a microSD card does provide more storage for your Android, using the storage can be problematic. See the nearby sidebar, "Why removable storage is unpopular."

Inserting a microSD card

To shove a microSD card into your Android, whether the device is on or off, heed these steps:

1. Locate the microSD card slot.

The slot is labeled as illustrated in Figure 19-6. It isn't the same as the SIM card slot.

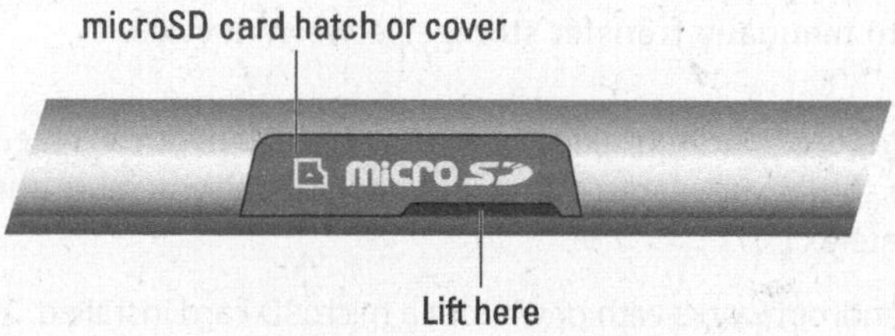

microSD card hatch or cover

FIGURE 19-6:
Opening the microSD card hatch

Lift here

2. Flip open the slot's teensy hatch.

Insert your thumbnail into the tiny slot and flip the hatch outward. It's attached on one end, so it may not completely pop off.

3. Insert the microSD card into the slot.

The card goes in only one way. If you're fortunate, a wee card silhouette illustrates the proper orientation. If you're even more fortunate, your eyes will be good enough to see the tiny silhouette.

TIP

You may hear a faint click when the card is fully inserted. If not, use the end of a paper clip or your fingernail to fully insert the card.

Upon success, you may see a notification detailing information about the card.

Removing a microSD card

To remove the microSD card, follow these steps:

1. Unmount the microSD card.

Directions are offered in the later section "Unmounting the microSD card."

2. Open the little hatch covering the microSD card slot.

Refer to the preceding section.

3. Using your fingernail or a bent paper clip, gently press the microSD card inward a tad.

The microSD card is spring-loaded, so pressing it in pops it outward. Stand by to catch it, should the ejection method prove aggressive.

4. Pinch the microSD card between your fingers to extract it.

After you've removed the card, you can continue using the phone or tablet. It works just fine without a microSD card.

WARNING

>> You can remove the microSD card at any time when the Android is turned off.

>> The microSD card is too tiny to leave lying around, lest you lose it. Put it into a microSD card adapter or its original plastic container. Try not to stick it in your ear.

Formatting microSD storage

Your Android instantly recognizes a microSD card after it's inserted. If not, you can try formatting the card to see whether that fixes the problem.

WARNING

All data on the microSD card is erased by the formatting process.

To format a microSD card, follow these steps:

1. Open the Settings app.

2. Choose Storage.

3. **Choose the action Format SD Card.**

    If necessary, tap the microSD card's item on the storage screen to locate the Format action.

4. **Tap the Format button or the Format SD Card button.**

5. **If prompted, tap the Delete All button to confirm.**

    The microSD card is unmounted, formatted, and then mounted again and made ready for use.

On Samsung devices, heed these directions:

1. **Open the Settings app.**

2. **Choose Device Care.**

3. **Choose Storage.**

4. **Tap the Action Overflow and choose Storage Settings.**

5. **Choose SD Card.**

6. **Tap the Format button.**

7. **Tap Format SD Card to confirm.**

    The microSD card is reformatted.

After the card is formatted, you can use it to store information, music, apps, photos, and stuff like that.

Unmounting the microSD card

When your Android is turned off, you can insert or remove the microSD card at will. Otherwise, to remove the microSD card when the Android is turned on, you must first unmount it. Obey these steps:

1. **Open the Settings app and choose Storage.**

    This item might be titled Storage & USB.

2. **Choose Unmount SD Card or tap the Eject button.**

    The button may be located by the USB storage item shown on the storage screen. Otherwise, the Unmount SD Card action is found near the bottom of the screen.

3. **Ignore the warning and tap the OK button.**

4. **Remove the microSD card.**

For Samsung devices, follow these directions:

1. **Open the Settings app.**

2. **Choose Device Care and then Storage.**

3. **Tap the Action Overflow and choose Storage Settings.**

4. **Choose SD Card.**

5. **Tap the Unmount button.**

6. **Remove the card.**

It's important that you follow these steps to safely remove the microSD card. If you don't, and you just pop out the card, it can harm the card and lose information.

REMEMBER

You can insert a microSD card at any time.

Android Storage Mysteries

Somewhere, nestled in your Android's bosom, lies a storage device. That storage works like the hard drive in a computer, and for the same purpose: to keep apps, music, videos, pictures, and a host of other information for the long-term.

>> Android phones and tablets come with a given quantity of internal storage. The amount is preset by the manufacturer, usually given as an option at purchase time.

>> Typical quantities of internal storage include 16GB, 32GB, 64GB, and more.

>> Removable storage in the form of a microSD card is available on some Androids.

TECHNICAL STUFF

>> *GB* stands for gigabyte, or 1 billion bytes (characters) of storage. A typical 2-hour movie occupies about 4GB of storage, but most items that you store on your Android — music and pictures, for example — occupy only a sliver of storage.

Reviewing storage stats

To see how much storage space is available on your Android, follow these steps:

1. **Open the Settings app.**

2. **Choose the Storage item.**

   This item might be titled Storage & USB on some devices. On some Samsung galactic gizmos, choose the Device Care (or Device Maintenance) category and then choose Storage.

Figure 19-7 shows a storage screen on a Pixel 4, which is close to stock Android, and on a Samsung phone. The information displays details about internal storage and, if available, the microSD card.

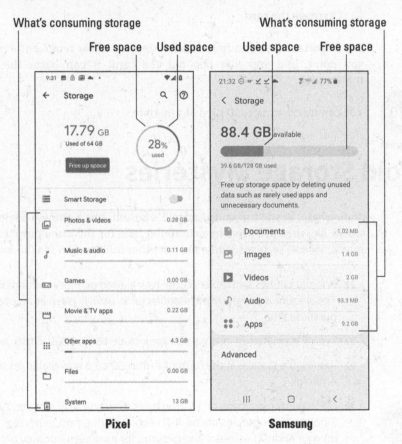

FIGURE 19-7:
Android storage
details

Tap the storage item or category to view details on how the storage is used or to launch an associated app. For example, tap the Photos and Videos item to see (and manage) photos and media storage on the device.

>> Things that consume the most storage space are videos, music, and pictures, in that order.

>> Most media is stored in the cloud and streamed from the Internet to your Android. If you're keeping media on the device (described in Chapter 17), you can remove it to free storage.

>> Don't feel ripped-off if the Total Space value is far less than the stated capacity of your Android. For example, your device may have 32GB of storage but the Storage screen reports only 29.85GB of total space. The missing space is considered overhead, as are several gigabytes taken by the government for tax purposes.

Freeing storage

Your Android is willing to help you when storage gets tight. Somewhere hidden on the Settings app's storage screen is a storage optimizer utility.

For stock Android, or similar devices such as the Pixel phone illustrated in Figure 19-7, tap the Free Up Space button. Peruse options on the Remove Items screen, placing a check in the box by items you desire the phone to "free up." Tap the Free Up Space button to remove the selected items.

On Samsung devices, choose Device Care from the Settings app's main screen, and then tap the OPTIMIZE NOW button. Your galaxy gadget doesn't offer additional options at this point. Instead, it dutifully removes what it believes are excess items.

>> If photos and videos you've recorded are consuming a lot of space, consider copying them to a computer for long-term storage. Refer to the earlier section "The USB Connection." After copying the files, remove them from your Android.

>> An excellent way to free storage on your Android is to remove media (movies, music, books) you've downloaded and saved on the device's storage. See Chapter 17.

Chapter **20**

Apps and Widgets

O f the gazillions of apps available for your Android, you probably want to keep a handful of your favorites ready and available. The best way to keep them accessible, neat, and tidy is to place their launcher icons on the Home screen. Indeed, the whole point of having a Home screen is to keep handy apps and widgets.

Apps and Widgets on the Home Screen

Your Android came with app launchers and perhaps some widgets affixed to the Home screen. You can keep those items, add your own, remove some, and change their locations. And when the Home screen brims with launchers like an over-flowing teacup, you can build folders to further organize and keep your apps neat and tidy.

Adding launchers to the Home screen

As you find yourself using an app frequently, consider slapping its launcher icon on the Home screen. Here's how that works:

1. **Visit the Home screen page on which you want to stick the launcher.**

   The page must have room for the launcher icon. If it doesn't, swipe the screen left or right to hunt down a page with room. Conversely, you can choose to add the launcher to a folder; see the later section "Working with folders."

   If you're organizing Home screen pages by app type, visit the proper page. For example, on my Android gizmos, the second Home screen page is just for games.

2. **Swipe upward to display the apps drawer.**

   If your Android features the Apps icon, tap it to view the apps drawer.

3. **Drag upward the launcher icon you want to add to the Home screen.**

   After a moment, the Home screen page you chose in Step 1 appears.

4. **Continue dragging the app to a position on the Home screen page.**

   Launchers are aligned to a grid. Other launchers may wiggle and jiggle as you find a spot. That's okay.

5. **Lift your finger to place the app.**

TIP

A quick shortcut on some Samsung devices is to long-press the launcher icon in the apps drawer and choose the Add to Home action. Unfortunately, adding a launcher in this manner sets its icon only on the far right Home screen page.

> » Home screen launchers are shortcuts only. You can still find the app in the apps drawer. In fact, you can set multiple copies of an app on the Home screen. It's dorky, but possible.

> » Newly installed apps often automatically affix a launcher to the Home screen. If you want to remove that launcher, see the later section "Evicting items from the Home screen."

> » The top row of the apps drawer may list frequently accessed apps. Review this list to consider adding a frequent app to the Home screen if its launcher isn't there already.

Placing a launcher on the favorites tray

The row of launcher icons at the bottom of the Home screen remains the same no matter which Home screen page you're viewing. It's called the *favorites tray*, and it's an ideal spot for apps you use most frequently.

To add a launcher to the favorites tray, first remove an existing icon: Drag it off the favorites tray, either to the Home screen page or to the Remove or Delete icon. This step makes room for a new launcher, which you can then drag from the Home screen or from the apps drawer.

>> If you drag an icon to the favorites tray without first making room, you may create a folder instead of replacing the existing icon. See the later section "Working with folders."

>> The best launchers to place on the Home screen are those that show notifications, as shown in the margin. The apps include Facebook, Twitter, Email, and others.

Slapping down widgets

Beyond launchers, the Home screen is also where you find widgets. A *widget* works like a tiny, interactive or informative window, often providing a gateway into another app, or it displays information such as status updates, the current song that's playing, or the current weather.

To add widgets to the Home screen, obey these steps:

1. Switch to a Home screen page that has enough room for the new widget.

Widgets come in a variety of sizes. The size is measured by launcher icon dimensions: A 1x1 widget occupies the same space as a launcher. A 2x2 widget is twice as tall and twice as wide as a launcher.

2. Long-press a blank part of the Home screen.

3. Choose Widgets.

A list of widgets appears, with each shown alphabetically along with preview images and the widget's dimensions. Widgets associated with apps, such as Calendar and Weather, appear under those names.

4. Long-press the widget you want to add.

5. Position the widget on the Home screen.

As you drag the widget, existing launcher icons and widgets jiggle to make room.

6. Lift your finger.

If the widget grows a border, it can be resized. See the next section.

After adding some widgets, you may be prompted for additional information — for example, a location for a weather widget or a contact name for a contact widget.

>> The variety of available widgets depends on the apps installed. Some apps come with widgets, some apps don't, and some widgets are independent of any app.

>> Fret not if you change your mind about the widget's location. See the later section "Moving launchers and widgets" for obtaining the proper feng shui.

>> To remove a widget, see the later section "Evicting items from the Home screen."

Resizing a widget

Some widgets are resizable. You can change a widget's size immediately after plopping it down on the Home screen — or at any time, really: The secret is to long-press the widget. If it grows a box, as shown in Figure 20-1, you can change the widget's dimensions.

Drag to resize

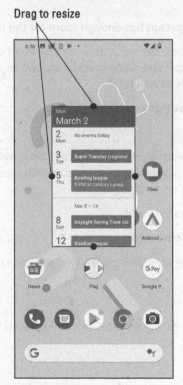

FIGURE 20-1:
Resizing a widget

244   PART 4 **Nuts and Bolts**

To resize, drag one of the resizing dots in or out. Tap elsewhere on the touchscreen when you're done.

Moving launchers and widgets

Launchers and widgets aren't fastened to the Home screen with anything stronger than masking tape. That's obvious because it's quite easy to pick up and move a launcher or widget, relocating it to a new position or removing it completely. To start, long-press an item, as illustrated in Figure 20-2.

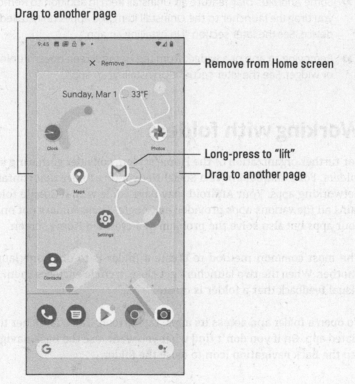

Drag to another page

Remove from Home screen

Long-press to "lift"

Drag to another page

FIGURE 20-2:
Moving a
launcher

Drag the item to another position on the Home screen. If you drag to the far left or far right of the screen, the icon or widget is sent to another Home screen page.

REMEMBER

>> When you long-press some launchers, action shortcuts appear. To move the launcher, ignore the shortcuts and drag your finger to relocate the launcher.

>> On some Samsung devices, long-pressing a launcher displays a pop-up x of actions for the icon. As with the shortcuts, drag your finger to make the pop-up vanish.

Evicting items from the Home screen

To banish a launcher or widget from the Home screen, move the launcher or widget to the Remove icon located atop the Home screen.

For some Samsung devices, long-press the app to view its shortcut menu. Choose the action Remove from Home or Remove Shortcut.

WARNING

>> The Remove icon may be an X or the word *Remove* (refer to Figure 20-2), though some devices show the Delete (trash) icon.

>> Some Androids may feature an Uninstall item in addition to Remove. When you drag the launcher to the Uninstall item, the app is uninstalled from your device. See the later section "Uninstalling an app."

>> Removing an app or a widget from the Home screen doesn't uninstall the app or widget. See the later section "Uninstalling an app."

Working with folders

For further organization of the Home screen, consider gathering similar apps into folders. For example, I have a Social Networking folder that contains all my social networking apps. Your Android may have come with a Google folder, which contains all the various apps provided by Google. These folders not only help organize your apps but also solve the problem of a crowded Home screen.

The most common method to create a folder is to drag one launcher on top of another. When the two launchers get close, a circle encloses them, which provides visual feedback that a folder is created.

To open a folder and access its apps, tap its icon. Tap a launcher to start the associated app. Or, if you don't find what you want, use the Back navigation gesture or tap the Back navigation icon to close the folder.

>> To add more app launchers to the folder, drag in their icons.

>> Some folders may feature a Plus (+) icon or the Add Apps button. Tap this icon or button to add more launchers.

>> Folders are organized just like other items on the Home screen. You drag folder icons around or delete them. When you delete a folder, you remove the launcher icons from the folder; deleting the folder doesn't uninstall the apps.

>> To change a folder's name, open the folder and tap the folder's name. Use the onscreen keyboard to type a new name.

>> Some Androids may display a palette in a folder, from which you can set the folder's background color.

>> To remove a launcher from a folder, open the folder and drag out the icon. When the second-to-last icon is dragged out of a folder, the folder is removed. If it isn't, drag the last icon out and then remove the folder, as you would any other item on the Home screen, as described in the preceding section.

App Management

The apps you install on your Android originate from the Play Store app. And that's where you can return for basic app management. The task includes reviewing apps you've downloaded, updating apps, and removing apps that you no longer want or that you severely hate.

>> Additional app management is provided in the Settings app, though for most app chores it's off to the Play Store.

>> Also see Chapter 17 for details on virus protection.

Reviewing your apps

To peruse the apps you've downloaded from Google Play, follow these steps:

1. **Open the Play Store app.**

2. **Tap the Side Menu icon.**

   If you don't see this icon (shown in the margin) at the top left corner of the app's screen, use the Back navigation gesture or tap the Back navigation icon until it appears.

3. **Choose My Apps & Games from the navigation drawer.**

Your apps are presented in three categories, shown on three tabs: Updates, Installed, and Library, illustrated in Figure 20-3. You might also see the Subscriptions tab, with recurring items, such as video and magazine subscriptions.

Apps updating   Apps installed on this device

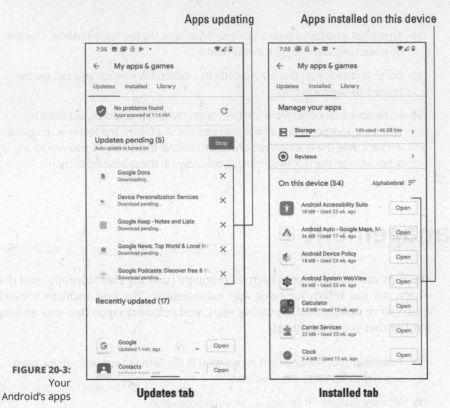

FIGURE 20-3:
Your
Android's apps

Updates tab   **Installed tab**

The difference between the Installed and Library tabs depends on the apps installed on the device. Only apps available on the device appear on the Installed tab. Apps you've obtained (even on other Android gizmos), but not installed on the device, are listed on the Library tab.

>> Tap an app in the list to view its details.

>> Uninstalled apps remain on the Library tab because you did, at one time, download the app.

>> To reinstall an app listed on the Library tab (and without paying a second time for paid apps), choose the app from the Library tab's list and tap the Install button.

Updating apps

New versions, or updates, of apps happen all the time. They're automatic. Occasionally, you're called upon to perform a manual update. How can you tell? The App Update notification appears, which is the generic Google Play Store notification, shown in the margin.

To deal with a manual update, open the Play Store app to view all your installed apps, as presented in the preceding section (see Figure 20-4, left side, shown later in this chapter). What you're looking for is the Update All button. Tap that button to apply necessary app updates. If prompted to accept the app's permissions, tap the Accept button. If the Update All button doesn't appear, your apps are up-to-date.

You can gaze upon the app update process in the Play Store app or wander off and do something else with your Android.

>> Yes, an Internet connection is required in order to update apps. If possible, try to use Wi-Fi so that you don't incur any data surcharges on your mobile-data bill. Android apps aren't superhuge in size, but why take the risk?

>> If the Internet connection is broken during an update, the update process continues after the connection is reestablished. Apps aren't messed up by the interruption.

Uninstalling an app

I can think of a few reasons to remove an app. It's with eager relish that I remove apps that don't work or that somehow annoy me. It's also perfectly okay to remove redundant apps, such as when you're trying to find a decent music-listening app and you end up with a dozen or so that you never use.

Whatever the reason, heed these steps to remove an app:

1. **Open the Play Store app.**

2. **Choose My Apps & Games from the navigation drawer.**

3. **Tap the Installed tab.**

4. **Choose the app that offends you.**

   Tap the app's card, not the Open button. You see the app's description from within the Play Store app.

5. **Tap the Uninstall button.**

6. **Tap the OK button to confirm.**

   The app is removed.

The app appears on the Library list even after the app has been removed. That's because you downloaded it once. That doesn't mean, however, that the app is installed.

» You can always reinstall paid apps that you've uninstalled. For paid apps, you aren't charged twice for doing so.

» On some Samsung galactic gizmos, long-press an app in the apps drawer. Choose the Uninstall action from the shortcuts pop-up.

WARNING

» You can't remove apps that are preinstalled by either the manufacturer or cellular provider. I'm sure there's a technical way to uninstall such apps, but seriously: Just don't use the apps if you want to remove them and discover that you can't.

Controlling app notifications

Some apps may harbor their own notification controls, which is messy. Before checking each app for notification settings, heed these directions to use the Settings app instead:

1. **Open the Settings app.**

2. **Choose Apps & Notifications, and then select Notifications; on Samsung devices, choose the Notifications item.**

   You see a list of apps that have recently generated notifications.

3. **Choose an app to set individual notification options.**

   For example, in Figure 20-4, notification options for the Gmail app appear. You can disable all notifications by switching the master control to the Off position. Or you can set individual notification options as offered by the specific app.

As an example, I disabled notifications on one app that kept bugging me all the time with trivial notices. The app still runs, albeit silently.

Selecting an open-by-default app

Every so often, you may see an Open With or Complete Action Using prompt, which may look like those shown in Figure 20-5. Regardless of its appearance, you're prompted to choose an app to complete an action and then given the choice of Just Once or Always.

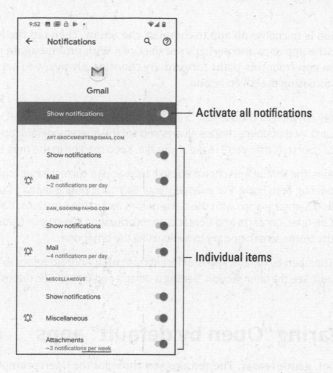

FIGURE 20-4:
App notifications

Activate all notifications

Individual items

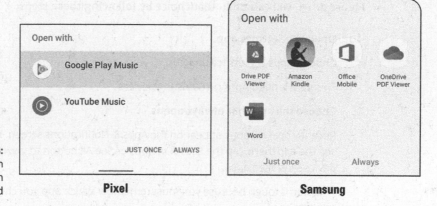

FIGURE 20-5:
The Open With
question
is posed

Pixel   **Samsung**

The apps listed are each capable of completing some action. On the left in
Figure 20-5, a sound file was chosen, and the apps listed can play the sound file.
On the right, a PDF file was chosen, and each app listed can open or view the
PDF. Sometimes, a recently used app appears atop the list.

Your job is to choose an app to complete the action. Then tap the Just Once button to use the app once and perhaps see the Open With prompt again or tap Always to use the app from this point forward. By choosing Always, you set the default app for completing the given action.

TIP

» My advice is to choose Just Once until you get sick of seeing the Open With card. At that point, choose Always and set the open-by-default app. The fear, of course, is that you'll make a mistake. Keep reading in the next section.

» Alas, the default app choice doesn't allow you to correct what I call the dueling-apps issue. For example, your Samsung phone features both Google and Samsung apps with the same names and same functions: Calendar and Calendar, Contacts and Contacts. In this situation, keep your favorite app on the Home screen and try to avoid using the other one.

» The open-by-default app is different from what Android refers to as a *default app*. See the later section "Setting a default app for specific duties."

Clearing "Open by default" apps

Fret not, gentle reader. The settings you chose for the Open prompt can be undone. For example, if you select the Drive PDF Viewer app from the right side in Figure 20-5, you can undo that choice by following these steps:

1. **Open the Settings app.**

2. **Choose Apps & Notifications.**

   This item is titled Apps on Samsung devices.

3. **Choose the app that always opens.**

   Recently opened apps appear on the Apps & Notifications screen. If you don't see the app there, tap the See All *xx* Apps or See All button to view all your device's installed apps.

   This step is tough because you must remember which app you chose to "always" open.

4. **On the App Info screen, choose Open by Default or Set as Default.**

   If you don't see this item, tap Advanced.

5. **Tap the Clear Defaults button.**

After you clear the defaults for an app, you see the Open With card again. The next time you see it, however, make a better choice.

Setting a default app for specific duties

Adding confusion to the already befuddling term *default*, your Android features a set of default apps. These are the apps designated to control specific device features, such as

>> The app to place phone calls on an Android phone

>> The app to send and receive text messages on an Android phone

>> The web browser app

>> The camera app

>> The Home screen app

>> Other things I can't think of

For example, if you want to use a different camera app or text messaging app, you can reset the default app by following these steps:

1. **Open the Settings app.**

2. **Choose Apps & Notifications.**

   On some devices, this item is titled Apps.

3. **Choose Default Apps.**

   You may need to expand the Advanced item: Tap the chevron to view the Default Apps item.

4. **Select a default app to reset.**

   For example, choose Browser App to set a web browser other than Chrome.

5. **Choose the default app.**

   Available apps appear in the list.

For Samsung galactic gizmos, choose the Apps item in the Settings app. Tap the Action Overflow and choose Default Apps. From this screen, choose a default app to reset.

>> Additional apps to carry out the "default" functions can be found at Google Play; see Chapter 17.

>> The most common default app to change is the text messaging app. Usually, a phone has two: the stock Android version and a crappy one supplied by your device's manufacturer. See Chapter 8.

>> The Home screen app is the one you see when you use the Home navigation gesture or tap the Home navigation icon. Yes, it can be changed. Many alternative Home screen apps are available, from those that display very basic uses to advanced and nerdy Home screen apps.

WARNING

>> I recommend not resetting default apps until you become comfortable using your Android. Most documentation and helpful resources such as this book assume that you're using the stock Android apps, such as Chrome for the web browser.

Reviewing app permissions

The Android operating system is completely open about which apps access which device features. That's the reason you see the various permission cards to allow or deny access. To review or reset those permissions, obey these directions:

1. **Open the Settings app.**

2. **Choose Apps & Notifications.**

   On Samsung gizmos, choose the Apps category.

3. **Choose Permission Manager.**

   You may need to choose the Advanced item to locate Permission Manager. On Samsung devices, tap the Action Overflow to locate the Permission Manager or similar item.

   You see a list of hardware and software items an app can access on your Android — for example: Location, Microphone, Storage, and so on.

4. **Tap a category.**

   A list shows apps that can access the resource.

5. **Choose an app to reset its permission.**

6. **Choose Allow to grant the app access or Deny to restrict access.**

   On some Androids, manipulate the master control to allow or deny access to the specific app.

Resetting the access permission doesn't prevent the app from asking again in the future. Some permission cards feature the Do Not Ask Again check box, which you can select to ensure that the question doesn't arise again. Still, other apps are persistent.

Shutting down an app run amok

Sometimes an app goofs up or crashes. You may see a warning message on the touchscreen, informing you that the app has been shut down. That's good. What's better is that you too can shut down apps that misbehave or those you cannot otherwise stop.

First, try dismissing the app from the Overview:

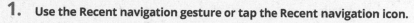

1. **Use the Recent navigation gesture or tap the Recent navigation icon.**

2. **Swipe away the miscreant app's thumbnail or tap the X button.**

   The app is closed.

When these steps don't work, more drastic measures are required:

1. **Open the Settings app.**

2. **Choose the Apps & Notifications category.**

   On Samsung devices, the category is titled Apps.

3. **Choose the errant app from the list of recently opened apps.**

   If the app isn't on this list, tap the See All *xx* Apps item.

4. **Tap the Force Stop button.**

   The app is terminated.

If the Force Stop button isn't available, the app isn't running.

WARNING

Use the Force Stop button only as a final act. Don't kill off any app or service unless the app is annoying or you are otherwise unable to stop it. Avoid killing off Google Services, which can change the device's behavior or render the Android operating system unstable.

Apps Drawer Organization

Some Androids offer tools for arranging apps on the apps drawer. These tools allow you to present the apps in an order other than alphabetical, rearrange the apps, or even collect apps into folders.

The key to organizing the apps drawer is to look for the Action Overflow or for specific icons on the screen. For example, some Samsung gizmos feature the EDIT button, which is used to arrange icons on the apps drawer. The A–Z command arranges apps in alphabetical order.

You may find a Folder action that lets you build apps drawer folders, or you might create folders by dragging icons over each other, similar to how folders work on the Home screen folder. Refer to the earlier section "Working with folders" for details.

IN THIS CHAPTER

» **Changing the background image**

» **Working with Home screen pages**

» **Setting orientation**

» **Changing the screen brightness**

» **Putting shortcuts on the lock screen**

» **Activating keyboard feedback**

» **Checking predictive text**

» **Setting sound options**

Chapter **21**

Customize and Configure

Customizing your Android doesn't involve sprucing up the case, so put away that Bedazzler™. The kind of customization this chapter refers to involves fine-tuning the way the Android operating system presents itself. You can modify the Home screen, adjust the display, customize the keyboard, and change sounds. The goal is to truly make the device your own.

It's Your Home Screen — and Lock Screen

The typical Android Home screen sports anywhere from three to nine pages and a specific background, or *wallpaper,* preset by the device's manufacturer or cellular provider. You're not stuck with this choice — both the Home screen and the lock screen are yours to change at your whim.

Accessing Home screen actions

To start your Home screen decoration project, long-press a blank part of the Home screen. Don't long-press an icon or a widget. Upon success, you see a single

Home screen management card or multiple icons, arranged differently depending on your device, as illustrated in Figure 21-1.

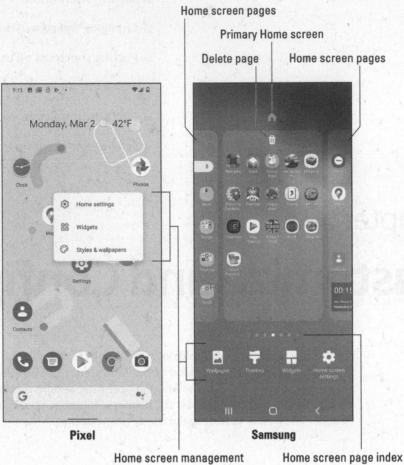

FIGURE 21-1:
Home screen actions

The icons or options presented for Home screen management include some or all of the following:

Settings: Control basic Home screen behavior and options.

Styles and Wallpaper: Change the background image and icon presentations.

Widgets: Add widgets to the Home screen.

The Styles and Wallpaper item is shown as two separate icons on Samsung devices: Wallpaper and Themes (refer to Figure 21-1).

Changing Home screen settings

Home screen settings items include activating notification dots on launcher icons, controlling how new app icons are added to the Home screen, changing Home screen orientation, and more. To set these items, long-press the Home screen and choose Home Settings or Home Screen Settings (refer to Figure 21-1).

Some Androids may offer Home screen options to change the layout, resize the app grid, show the Apps drawer button, and make other interesting and obscure settings. For example, on Samsung devices you can choose a high-density app grid to allow for more launchers and folders on the Home screen.

Choosing a new style or wallpaper

Home screen styles control elements such as the font, icons, colors, shapes, and other elements that complete the Home screen presentation. Styles are chosen by long-pressing the Home screen and choosing Styles & Wallpaper and then tapping the Style tab. On Samsung devices, choose the Themes item to choose from a variety of Home screen delights.

The *wallpaper,* or Home screen background, might be included as part of a style package, or it can be set separately. Two styles of wallpaper are available: traditional and live. *Traditional* wallpaper can be any image, such as a picture you've taken or an image provided by the device's manufacturer. *Live* wallpaper is animated or interactive.

To set a new wallpaper for the Home screen, obey these steps:

1. **Long-press the Home screen.**

2. **Choose Styles & Wallpapers or Wallpaper.**

3. **Ensure that you're viewing the Wallpaper tab.**

   The other tab is Style. Some devices show only wallpaper settings.

4. **Choose a wallpaper category.**

   To choose your own images, tap the My Photos or Gallery button.

5. **Tap a wallpaper to see a preview.**

6. **Tap the Set Wallpaper button to confirm your choice.**

   Some devices may prompt you to set the wallpaper for the Home screen, lock screen, or both.

When choosing your own photo or image, you might be given the opportunity to crop the image before setting the wallpaper. Unlike cropping a photo (covered in

Chapter 14), you may see two rectangles for cropping in both landscape and portrait orientations.

TIP

>> Some wallpapers come with advertising. Others are available for a fee.

>> Another way to set the wallpaper is to view an image in the Photos app. Select the image and tap the Action Overflow. Choose the Use As action and then Wallpaper.

Managing Home screen pages

The number of pages on the Home screen isn't fixed. You can add pages. You can remove pages. You can even rearrange pages. This feature might not be available to all Androids and, sadly, it isn't implemented in exactly the same way.

The stock Android method of adding a Home screen page is to drag an icon right, just as though you were positioning that icon on another Home screen page. When a page to the right doesn't exist, a new page is added automatically.

Some Androids may be more specific in how pages are added. For example, you can choose a Page command from the Home screen menu.

On Samsung devices, use the Delete icon (refer to Figure 21-1) to remove a Home screen page. Use the Add (plus) icon on the Home screen page index to add a new page.

>> The maximum number of Home screen pages may be three, five, seven, or nine, depending on your device. The minimum is one.

>> Older Androids let you add pages left or right and rearrange the pages. Since Android version 8.0 (Oreo), the far left Home screen page is reserved for the Google Assistant app. On Samsung devices, the far left Home screen page is reserved for its Bixby assistant.

>> Samsung devices let you reset the primary Home screen page, which need not be the center Home screen page. I've seen different ways to accomplish this task. The most common one is to tap the Home icon in a thumbnail's preview, which is illustrated earlier, in Figure 21-1.

Adding lock screen launchers

Some Androids feature lock screen launchers, such as a Camera launcher in the lower right corner of the lock screen. Swipe that icon to run the Camera app without fully unlocking the device. It's a quick way to take a picture.

To see whether your Android lets you customize or add lock screen launchers, heed these steps:

1. **Open the Settings app.**

2. **Choose Lock Screen or Lock Screen and Security.**

If you can't find the Lock Screen item, your Android lacks the capability to modify lock screen launchers.

3. **Choose Shortcuts or Apps Shortcuts.**

4. **Select the apps to place on the lock screen.**

You may see one or more app screen shortcuts for launchers along with the Camera app. I've seen devices that let you line up five launchers at the bottom of the lock screen. Because this feature isn't a part of stock Android, it can vary.

REMEMBER

>> When you use a lock screen launcher (shortcut) to start an app, the device isn't fully unlocked. To access other features, you must work the screen lock.

>> The lock screen shortcuts might not be available if you've not set the screen lock for your Android.

>> See Chapter 22 for details on screen locks and lock screen notifications.

Display Settings

The Display item in the Settings app deals with touchscreen settings. Items worthy of your attention include screen orientation (or rotation), display brightness, and the screen timeout options.

Saving your eyeballs

To help you smoothly transition to sleep while using your Android at night (and admit it — you use the thing in bed), consider activating the Blue Light filter:

1. **Open the Settings app.**

2. **Choose Display.**

3. **Choose Night Light.**

   On Samsung devices, by the Blue Light Filter item, set the master control to the On position.

4. **Choose the Night Light or Blue Light Filter item to make further adjustments, set a schedule, and so on.**

The Night Light filter eliminates the blue end of the visible light spectrum, rendering the screen a warm yellow color. This change helps your eyes adapt at night. Options on the Blue Light Filter screen direct your Android to turn on the filter from dusk to dawn, which is ideal. (You must allow the app permission to access your device's location to ensure that sunset-to-sunrise times are properly set.)

Another eyeball-saving setting is Dark Theme or Dark Mode. When it's active, some apps switch their color scheme from dark text on a light background to light text on a dark background, which many folks find easier on the eyes. Look for the Dark Theme or Dark Mode item on the display screen in the Settings app (follow Steps 1 and 2 in this section).

Setting orientation

Many apps, and perhaps the Home screen itself, can change their presentation as you switch the Android between portrait and horizontal orientations. You can lock that presentation, if you like. Heed the directions:

1. **Open the Settings app and choose Display.**

2. **Choose Auto-Rotate Screen or Device Rotation.**

   If necessary, choose the Advanced item to locate this item.

This item may present itself as a master control, though you might see options for locking in an orientation.

REMEMBER

>> Even if this setting isn't available for your Android, remember to look on the quick settings drawer. The Rotation icon is found there, which lets you switch between freely rotating the touchscreen and locking it into one position or the other. This setting may not apply to the Home screen.

TIP

>> The Play Books app offers its own screen orientation controls, which make it easier (and more predictable) to read an eBook. See Chapter 16.

Adjusting display brightness

The touchscreen can be too bright, too dim, or just right. Which setting is best? That's up to you. Follow these steps:

1. **Open the Settings app.**

2. **Choose Display.**

3. **Choose Brightness Level.**

    This item might not appear in some Settings apps. Instead, you immediately see the Brightness slider.

4. **Adjust the slider to set the touchscreen's intensity.**

If you'd rather have the Android's brain and secret eyeball adjust the brightness for you, use the Adaptive Brightness item to set the display's brightness based on your location's ambient light.

TIP

>> The Adaptive Brightness setting might be called Auto Brightness or Automatic Brightness.

>> You also find the Brightness setting in the quick settings drawer. See Chapter 3.

Setting the screen lock time-out

Unless you press the Power/Lock key, the touchscreen automatically locks itself after a given period of inactivity. To adjust that period, obey these steps:

1. **Open the Settings app and choose Display.**

2. **Choose Screen Timeout or Sleep.**

3. **Select a time-out value from the list.**

    The standard value is 1 minute.

The sleep timer measures inactivity; after you last touch the screen, the timer starts ticking. About 5 seconds before the touchscreen locks, the screen dims. Then the touchscreen turns off and the device locks. If you tap the screen before then, the timer is reset.

TECHNICAL
STUFF

The lock screen has its own time-out. If you unlock the Android but don't work the screen lock, the device locks itself automatically after about 10 seconds. This time-out is not adjustable.

Configuring the always-on touchscreen

Many Androids feature an always-on or wake-up display. Called Screen Saver, this feature shows the current time and perhaps a few notifications, even when the device is locked. This convenience doesn't affect battery life. Obey these steps:

1. **In the Settings app, choose Display.**
2. **Choose Screen Saver.**

Options available include setting the type of screen saver, though the Clock is the most popular. You control when the screen saver starts, such as when the device is docked or charging.

Setting the clock screen saver while charging turns your phone into a convenient bedside clock.

Keyboard Settings

Quite a few options are available for the Google keyboard, the Gboard. Some of these settings enable special features, and others supposedly make the onscreen typing experience more enjoyable. I'll leave it up to you to determine whether that's true.

To examine or change a keyboard setting, you must visit the Settings app. Specifically, these steps get you to the Keyboard Settings screen:

1. **Open the Settings app.**
2. **Choose System or, on Samsung devices, choose General Management.**
3. **Choose Language & Input.**
4. **Choose Virtual Keyboard, which is titled On-Screen Keyboard on Samsung phones and tablets.**
5. **Choose Gboard or — you guessed it — Samsung Keyboard.**
6. **Choose Preferences.**

   Abuse the settings as described in the following sections.

Customizing the keyboard layout

Here are several items you can change from the default keyboard presentation:

Add a number row. On the keyboard preferences screen (refer to the preceding section), set the Number Row master control to the On position. For Samsung devices, choose the Keyboard Layout option and ensure that the master control by the Number Keys option is set to the On position.

Add quick access to emojis. Activate the Show Emoji Switch Key setting; set its master control to the On position. For the Samsung Keyboard, set the master control by the Keyboard Toolbar option to the On position.

Adjust the keyboard height. Choose the Keyboard Height item and select from one of several options from Extra-Short to Extra-Tall. The default setting is Normal. On a Samsung device, choose the Size and Transparency option, and then use the resizing bars to adjust the keyboard's width and height.

Generating keyboard feedback

The onscreen keyboard can assist your typing by generating haptic feedback. This feedback is in the form of either a pleasing click sound or the vibrating of the device.

To check keyboard feedback settings, follow the steps, earlier in this section, to visit the Gboard preferences screen in the Settings app. The two items you can check are Sound on Keypress and Haptic Feedback on Keypress.

For Samsung's keyboard, follow Steps 1 through 5 earlier in this section, and then continue with these steps:

1. **Choose Swipe, Touch, and Feedback.**

2. **Choose Touch Feedback.**

3. **Set the master controls by the Sound and Vibration items.**

Not every Android tablet features vibration.

Ensuring that predictive text is active

Predictive text is on all the time when you use the Gboard. To ensure that the feature is active, follow Steps 1 through 5 earlier in this chapter, in the section "Keyboard Settings," and then continue with the following two steps:

1. **Choose Text Correction.**

2. **Ensure that all the master controls are set to the On position.** On Samsung devices, follow Steps 1 through 4 and then continue with these steps:

1. **Choose Smart Typing.**

2. **Set the master control by Predictive Text to the On position.**

Some of these items you might consider disabling. For example, Auto-Correction or Auto-Replace is the bane of folks who enjoy texting. If so, disable that option; slide the master control to the Off position.

Refer to Chapter 4 for details on using the predictive text feature.

Activating glide typing

Once known as *gesture* typing, *glide* typing allows you to swipe your finger over the onscreen keyboard to create text. Chapter 4 explains the details, although this feature may be inactive on your phone or tablet.

To enable glide type, visit the Keyboard Settings screen as described earlier, in the section "Keyboard Settings," Steps 1 through 5, and choose Glide Typing instead of Preferences in Step 6. Ensure that the item Enable Glide Typing is active.

For Samsung Keyboards, follow Steps 1 through 5 from earlier and choose Swipe, Touch, and Feedback in Step 6. Choose Keyboard Swipe Controls and ensure that the item Swipe to Type has its master control set to the On position.

Audio Adjustments

Yes, your Android makes noise. Incoming calls ring; you hear music, alarms sound; and games go "beep," "bleep," and "blort." The Settings app is the place to go when the sound needs fine-tuning.

Setting the volume

The Volume key on the side of your Android sets the volume as sound is generated. To preset the sound levels, follow these steps:

1. **Open the Settings app.**

2. **Choose Sound or Sounds and Vibration.**

3. **On Samsung gizmos, choose Volume.**

4. **Adjust the sliders to set the volume for various noise sources.**

   The common volume sliders are

   > *Media Volume or Media:* Controls the sound for movies, videos, audio in the web browser, and so on.

   > *Call Volume:* Sets the levels while you're listening to a phone call.

   > *Alarm Volume or Notifications:* Sets the intensity used for the Clock app's alarm or generally for all notifications.

   > *Ring Volume or Ringtone:* Sets an Android phone's ringtone volume. This category includes incoming calls and notifications, although some phones may feature a separate slider for notifications.

   Other sliders may appear, such as System to adjust any volume not covered by the other categories.

5. **Move the slider to the left to make a sound quieter; slide to the right to make a sound louder.**

   When you lift your finger, you hear a sound preview.

TIP

If you'd like your phone to vibrate on an incoming call, enable the option Vibrate for Calls. This item might be titled Vibrate When Ringing.

Selecting a ringtone

The term *ringtone* applies to any sound an Android uses for certain activities. Yes, on an Android phone, the ringtone sounds for an incoming call. The device also features a notification ringtone. The Clock app also uses a ringtone for various alarms.

To review and set the various ringtones, follow these steps:

1. **Open the Settings app.**
2. **Choose Sound or Sounds and Vibration.**
3. **Choose Phone Ringtone or Ringtone.**

   The Phone Ringtone item is made visible by first choosing the Advanced item.

   If confronted by the Complete Action Using prompt, select the Sounds or Media Storage item for now. (Refer to Chapter 20 for details on using the Complete Action Using card or Open With card.)

4. **Select a ringtone from the list.**

You may first see a list of categories, including the My Sounds item for sounds you've saved to your Android.

Upon choosing a potential ringtone, you hear a preview.

5. **Tap the Save or OK button to set the new ringtone.**

On some devices, the new ringtone is set after you choose it in Step 4.

Repeat Steps 4 and 5 for the Default Notification Sound and Default Alarm Sound items. You may need to tap the Advanced item (tap the chevron) to view these two items. On Samsung devices, choose Notification Sound instead.

>> Various apps may set their own ringtones, such as text messaging ringtones, alerts for Calendar events, and alert sounds for Facebook. These ringtones are set within the given app: Look for a Settings action in the app, either found on the navigation drawer or accessed by tapping the Action Overflow icon. The ringtones might also be set from the Settings app: Choose the app from the Apps & Notifications or Apps category. On the App's settings screen, choose Notifications.

TIP

>> To disable a ringtone, choose None in Step 4. Do keep in mind that it's possible to temporarily disable sound on your Android. Refer to Chapter 3.

Chapter **22**

Security and Privacy

As more and more of your life is surrendered to the digital realm, the topic of security grows in importance. This concern extends directly to your Android mobile device, which is often home to your email, social networking, and other online accounts — including, potentially, important files and financial information. Don't take Android security lightly.

Also refer to Chapter 17 for information on fighting malicious Android apps.

Lock Your Android

The first line of defense for your Android is the screen lock. It can be simple, complex, or nonexistent. The choice is yours.

Finding the screen locks

All screen locks on your Android are found in the Settings app, on the Choose Screen Lock screen. Heed these steps to visit this screen:

1. **Open the Settings app.**

2. **Choose Security & Location or, on Samsung devices, choose Lock Screen.**

   This item may have another title, though Security is in there somewhere.

3. **Choose Screen Lock or Screen Lock Type.**

4. **Work any existing secure screen lock to continue.**

   Eventually, you see the Choose Screen Lock screen, which might instead be called Screen Lock Type.

The Choose Screen Lock screen lists several types of screen locks. Some are unique to your device, and others are common Android screen locks, which include

None: This choice is no screen lock at all. You unlock the device by pressing the Power/Lock key or swiping the screen.

Swipe: Unlock the device by swiping your finger across the touchscreen. This item might also be titled Slide.

Pattern: Trace a pattern on the touchscreen to unlock.

PIN: Type a personal identification number (PIN) to unlock the touchscreen.

Password: Type a password to unlock.

Some devices feature additional lock types, including face unlock, fingerprint, and so on. These items might appear on a different screen.

REMEMBER

>> The most secure lock types are the PIN and password. Either screen lock type is required if the Android has multiple users, has a kid's account, or accesses a secure email server.

>> The fingerprint lock is also considered secure, though it often uses a secondary secure lock as a fallback.

>> Some of the less secure choices on the Choose Screen Lock screen are disabled when your device's security is set to High.

TIP

>> I recommend writing down your PIN or password in a secure location, just in case.

>> The screen lock doesn't appear on an Android phone when you answer an incoming call. You're prompted, however, to unlock the phone if you want to use its features while you're on a call.

WARNING

>> The screen lock appears when you first power-on the device or after a restart or an update to the Android operating system.

>> If you're in a panic, you can tap the Emergency Call button on the phone's lock screen to bypass the screen lock and dial 911 or another emergency number.

>> I know of no recovery method available should you forget your Android's PIN or password screen locks. If you use either one, write it down in an inconspicuous spot, just in case.

Removing a screen lock

You don't remove the screen lock on your Android. Instead, you replace it with a non-lock, such as Swipe or None. Follow the directions in the preceding section to get to the Choose Screen Lock screen. Then switch from the Pattern, PIN, or Password screen lock to Swipe or None.

>> You may be prompted for confirmation if you're opting to reset a secure screen lock to one that's less secure.

>> You're prohibited from removing a secure screen lock if the device's storage is encrypted or accesses secure email or when other security features are enabled.

Setting a PIN

The PIN lock assigns a 4- to 16-digit code to the lock screen. You must type the PIN (*personal identification number*) to gain access to the device. This type of screen lock is often employed as a backup for the less secure screen-unlocking methods.

To set the PIN lock, follow the directions in the earlier section "Finding the screen locks" to reach the Choose Screen Lock screen. Choose PIN from the list of locks. You're required to type the PIN twice — once to set it and again to confirm.

Applying a password

The most secure way to lock an Android is to apply a full-on password. Unlike a PIN, a password contains more than digits, including a combination of numbers, symbols, and uppercase and lowercase letters.

Choose Password from the Choose Screen Lock screen to set the password; refer to the earlier section "Finding the screen locks." The password must be at least four characters long, though keep in mind that longer passwords are more secure.

You're prompted to type the password whenever you unlock your Android, initially turn on the device, restart, or try to change the screen lock. Tap the OK button to accept the password and use your gizmo.

Creating an unlock pattern

Perhaps the most popular, and certainly the most unconventional, screen lock is the Pattern lock. You must trace a pattern on the touchscreen to unlock the device. To create a Pattern lock, follow these steps:

1. **Summon the Choose Screen Lock screen.**

Refer to the earlier section "Finding the screen locks."

2. **Choose Pattern.**

If you haven't yet set a pattern, you may see the tutorial describing the process; feel free to skip merrily through the dreary directions.

3. **If you're prompted for Secure Start-up, tap the Yes button.**

I strongly recommend using the Secure Start-up feature.

4. **Trace an unlock pattern.**

Use Figure 22-1 as your guide. You can trace over the dots in any order, but you can trace over a dot only once. The pattern must cover at least four dots.

5. **Tap the Next or Continue button.**

6. **Redraw the pattern.**

7. **Tap the Confirm button.**

You may be required to type a PIN or password as a backup to the Pattern lock. If so, follow the onscreen directions to set that lock as well.

 TIP After the Pattern screen lock is set, the Settings icon appears to the right of its item on the Screen Lock option. Tap that icon and ensure that the setting Make Pattern Visible is chosen. For even more security, you can disable this option, but you must remember how — and where — the pattern goes.

Also: Clean the touchscreen! Smudge marks can betray your pattern.

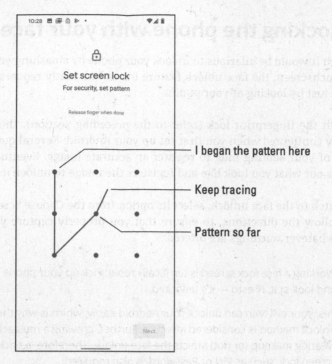

I began the pattern here

Keep tracing

Pattern so far

FIGURE 22-1:
Set the unlock
pattern

Using a fingerprint lock

It's trendy for a smartphone to feature a fingerprint scanner. It's often found on the back of the device, right near where you can smudge the rear camera lens. Tap the scanner to instantly unlock the phone.

The fingerprint scanner is usually configured when you first set up the device. As part of the initial setup, you're prompted to tap the fingerprint scanner multiple times to register a specific digit.

>> To keep ambidextrous humans pleased, some Androids let you register multiple fingers.

>> To work the fingerprint scanner, tap your finger on the sensor. Ensure your finger covers the entire sensor.

>> Backup security is required for the fingerprint scanner, such as a pattern, PIN, or password.

REMEMBER

>> The Fingerprint screen lock is *not* considered secure.

Unlocking the phone with your face

Though it would be hilarious to unlock your phone by smashing your face against the touchscreen, the face unlock feature instead instantly renders access to your device just by looking at your punim.

As with the fingerprint lock (refer to the preceding section), the face unlock is usually configured when you first set up your Android: Several quick pictures are taken of your adoring mug to register an accurate image. Eventually, the device figures out what you look like and registers the image to unlock itself.

To switch to the face unlock, select its option from the Choose Screen Lock screen and follow the directions, to ensure that you properly capture your visage and heed whatever warnings are offered.

>> Working a face lock screen is terrifically rapid: Pick up your phone or tablet and look at it. Presto — it's unlocked.

>> Yes, your evil twin can unlock your Android easily, which is why the face unlock method is considered insecure. Further, growing a mustache or wearing makeup (or not) affects the face unlock. Therefore, a backup screen lock, such as PIN or Password, is also required.

Other Security Features

Beyond locking the screen, other tools are available to help you thwart the Bad Guys and keep safe the information in your mobile device. Tools are also available to help locate a lost or stolen phone or tablet and to wipe your personal data, should you ever need to depart with your Android pal.

Controlling lock screen notifications

Lock screen notifications can be handy — unless you're haggling over the price of a used car and the seller sees a notification from your bank showing how much you can spend. Some notices are innocent, but some are sensitive. To control how all notifications appear on the lock screen, follow these steps:

1. **Open the Settings app.**
2. **Choose Apps & Notification or, on Samsung gizmos, choose Lock Screen.**

   Some devices may title this item Sound & Notification or something similar.

3. Choose Notifications.

On Samsung devices, disable lock screen notifications by deactivating the master control. Otherwise, choose the Notifications item by the master control to configure lock screen notifications. You're done.

4. Choose Notifications On Lockscreen.

The wording for this item may not exactly match this title.

5. Select a lock screen notification level.

Up to three settings are available:

- Show alerting and silent notifications
- Choose alerting notifications only
- Don't show notifications

The names of these settings may be subtly different on your device.

6. Choose a notification level.

The Choose Alerting Notifications Only option (refer to Step 5) appears only when a secure screen lock is chosen. When active, only the app's icon appears on the lock screen; text previews are suppressed.

When lock screen notifications are abbreviated or hidden, double-tap the notification to open its related app and view more details. You must unlock the device first, and then the app opens.

Adding owner info text

Suppose that you lose your phone or tablet. A kind person finds it. (I know, bear with me here.) She looks on the touchscreen to see who owns the device. How would she know? Because you followed these steps to add the owner info text on your Android's lock screen:

1. Open the Settings app.

2. Choose Display.

On older Androids, choose the Security category.

3. Choose Lock Screen Display.

You may need to tap the chevron by the Advanced item to locate Lock Screen Display.

4. Choose Lock Screen Message.

5. **Type text in the box.**

For example, type **This phone belongs to Arius Sterling** — if your name is Arius Sterling.

6. **Tap the Save or Done button.**

On Samsung devices, in the Settings app, choose Lock Screen and then choose Contact Information. Type your owner info text into the box, as directed by Step 6 in the first step list in this section.

REMEMBER

Whatever text you type in the box appears on the lock screen, usually as only one line. Be brief and succinct. I recommend typing something useful: your name, another phone number, an email address, or similar vital information. This way, should someone find your Android, he or she can easily contact you.

WARNING

>> The owner info may not show up when None is selected as a screen lock.

>> Avoid using your Gmail address in the owner info text. An unscrupulous person can use this address to unlock and gain access to your phone.

Finding a lost device

Someday, you may lose your beloved Android. It might be for a few panic-filled seconds, or it might be for forever. The hardware solution is to chain a heavy object to the phone, such as an anvil. Alas, that strategy kind of defeats the entire mobile/wireless paradigm.

To quickly locate your Android, follow these steps:

1. **Open a web browser, such as Google Chrome.**

Oops! You can't use your missing phone. Better complete these steps on a computer.

2. **Visit the main Google search page:** www.google.com.

3. **Type** find my phone **or** find my tablet **and press the Enter key.**

4. **If prompted, sign in to your Google (Gmail) account.**

Your phone or tablet's location appears on the screen.

To ensure that this system works best, complete these steps on your phone or tablet:

1. **Open the Settings app.**

2. **Choose Security or, on Samsung devices, choose Biometrics and Security.**

3. **Choose Find My Device.**

4. **Ensure that the master control is set to the On position.**

TIP

To remotely erase your Android, obtain the app named Google Find My Device from the Google Play Store. Install this app and heed the directions. Its features include finding your device, sounding the ringtone, and remotely erasing all the device's data.

Encrypting storage

Encrypting an Android's storage seems drastic, but it's highly secure, and some devices come with this feature activated right out of the box. The encryption process ensures that if a Bad Guy finds your phone or tablet and somehow manages to bypass all the device's security features, he still can't access any information.

WARNING

It's not currently possible to remove encryption from an Android mobile gizmo. After encryption is applied, it's stuck forever, like a regrettable, drunken tattoo of that girl you met in Ensenada.

To start the encryption process, follow these steps:

1. **Ensure that the device has a secure screen lock — a PIN or password.**

   Refer to the first part of this chapter for details.

2. **Connect the Android to a power source, or ensure that it's fully charged.**

   Encryption can take as long as several hours if your device's storage is rather full.

3. **Open the Settings app and choose Security.**

4. **Look below the heading Encryption & Credentials.**

   Tap the Advanced item if you don't first see Encryption & Credentials.

   If the text below this item reads *Device encrypted,* you're done; the device is already encrypted. Otherwise, continue with Step 5.

5. **Choose Encryption & Credentials.**

6. **Choose Encrypt Phone or Encrypt Tablet.**

7. **Tap the Encrypt Phone or Encrypt Tablet button.**

8. **Wait.**

On Samsung devices, in the Settings app, choose Biometrics and Security, and then Other Security Settings, and, finally, Strong Protection. Ensure that the master control is in the On position.

Performing a factory data reset

The most secure thing you can do with the information on your Android is to erase it all. The procedure, known as a *factory data reset*, effectively restores the device to its original state, fresh out of the box.

WARNING

A factory data reset is a drastic thing. It not only removes all information from storage but also erases all your accounts. Don't take this step lightly! In fact, if you're using this procedure to cure an ill, I recommend first getting support. See Chapter 24.

When you're ready to erase all the device's data, follow these steps:

1. **Open the Settings app.**

2. **Choose System.**

If you're using a Samsung galactic gadget, choose General Management and then Reset. Skip to Step 4.

3. **Choose Reset Options.**

You may need to choose the Advanced item to find Reset Options.

4. **Choose Erase All Data (Factory Reset), which is titled Factory Data Reset on Samsung devices.**

5. **Review the data presented.**

Everything gets wiped, so the reminder screen reinforces the extreme measures taken in a factory data reset.

6. **Tap the button Erase All Data, Reset (or a similarly named button).**

7. **If prompted, work the screen lock.**

This level of security prevents others from idly messing with your beloved gizmo.

8. **Tap the Erase All Data, Erase Everything, or Delete All button to confirm.**

All the information you've set or stored on the device is purged, including all your accounts, any apps you've downloaded, music — everything.

TIP

Practical instances when this action is necessary include selling your Android, giving it to someone else to use, and upgrading to a new phone or tablet.

This process doesn't erase removable storage data. You must reformat the microSD card or otherwise subject it to some form of destruction. Refer to Chapter 19 for details on formatting microSD card storage.

Erasing all the data from an Android phone doesn't reset the phone number. You must remove the SIM card to disassociate the phone number from that phone. Or you can replace the SIM card to use another phone number with the phone.

Privacy

Does your phone spy on you? The answer is unclear, but the point is that it has the potential to. Your Android device has a camera and microphone. It features a GPS radio that can track your position. It can communicate this data to the Internet. Spy? Yep.

The good news is that *you* are in control. You can allow or deny apps to access the device's hardware features. These features are a new and welcome addition with the latest version of the Android operating system.

Hiding your location

In the Settings apps, choose Location to access the list of apps that have been granted permission to access the Android's GPS radio and read your location on Planet Earth. Choose the App Permission item to witness the list.

For each app granted access, you can adjust the setting to allow access only while using the app or to deny access outright. Further, you can disable the Use Location master control on the main location screen to deny access to the GPS radio for all apps.

» Disabling access to the device's GPS radio doesn't prevent some apps from asking again for access.

» Location options for a child's phone, or a child's account when using your Android, are configured when the child's account is added to the device. See Chapter 25 for information about creating a child's account on an Android.

Controlling permissions

All current Android apps must ask permission before accessing device hardware features, such as the microphone or camera, as well as software features such as your contacts list. In the latest version of the Android operating system, permissions details are kept in a single location in the Settings app. To visit this place, heed these directions:

1. **Open the Settings app.**

2. **Choose Privacy.**

3. **Choose Permission Manager.**

   You see a list of device features, below which you see information on how many apps have permission to access the named feature.

4. **Choose a feature.**

   For example, select Microphone to see which apps have permission to use the device's microphone and which have been denied.

To reset permissions, choose an app from the list (in Step 4) and select either Allow or Deny. While vising this screen, choose the option See All *App's* Permissions to view which other Android features the named app is either allowed or denied access.

WARNING

Suspect apps are notorious for asking permission to access features that have little to do with the app's given function — for example, a flashlight program that wants access to your Android's microphone and contacts list.

Thwarting ads

Most free or "lite" versions of a paid app vex you by displaying advertisements. Games are notorious this way. Though you can't banish all ads, you can halt them from being targeted toward you based on information the phone gathers. Follow these directions:

1. **Open the Settings app and choose Privacy.**

2. **Choose the Ads category.**

   You may need to first choose Advanced to reveal the Ads item.

3. **By the item Opt Out of Ads Personalization, slide the master control to the On position.**

   Yes, this item is off by default.

REMEMBER

Activating the opt-out is no guarantee that non-Google apps and social networking sites won't continue to track your personal choices or monitor other behavior in their efforts to direct advertising your way.

Chapter **23**

On the Road Again

Y ou're in a land far, far away. The sun shines warmly upon your face. A gentle breeze wafts over crashing waves. You wiggle your toes in the soft, grainy sand. And the number-one thought on your mind is, "Can my Android phone get a signal?"

For an Android tablet, the question is the same: "Do they have Wi-Fi on this beach?" Funny as it sounds, they probably do.

As a mobile device, your Android is designed to go wherever you go. And if you give the thing a good throw, it can go beyond where you go, but that's not my point. Because it is wireless and has a generous battery, an Android mobile device is built to go on the road. Where can you take it? How can it survive? What if it runs off by itself? Does it need wheels? These are some of the issues regarding taking your Android elsewhere.

Where the Android Roams

The word *roam* takes on an entirely new meaning when applied to an Android phone or LTE tablet. It means that your device receives a cell signal whenever you're outside the service provider's operating area. In that case, your Android is roaming.

Roaming sounds handy, but there's a catch: It almost always involves a surcharge for using another cellular service — an unpleasant surcharge.

Detecting phone service roaming

Relax: Your Android alerts you whenever it's roaming. The Roaming icon appears at the top of the screen, in the status area, whenever you're outside your cellular provider's signal area. The icon differs from device to device, but generally the letter *R* figures in it somewhere, as in the margin.

On an Android phone, you might even see the alien cellular provider's name appear on the lock screen.

To avoid roaming surcharges when making phone calls, wait until you're back in an area serviced by your primary cellular provider.

TIP

If you're concerned about roaming while overseas, place the phone into Airplane mode, as discussed elsewhere in this chapter.

Stopping MMS when roaming

Another network service you might want to disable while roaming has to do with multimedia, or MMS, text messages. To avoid surcharges from another cellular network for downloading an MMS message, follow these steps when using the stock Android Messages app:

1. **Ensure that you're viewing the main screen, not an individual message thread.**

2. **Tap the Action Overflow icon.**

3. **Choose Settings.**

4. **Choose Advanced or More Settings.**

5. **Ensure that the Auto-Download MMS setting is off or disabled.**

   This item might also be called Auto-Retrieve or Roaming Auto Retrieve.

For Samsung's Message+ app, follow these steps:

1. **Tap the Side Menu icon to show the navigation drawer.**

2. **Choose Settings.**

3. **Choose Application.**

4. **Choose When Roaming.**

5. **Ensure that all the items are unchecked.**

Other text messaging apps feature similar controls. View the app's Settings screen to hunt for the Roaming item.

Disabling data roaming

Data roaming is like phone service roaming, though it applies only to the data signal. As with the phone signal, when you and your mobile device wander from the provider's coverage area, that data signal roams. To prevent it, work through these steps:

1. **Open the Settings app.**

2. **Choose Network and Internet.**

3. **Choose Mobile Network or Cellular Networks.**

4. **Ensure that the Roaming setting is disabled or denied.**

On Samsung gizmos, follow these steps:

1. **Open the Settings app.**

2. **Choose Connections.**

3. **Choose Mobile Networks.**

4. **By the item Data Roaming Access, switch the master control to the Off position.**

REMEMBER

Your Android can still access the Internet over the Wi-Fi connection when it roams. Setting up a Wi-Fi connection doesn't affect the mobile data network connection, because the device prefers to use Wi-Fi. See Chapter 18 for more information about Wi-Fi.

International Calling

A phone is a bell that anyone in the world can ring. To prove it, all you need is the phone number of anyone in the world. Use your Android phone to dial that number and, as long as you both speak the same language, you're talking!

To make an international call with your Android phone, you must know the foreign phone number. The number is prefixed by the international country-code prefix. For example:

01-234-56-789

Before dialing the international country-code prefix (01, in this example), you must first type a plus (+). The + symbol is the *country exit code*, which must be dialed in order to flee the national phone system and access the international phone system. For example, to dial Finland on your phone, type +358 and then the number in Finland. The +358 is the exit code (+) plus the international code for Finland (358).

To type the + character, press and hold down the 0 key on the Phone app's dialpad. Then type the country prefix and the phone number. Tap the Dial icon to place the call.

REMEMBER

>> In most cases, dialing an international number involves a time zone difference. Before you dial, be aware of what time it is in the country or location you're calling. The Clock app can handle that job for you: Summon a clock for the location you're calling and place it on the Clock app's screen.

>> Dialing internationally involves surcharges, unless your cellular plan provides for international calling.

>> International calls fail for several reasons. One of the most common is that the recipient's phone service blocks incoming international calls.

>> Another reason that international calls fail is the zero reason: Oftentimes, you must leave out any zero in the phone number that follows the country code. So, if the country code is 254 for Kenya and the phone number starts with 012, you dial +254 for Kenya and then 12 and the rest of the number. Omit the leading zero.

>> Know which type of phone you're calling internationally — cell phone or landline. The reason is that an international call to a cell phone might involve a surcharge that doesn't apply to a landline.

WARNING

>> The + character isn't a number separator. When you see an international number listed as 011+20+xxxxxxx, do not insert the + character in the number. Instead, type +20, where the + represents dialing 011, and then the rest of the international phone number.

>> Most cellular providers add a surcharge when sending a text message abroad. Contact your cellular provider to confirm the text message rates. Generally, you find two rates: one for sending and another for receiving text messages.

>> If texting charges vex you, remember that email has no associated per-message charge, nor does using a social networking app to send an instant message.

An Android in Your Car

Your car may feature Android technology, but more importantly your phone comes with an app called Android Auto. It's a revival of a very ancient Android feature called the Car Home, a customized and easy-to-use Home screen for operating an Android phone in your motor vehicle.

Figure 23-1 illustrates what the Android Auto app's screen might look like. Driving destinations appear for nearby locations and places you frequent, or you may see the current time as shown in the figure.

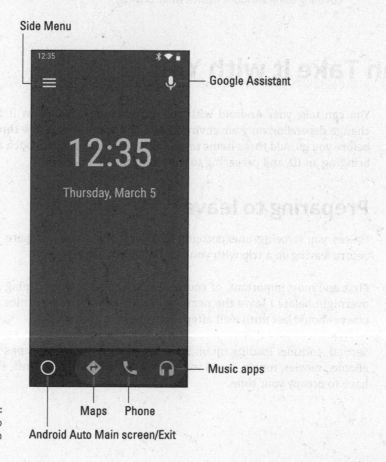

FIGURE 23-1:
Android Auto
in action

Side Menu

Google Assistant

Music apps

Maps   Phone

Android Auto Main screen/Exit

Some cars may recognize the Android Auto app and instantly coordinate with it. If not, obtain a phone mount for your car and use your phone and Android Auto independently to assist you. Ensure that you connect your phone to a power source when using this app.

>> Refer to Chapter 18 for details on using Bluetooth, which is how you connect your Android phone to an Android-enabled vehicle.

>> If your car doesn't feature a connection to Android Auto, consider upgrading the car's radio. Many car radios manufacturers offer products that work with Android Auto.

>> Android Auto has its own apps (sub-apps?) you can obtain from Google Play. Tap the side menu icon and choose Apps for Android Auto.

WARNING

>> Do not text and drive.

>> Using your phone with Android Auto might be considered a moving violation in some states. Check with your jurisdiction for a review of laws (and fines) covering using a mobile device while driving.

You Can Take It with You

You can take your Android with you anywhere you like. How it functions may change depending on your environment, and you can do a few things to prepare before you go. Add these items to your other travel checklists, such as taking cash, bringing an ID, and preparing to wait in inspection lines.

Preparing to leave

Unless you're being unexpectedly abducted, you should prepare several things before leaving on a trip with your Android phone or tablet.

First and most important, of course, is to charge the thing. I plug in my Android overnight before I leave the next day. The device's battery is nice and robust, so power should last until well after you reach your destination.

Second, consider loading up on some media, plus a few new apps before you go: eBooks, movies, music, saved web pages, games. The more stuff, the more you'll have to occupy your time.

Finally, don't forget your tickets! All major airlines offer apps. The apps may make traveling easy because they generate notifications for your schedule and provide timely gate changes or flight delays — plus, you can use the touchscreen as your e-ticket. Search Google Play to see whether your preferred airline offers an app.

TIP

>> In addition to charging your Android, consider charging your wireless, noise-canceling headphones as well.

>> If you plan to read eBooks, listen to music, or watch a video while on the road, consider downloading that media to your Android before you leave. See Chapter 16 for information on keeping media on your device.

>> I save a few of my regular morning web pages for offline reading before I go. See Chapter 10 for details on saving web pages in the Chrome app. To access saved web pages, tap the Action Overflow and choose Downloads.

>> I usually reward myself with a new game before I go on a trip. Visit Google Play and see what's hot or recommended. A good puzzle game can make a nice, long international flight go by a lot quicker.

Arriving at the airport

I'm not a frequent flier, but I am a nerd. The most amount of junk I've carried with me on a flight is two laptop computers and three cell phones. I know that's not a record, but it's enough to warrant the following list of travel tips, all of which apply to taking an Android phone or tablet with you on an extended journey:

>> Take the Android's AC adapter and USB cable with you. Put them in your carry-on luggage or backpack.

>> All major airports feature USB chargers, so you can charge the Android in an airport, if you need to. Even though you need only the cable to charge, bring along the AC adapter anyway.

>> Most newer planes provide charging ports in-flight.

>> At the security checkpoint, place your Android phone or tablet in a bin by itself or with other electronics. You might be able to get away with leaving the tablet inside a pouch or backpack, though first confirm that possibility with the security personnel.

>> You can never walk through the metal detector or scanner wearing a cell phone. Well, you can, but you'll be directed to secondary search and get dirty looks from others waiting in line. (Yeah, I've done that.)

TIP

» Use the Calendar app to keep track of your flights. If you use the airline's app, calendar information may be provided automatically. Otherwise, create an event for each flight. See Chapter 16 for more information on the Calendar app.

» Scan for the airport's Wi-Fi service. Most airports don't charge for the service, though you may have to use the web browser app to agree to terms before getting full access.

Flying with an Android

Readers of the future: The title of this section applies to mobile Android devices, popular in the first part of the 21st century. What you probably want is the title *Personal Robots For Dummies*, published in 2049.

It truly is the trendiest of things to be aloft with the latest mobile gizmo. Still, you must follow some rules:

1. **Obey the flight crew.**

Pay attention to the safety instructions. Don't pretend to be cool and thumb-out a text message during the safety presentation.

2. **Place your device into Airplane mode.**

This direction applies to both phones and tablets. The easy way is to use the quick settings and tap the Airplane Mode icon. See Chapter 3 for details on using the quick settings.

3. **If you want to use the in-flight Wi-Fi, turn on Wi-Fi after the service is available.**

Yes, it's possible to have the device's Wi-Fi radio on while Airplane mode is active. Ditto for Bluetooth and the connection to your noise-canceling wireless headphones. GPS, however, is verboten in-flight.

When the Android is in Airplane mode, a special icon appears in the status area, similar to the one shown in the margin.

To exit Airplane mode, tap the Airplane Mode icon on the quick settings drawer.

Getting to your destination

After you arrive at your destination, the Android may update the date and time to the local time zone. One additional step you may want to take is to set the time zone. By doing so, you ensure that your schedule adapts properly to your new location.

To change or confirm the device's time zone, follow these steps:

1. **Open the Settings app.**

2. **Choose System or, on Samsung devices, choose General Management.**

3. **Choose Date & Time.**

4. **If you find an automatic date-and-time setting, ensure that it's active.**

This setting might be titled Use Network-Provided Time Zone.

If the time zone remains incorrect, on the Date & Time screen, disable the item to use the network-provided time zone and choose the Time Zone item to manually set the time zone based on your current city.

TIP

>> If you've set appointments for your new location, visit the Calendar app to ensure that their start and end times have been properly adjusted. If you're prompted to update appointment times based on the new zone, do so.

REMEMBER

>> When you're done traveling or you change your time zone again, make sure that the Android is updated as well.

The Android Goes Abroad

Yes, your Android works overseas. The two resources you need to consider are how to recharge the battery and how to access Wi-Fi. As long as you have both, you're pretty much set. You also must be careful about mobile-data (cellular) roaming surcharges when using an Android phone or LTE tablet.

Calling with your Android phone overseas

The easiest way to use a cell phone abroad is to rent or buy one in the country where you plan to stay. I'm serious: Often, international roaming charges are so high that it's cheaper to simply buy a temporary cell phone wherever you go, especially if you plan to stay there for a while.

When you opt to use your own phone rather than buy a local phone, things should run smoothly — if a compatible cellular service is in your location. Not every Android phone uses the same mobile network type and, of course, not every foreign country uses the same cellular network. Things must match before the phone can work. Plus, you may have to deal with foreign carrier roaming charges.

The key to determining whether your phone is usable in a foreign country is to turn it on. The name of that country's compatible cellular service shows up on the phone's lock screen. So, where your phone once said *Verizon Wireless*, it may say *Wambooli Telcom* when you're overseas.

REMEMBER

>> You receive calls on your cell phone internationally if the phone can access the network. Your friends need only dial your cell phone number as they normally would; the phone system automatically forwards your calls to wherever you are in the world.

>> The person calling you pays nothing extra when you're off romping the globe with your Android phone. Nope — *you* pay extra for the call.

>> While you're abroad, you must dial internationally. When calling home (for example, the United States), you need to use a 10-digit number (phone number plus area code). You may also be required to type the country exit code when you dial. See the earlier section "International Calling."

>> When in doubt, contact your cellular provider for tips and other information specific to whatever country you're visiting.

Using overseas power

You can easily attach a foreign AC power adapter to your Android's AC power plug. You don't need a voltage converter — just an adapter. After it's attached, you can plug your phone or tablet into those weirdo overseas power sockets without facing the risk of blowing up anything. I charged my Android nightly while I spent time in France, and it worked like a charm.

Accessing Wi-Fi in foreign lands

Wi-Fi is universal. The same protocols and standards are used everywhere, so if your Android can access Wi-Fi at your local Starbucks, it can access Wi-Fi at the Malted Yak Blood Café in Wamboolistan. As long as Wi-Fi is available, your Android can use it.

>> Internet cafés are more popular overseas than in the United States. They're the best locations for connecting to the Internet and catching up on life back home.

» Many overseas hotels offer free Wi-Fi service, although the signal may not reach into every room. Don't be surprised if you can use the Wi-Fi network only while you're in the lobby.

» The Skype app is excellent for placing phone calls overseas. You must first obtain Skype Credit to place phone calls; Skype's international rates are quite reasonable. The calls are made over the Internet, so when the Android has Wi-Fi access, you're good to go. See Chapter 11 for more information on making Skype calls.

IN THIS CHAPTER

» **Cleaning an Android**

» **Checking on the battery**

» **Saving battery power**

» **Solving annoying problems**

» **Searching for support**

» **Troubleshooting issues**

» **Getting answers**

Chapter **24**

Maintenance, Troubleshooting, and Help

Maintenance is that thing you were supposed to remember to do but you didn't do, and that's why you need help and troubleshooting advice.

Don't blame yourself; no one likes to do maintenance. Okay, well, I like maintaining my stuff. I even change the belt on my vacuum cleaner every six months. Did you know that the vacuum cleaner manual tells you to do so? Probably not. I read that in *Vacuum Cleaners For Dummies*. This book is *Android For Dummies*, which is why it contains topics on maintenance, troubleshooting, and help for Android mobile devices, which lack belts that you should change every six months.

The Maintenance Chore

Relax. Unlike draining the lawnmower's oil once a year, regular maintenance of an Android phone or tablet doesn't require a drip pan or a permit from the EPA. In fact, an Android requires only two basic regular maintenance tasks: cleaning and backing up.

Keeping it clean

You probably already keep your Android clean. Perhaps you're one of those people who uses their sleeves to wipe the touchscreen. Of course, better than your sleeve is something called a *microfiber* cloth. This item can be found at any computer or office-supply store.

WARNING

>> Never use ammonia or alcohol to clean the touchscreen. These substances damage the device. If you must use a cleaning solution, select something specifically designed for touchscreens.

>> Touchscreen-safe screen cleaners are available for those times when your sleeve or even a microfiber cloth won't cut it. Ensure that you get a screen cleaner designed for a touchscreen.

>> If the touchscreen keeps getting dirty, consider adding a screen protector: This specially designed cover prevents the glass from getting scratched or dirty but still allows you to use your finger on the touchscreen. Be sure that the screen protector is designed for use with the specific brand and model of your phone or tablet.

>> For an Android phone, consider a phone case, belt clip, or another protector, which can help keep the phone looking spiffy. Be aware that these items are mostly for decorative or fashion purposes and don't even prevent serious damage should you drop the phone.

>> Android tablets offer special cases or folios. Some are even combination case-keyboards, which eases the frustration of typing with the onscreen keyboard.

Backing up your stuff

For most of the information on your Android, backup is automatic. Your Google account takes care of Gmail, the calendar, your contacts, music, eBooks, movies, and apps. This stuff is synchronized and backed up automatically.

To confirm that your account's media is synchronized and other information is backed up, heed these steps:

1. **Open the Settings app.**

2. **Choose Accounts or, on Samsung devices, choose Accounts and Backup.**

   This item may be titled Users & Accounts.

3. **Tap your Google account in the list.**

   If you don't see your Google account (or any accounts), choose the Accounts item.

4. **Choose Account Sync or Sync Account.**

5. **Ensure that the master control by each item is on.**

   These are the items that synchronize between the device and your Google account on the Internet.

6. **Use the Back navigation gesture or tap the Back navigation icon until you see the main Settings app screen.**

7. **Choose System and then Backup.**

   You may need to choose Advanced to display the Backup item.

   On Samsung devices, the item is titled Accounts and Backup (the same as in Step 2). After choosing it, tap the Backup and Restore item.

8. **Ensure that the master control by Back Up to Google Drive is on.**

   This item is titled Back Up My Data on Samsung gizmos.

Specific items from your device can be backed up manually. For example, if you download a PDF and want to keep a backup, copy that file from the device to a computer. Chapter 19 covers options for getting files out of your Android.

Some apps feature options to back up specific files and media. For example, One-Drive and Dropbox feature options to duplicate to their cloud storage any photos you take or movies you record.

Updating the system

Every so often, your Android signals that a system update is available. Android operating system security updates occur about once a month. The device's manufacturer may release an update as well. And Google occasionally releases a new version of the Android operating system.

When an update is available, you see the System Update notification icon, as shown in the margin. Choose that notification to apply the update.

You might also see a pop-up message, or "toast," appear on the screen when an update is available. Your options are to immediately update or postpone. My advice is to apply the update immediately, as long as the Android has sufficient battery life left (or you can connect to a power supply) and you're not expecting to do anything major with your Android during the next few minutes, such as receive an important phone call.

You can also manually check for an update. Heed these directions:

1. **Open the Settings app.**

2. **Choose System or, on Samsung devices, choose System Updates.**

3. **Choose System Update, which is titled Check for System Updates on Samsung phones and tablets.**

   If this item isn't visible, tap the Advanced item.

4. **Tap Check for Update.**

   If an update is pending, you see it listed.

In older versions of the Android operating system, choose About Phone or About Tablet in Step 2. The System Updates item is located on that screen.

> » Android versions 8.0 "Oreo" and later fetch an update if one is pending. Older versions of the Android operating system allow updates by quota — if they allow updates at all. So, manually checking for an update, even when one is pending, may not result in updating the device.

REMEMBER

> » Connect your device to a power source during a software update. You don't want the battery to die in the middle of the operation.

Battery Care and Feeding

Perhaps the most important item you can monitor and maintain on your Android is its battery. The battery supplies the necessary electrical juice by which the device operates. Without battery power, your gizmo is basically an expensive drink coaster or trivet. Keep an eye on the battery.

Monitoring the battery

Your Android displays its current battery status at the top of the screen, in the status area, next to the time. The icons used are similar to those shown in Figure 24-1. They can appear white-on-black or use a charming color scheme with the battery level tending to the red end of the spectrum as circumstances grow dire.

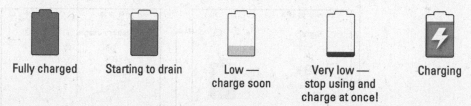

FIGURE 24-1: Battery status icons

Fully charged   Starting to drain   Low — charge soon   Very low — stop using and charge at once!   Charging

You might also see an icon for a dead battery, but for some reason I can't get my Android to turn on and display that icon.

>> Heed those low-battery warnings! You hear a warning sound and see a notification whenever the battery power gets low. Another sound chimes whenever the battery gets very low.

>> When the battery level is too low, the device shuts itself off — and it doesn't turn back on again until you give it a modicum of charge.

TIP

>> The best way to deal with low battery power is to connect the Android to a power source: Either plug it into a wall socket or use the USB cable to connect it to a computer. The phone or tablet begins charging itself immediately; plus, you can use the device while it's charging.

>> Android devices charge more efficiently when plugged into a wall socket rather than a computer.

>> You aren't required to fully charge the battery. For example, if you have only 20 minutes before the next flight, and you get only a 70 percent battery level, that's great. Well, it's not great, but it's far better than a lower battery level.

TECHNICAL STUFF

>> Battery percentage values are best-guess estimates. Just because you get 8 hours of use from the device and the battery meter shows 20 percent remaining doesn't imply that 20 percent equals 2 more hours of use. In practice, the amount of time you have left is much less than that. As a rule, when the battery percentage value gets low, the battery appears to drain faster.

Determining what is drawing power

The Battery screen in the Settings app informs you of the device's battery usage over time, as well as which apps have been consuming power, as illustrated in Figure 24-2.

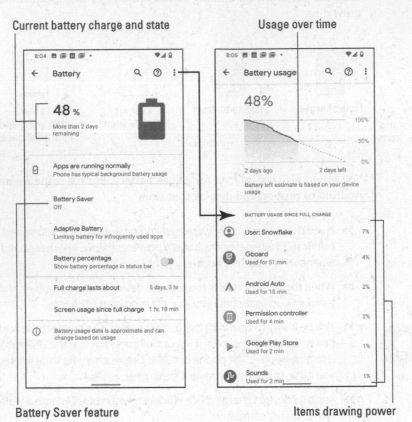

FIGURE 24-2:
Power
consumption
details

To view the battery usage, follow these steps:

1. **Open the Settings app.**

2. **Choose Battery.**

   On Samsung devices, choose the Device Care item and then choose Battery.

   You see general information about battery usage, plus some power-saving tools, shown on the left in Figure 24-2.

3. **Tap the Action Overflow and choose Battery Usage to view details.**

You see a charge illustrating battery power over time plus which apps are using the most power, shown on the right in Figure 24-2.

The number and variety of items shown on the battery usage screen depend on what you've been doing with your Android between charges. Don't be surprised if an item doesn't show up in the list; not every app consumes a lot of battery power.

Extending battery life

Most Android gizmos feature a smart battery feature, which monitors battery usage. This feature modifies various settings and closes certain apps based on battery usage. Further power-savings features cut back drastically on power settings, extending battery life for hours, if need be.

To activate the battery saver on your Android, heed these steps:

1. **Open the Settings app.**
2. **Choose Battery.**
3. **Choose Battery Saver.**
4. **Tap the button Turn On Now.**

On Samsung devices, follow these directions:

1. **Open the Settings app.**
2. **Chose Device Care.**
3. **Tap the Battery category.**
4. **Choose Power Mode.**
5. **Select a power mode from the list.**

Categories range from High Performance (drain that battery!) to Maximum Power Savings (make the battery last!).

Upon activating a battery-saving option, you may notice Dark mode activated instantly, which saves power by reducing screen illumination. Behind the scenes, the Android deactivates certain services when the device is locked, restricts background activity for certain apps, and may delay certain notifications. You can easily tolerate these changes when your priority is to maintain or extend battery life.

Help and Troubleshooting

Getting help with technology today isn't as bad as it was years back. I remember only two sources for help: the atrocious manual that came with your electronic device and a phone call to the guy who wrote the atrocious manual. It was unpleasant. Today, the situation is better. You have many resources for solving issues with your gizmos, including your Android.

Also see Chapter 17 for information on protecting your Android against malicious apps.

Fixing random and annoying problems

Aren't all problems annoying? A welcome problem doesn't exist, unless the problem is welcome because it diverts attention from another, preexisting problem. And random problems? If problems were predictable, they would serve in office.

General trouble

For just about any problem or minor quirk, consider restarting the phone or tablet: Hold the Power/Lock key. The device options menu may feature a Restart action. If so, use it. Otherwise, turn off your Android and then turn it on again. This procedure fixes most of the annoying problems you encounter.

See Chapter 2 for basic Android on–off instructions.

Connection woes

As you move about, the cellular signal can change. In fact, you may observe the status icon change from 4G LTE to 3G to even the dreaded 1X or — worse — nothing, depending on the strength and availability of the mobile data network.

My advice for random signal weirdness is to wait. Oftentimes, the signal comes back after a few minutes. If it doesn't, the mobile data network might be down, or you may just be in an area with lousy service. Consider changing your location.

For Wi-Fi connections, ensure that Wi-Fi is set up properly and working. This process involves pestering the person who configured the Wi-Fi router or, in a coffee shop, bothering the cheerful person with the tattoos and piercings who serves you coffee.

WARNING

Be aware that some Wi-Fi networks have a "lease time" after which your device is disconnected. If so, follow the directions in Chapter 18 for turning off the Wi-Fi radio and then turn it on again. That often solves the issue. Also refer to Chapter 18 for details on metered Wi-Fi connections.

Another problem I've heard about is that the Wi-Fi router doesn't recognize your Android. In this case, the router might use older technology and it needs to be replaced.

Music is playing and you want it to stop

It's awesome that your Android continues to play music while you do other things. Getting the music to stop quickly, however, requires some skill. You can access the Play controls for the Play Music app from a number of locations. They're found on the lock screen, for example. You can also find them in the notifications drawer.

Be aware that media playing on your phone halts for an incoming call. Media that's broadcast to another device, however, continues to play. Refer to Chapter 19 for information on streaming media.

An app has run amok

Sometimes, apps that misbehave let you know. You see a warning on the screen announcing the app's stubborn disposition. When that happens, tap the Force Quit button to shut down the app. Then say, "Whew!"

To manually shut down an app, refer to Chapter 20.

You've reached your wit's end

When all else fails, you can do the drastic thing and perform a factory data reset on your device. Before committing to this step, you should contact support as described in the next section.

Refer to Chapter 22 for details on the factory data reset.

Getting help and support

Never discount your Android device's manufacturer for assistance when you need it. If you have an Android phone or LTE tablet, consider contacting the cellular provider. Between the two, I recommend contacting the cellular provider first, no matter what the problem. Beyond these resources, you can read the information I've presented in this section.

The Help app

Some manufacturers include a Help app or Getting Started app with their devices. They may offer pop-up toasts, which present tips as you explore new features on your phone or tablet.

Google Support is available in the Settings app, though this feature was added only with newer releases of the Android operating system. Follow these steps:

1. **Open the Settings app.**

2. **Choose Tips & Support, which may be titled Tips and Help.**

The options on the support screen include phoning or chatting with a Google support person, as well as searching online Help. An option for reviewing tips and tricks is also presented.

>> Also look for a Help eBook in the Play Books app.

>> The Settings app features the Search icon, which helps you locate specific settings without knowing exactly under which category the item might be found.

Cellular support

Contact information for both the cellular provider and device manufacturer is found in the material you threw out with your Android's box. In Chapter 1, I recommend that you save those random pieces of paper. Never mind — that's why you're reading here.

Table 24-1 lists contact information for US cellular providers. The From Cell column lists the number you can call by using your Android phone; otherwise, you can use the toll-free number from any phone.

TABLE 24-1   ## US Cellular Providers

Provider	From Cell	Toll-Free	Website
AT&T	611	800-331-0500	www.att.com/esupport
Sprint	*2	888-211-4727	sprint.com
T-Mobile	611	800-866-2453	www.t-mobile.com/Contact.aspx
Verizon	611	800-922-0204	verizonwireless.com/support

Manufacturer support

Another source of support for your device, or the only source if you have a Wi-Fi-only tablet, is the manufacturer, such as Samsung or LG. Information about support can be found in those random papers and pamphlets included in the device's box. If not, refer to Table 24-2 for contact information.

TABLE 24-2 ### Android Manufacturers

Manufacturer	Website
HTC	www.htc.com/us/support
LG	www.lg.com/us/support
Motorola	www.motorola.com
Samsung	samsung.com/us/mobile/phones or samsung.com/us/mobile/tablets

App support

For app issues, contact the developer. Follow these steps:

1. **Open the Play Store app.**

2. **Tap the Side Menu icon to display the navigation drawer.**

3. **Choose My Apps & Games.**

4. **Tap the Installed tab.**

5. **Tap the entry for the specific app, the one that's bothering you.**

6. **Choose the Email item.**

   It's located below the Developer Contact heading.

7. **Craft your email message.**

REMEMBER

Contacting the developer is no guarantee that they'll respond.

Google Play support

For issues with Google Play itself, contact Google at

support.google.com/googleplay

Valuable Android Q&A

I love Q&A! Not only is it an effective way to express certain problems and solutions, but some of the questions might also cover things I've been wanting to ask.

"I can't turn the thing on (or off)!"

Sometimes, an Android locks up. It's frustrating, but I've discovered that if you press and hold the Power/Lock key for about 8 seconds, the device turns either off or on, depending on which state it's in.

If waiting 8 seconds doesn't work, let the phone or tablet sit for 10 minutes or so. Try again.

REMEMBER

Ensure that the Android is properly charged or else it won't turn on.

"The touchscreen doesn't work!"

A touchscreen requires a human finger for proper interaction. The screen interprets the static potential between the human finger and the device to determine where the touchscreen is being touched. The touchscreen will not work if the screen is damaged. It will not work when you're wearing gloves, unless they're specially designed touchscreen gloves. The touchscreen might fail also when the battery power is low.

"The screen is too dark!"

Android devices feature a teensy light sensor on the front. If the Adaptive Brightness or Auto Brightness feature is active, the sensor adjusts the touchscreen's brightness based on the amount of ambient light at your location. If the sensor is covered, the screen can get very, very dark.

Ensure that you don't unintentionally block the light sensor. Avoid buying a case or screen protector that obscures the sensor.

The automatic brightness setting might also be vexing you. See Chapter 21 for information on setting screen brightness.

"The battery doesn't charge!"

Start from the source: Is the wall socket providing power? Is the cord plugged in? The cable may be damaged, so try another cable.

When charging from a USB port on a computer, ensure that the computer is turned on. Most computers don't provide USB power when they're turned off. Also, some USB ports may not supply enough power to charge the battery. If possible, use a port on the computer console (the box) instead of a USB hub.

TIP

>> New computers and laptops feature a USB port that's color-coded yellow. This designation indicates that the port is designed to charge a mobile device when the computer or laptop is turned off. If the laptop isn't connected to a power source, the yellow USB port uses the laptop's battery to charge your Android.

>> Some Android tablets charge from a special cord, not the USB cable. Check to confirm that your tablet is able to take a charge from the USB cable.

"The gizmo gets so hot that it turns itself off!"

Yikes! An overheating gadget can be a nasty problem. Can you hold the Android in your hand, or is it too hot to hold? When it's too hot to hold, turn off the power. Disconnect it from the power supply. Let it cool.

If the overheating problem continues, have the Android looked at for potential repair. The battery might need to be replaced.

>> It's normal for a phone to get warm (not hot) as you use it. If you blab for an hour or so, the phone will seem warmer than normal. That's just the battery doing its job.

>> It's also normal for an Android to be warm as it's charging. If the device is too hot to hold, you need to disconnect the power cord and let the gizmo cool down.

WARNING

>> Do not continue to use any device that's too hot! The heat damages the electronics. It can also start a fire.

"The screen doesn't do Landscape mode!"

Not every app can change its orientation between Portrait and Landscape modes — or even Upside-Down mode. For example, many games present themselves in one orientation only. Some Androids don't rotate their Home screens. So, just because the app doesn't go into Horizontal or Vertical mode doesn't mean that anything is broken.

Confirm that the orientation lock isn't on: Check the quick settings. Ensure that the Auto-Rotate or Screen Rotation item is properly set. Also, some eBook reader apps sport their own screen rotation lock feature. Tap the Action Overflow to determine whether it's enabled.

5

The Part of Tens

Chapter **25**

Ten Tips, Tricks, and Shortcuts

A *tip* is a small suggestion, a word of advice often spoken from bruising experience or knowledge passed along from someone with bruising experience. A *trick,* which is something not many know about, usually causes amusement or surprise. A *shortcut* is a quick way to get home, even though it crosses the old graveyard and you never quite know whether Old Man Witherspoon is the groundskeeper or a zombie.

I'd like to think that just about everything in this book is a tip, trick, or shortcut for using an Android mobile gizmo. Even so, I've distilled items in this chapter into a list that is definitely worthy of note.

Switch Apps Quickly

REMEMBER

Android apps don't quit. Sure, some of them have a Quit action or Sign Out option, but most apps loiter in the device's guts while you do other things. The Android operating system may eventually kill off a stale app. Before that happens, you can deftly and quickly switch between all running apps.

The key to making the switch is to use the Recent gesture or tap the Recent navigation icon, found at the bottom of the touchscreen and shown in the margin. When you see the *Overview*, or list of open apps, swipe the screen up or down to peruse what's available. To dismiss the list, use the Back or Home navigation gestures or navigation icons.

TIP

» To remove an app from the list of recent apps, swipe it from the list (up, down, left, or right). This technique is effectively the same thing as quitting an app.

» For devices with the Recent navigation icon, double-tap this icon to switch between the two most recently used apps.

Deploy the Flashlight

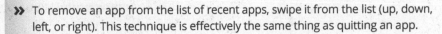

One of the first "killer apps" on mobile devices is the flashlight. It uses the camera's LED flash to help you see in the dark. For a while, everyone had to get a flashlight app, but today the flashlight feature is frequently found on the quick settings drawer.

Use two fingers to swipe down the screen and display the quick settings. If one of the icons looks like a flashlight (see the margin), tap it to activate the flashlight feature. Tap again to turn off the flashlight.

» The flashlight feature might also appear as a lock screen app, or you might be able to place it on the lock screen as an option. Refer to Chapter 21.

» Be aware that keeping the LED lamp on for extended durations drains the battery.

WARNING

» Use the Flashlight quick setting instead of obtaining a flashlight app. Though it may no longer be the case, at one time flashlight apps spied on their users. The apps collected data and beamed it back to a remote server somewhere. Such malicious apps were purged from Google Play long ago. In any event, the availability of the quick settings feature has rendered such apps unnecessary.

Improve the Display

Two things to consider helping your eyeballs when looking at your pet Android are to enable the dark theme and activate the night light feature.

Dark theme inverses the color scheme of many apps, replacing the obnoxious, glaring, white background with a gentle, power-saving, dark background.

The night light feature removes the blue end of the spectrum from the display, which provides for an easy transition to sleep during the night hours.

Both eyeball-saving features are covered in Chapter 21.

Avoid Data Surcharges

An important issue for anyone using an Android phone or LTE tablet is whether you're about to burst through your monthly data quota. Mobile data surcharges can pinch the wallet, but your Android has a handy tool to help you avoid data overages. In the Settings app, you can use the data usage screens, illustrated in Figure 25-1.

FIGURE 25-1: Data usage screens and settings

Mobile data usage   **Data limits screen**   **Wi-Fi data usage**

To access the data usage screens, open the Settings app and choose Network & Internet. Tap the Mobile network item to view cellular data information, as shown on the far left in Figure 25-1.

To view the Wi-Fi usage screen (shown on the far right in Figure 25-1), from the Network & Internet screen, choose Wi-Fi and then Wi-Fi Data Usage.

On Samsung devices, in the Settings app, choose Connections and then choose Data Usage.

The data usage screens show how much data your device has consumed for both mobile data and Wi-Fi connections. A list of data-consuming apps is also presented.

Showing the details is interesting, but what's useful is setting warnings and limits on mobile data. Follow these steps:

1. **Open the Settings app.**

2. **Choose Network & Internet.**

3. **Choose Data Saver.**

4. **Ensure that the master control by Use Data Saver is in the On position.**

5. **Use the Back gesture or tap the Back navigation icon to return to the Network & Internet screen.**

6. **Choose Mobile Network.**

7. **Choose Data Warning & Limit.**

   The Data Warning & Limit screen appears (refer to the center of Figure 25-1).

8. **Tap Set Data Warning.**

9. **Choose Data Warning and use the slider to set the data warning limit.**

   Say your plan allows for 3.0GB (gigabytes) of mobile data per billing cycle. Set the warning at 2.5GB. Tap the Set button.

10. **Ensure that the master control by Set Data Limit is in the On position.**

11. **Tap Data Limit and set a limit.**

    This value should be just below your allowed usage — say, 2.8GB for a plan that allows 3.0GB per month.

On a Samsung device, follow these steps:

1. **Open the Settings app.**

2. **Choose Connections.**

3. **Choose Data Usage.**

4. **Activate the setting Alert Me About Data Usage.**

5. **Choose the item Mobile Data Usage.**

6. **Tap the Settings icon.**

7. **Continue with Step 8 in the preceding set of steps.**

REMEMBER

It's important to remember that your device and the cellular provider monitor data usage differently. For example, your monthly quota may be 5GB, but if you set the limit (when the device stops using the mobile-data network, in Step 5) to 5GB, you may still be surcharged. That's why I recommend (in Step 5) to set a limit below your maximum allowed monthly usage.

Watch Your Android Dream

After the touchscreen time-out kicks in, the apps keep running and activity goes on, but does the device dream?

Well, of course it does! You can even see the dreams, if you activate the Daydream feature — and if you keep a power source connected. Heed these steps:

1. **Start the Settings app.**

2. **Choose Display.**

3. **Choose Screen Saver.**

   You may need to tap the Advanced item to find Screen Saver.

4. **Tap the Current Screen Saver item to choose a screen saver.**

   On Samsung devices, the list of screen savers is shown instantly.

   Some daydream options feature the Settings icon, which customizes the daydream's appearance.

5. **Choose When to Start.**

   If this item is unavailable, the screen saver is activated only when the device is charging.

6. **Select an option, such as While Charging or While Docked.**

   Choosing the Never option disables the screen saver.

The daydreaming begins when the screen would normally time-out and lock. For some Androids, the device must be receiving power for the screen saver to activate: when charging, when docked, or both.

Bring Back the Navigation Buttons!

Using gestures for the Home, Back, Recent, and other activities can be useful, but as an old-timer, I like having navigation buttons. To me, they bring a consistency to the interface and are welcome, like familiar friends.

To restore the navigation buttons, heed these directions:

1. **Open the Settings app.**
2. **Choose System.**
3. **Choose Gestures.**
4. **Choose System Navigation.**
5. **Select 3-Button Navigation.**

The three familiar navigation icons appear at the bottom of the screen. Use them to navigate your Android when the gestures are disabled.

Add Spice to Dictation

If you've used dictation, you might notice that it occasionally censors some of the words you utter. Perhaps you're the kind of person who doesn't put up with that kind of s***.

Relax. You can follow these steps to lift the vocal censorship ban:

1. **Start the Settings app.**
2. **Choose System and then choose Languages & Input.**

   On Samsung devices, choose General Management and then choose Language & Input.

3. **Choose Virtual Keyboard and then choose Google Voice Typing.**

On Samsung devices, choose On-Screen Keyboard and then choose Google Voice Typing.

4. **Disable the option Hide Offensive Words.**

And just what are offensive words? I would think that *censorship* is an offensive word. But no — apparently, only a few choice words fall into this category. I won't print them here.

Visit the Dictionary

Betcha didn't know that your Android sports a dictionary. The dictionary keeps track of words you type that may not be recognized as being spelled properly.

Unrecognized words are highlighted on the screen. Sometimes the word is shown in a different color or on a different background, and sometimes it's underlined in red. To add that word to the internal dictionary, tap it and choose Add to Dictionary.

To review or edit the dictionary, follow these steps:

1. **Start the Settings app.**

2. **Choose System and then Languages & Input.**

3. **Choose Virtual Keyboard.**

4. **Choose Gboard.**

5. **Choose Dictionary.**

6. **Choose Personal Dictionary.**

7. **Choose English.**

Behold your added words, if any.

With the dictionary visible, you can review words, edit them, remove them, or manually add new ones. Tap a word to edit or delete.

 To add a new word to the list, tap the Add icon.

As this book goes to press, Samsung devices (which use the Samsung Keyboard instead of the Gboard) lack an editable dictionary. This situation may change in the future.

Add Useful Widgets

Your Android features a wide assortment of widgets with which to festoon the Home screen. They can be exceedingly handy, though you may not realize it because the sample widgets that are preset on the Home screen are weak and unimpressive.

Good widgets to add include navigation, contact info, eBook, and web page favorites. Adding any of these widgets starts out the same. Here are the brief directions:

1. Long-press a Home screen page that has room for a widget.

2. Choose Widgets.

3. Drag a widget to the Home screen.

4. Complete the process.

The process is specific for each type of widget suggestion in this section.

Refer to Chapter 20 for specifics on managing widgets.

Direct Dial widget

Use the Contacts/Direct Dial widget on an Android phone to access those numbers you dial all the time. After adding the widget, choose a contact from the address book. Tap this widget to dial the contact's default number instantly.

Directions widget

The Maps/Directions widget allows you to quickly summon directions to a specific location from wherever you happen to be. After you add the widget to the Home screen, select a traveling method and destination. You can type a contact name, an address, a business name, and so on. Add a shortcut name, which is a brief description to fit under the widget on the Home screen. Tap the SAVE button.

Tap the Directions widget to use it. Instantly, the Maps app starts and enters Navigation mode, steering you from wherever you are to the location referenced by the widget.

eBook widget

When you're mired in the middle of that latest potboiler, put a Google Play Books/Book widget on the Home screen: Choose the Book widget and then select which eBooks in your digital library you want to access. Tap the widget to open the Play Books app and jump right into the book at the spot where you were last reading.

Web bookmark widget

If you collect bookmarks in the Chrome app, add their list to the Home screen. Choose the Chrome Bookmarks widget. For a specific web page, however, open the Chrome app and visit the page. Tap the Action Overflow and choose Add to Home Screen, edit the web page name (if necessary), and then tap the Add button. A widget is created to access that specific page.

Take a Screen Shot

A *screen shot*, also called a *screen cap* (for *cap*ture), is a picture of your Android's touchscreen. If you see something interesting on the screen or you just want to take a quick pic of your digital life, you take a screen shot.

The stock Android method of shooting the screen is to press and hold both the Volume Down and Power/Lock keys at the same time. Upon success, the touchscreen image reduces in size, you may hear a shutter sound, and the screen shot is saved.

TECHNICAL
STUFF

>> Screen shots are accessed through the Photos app or from a screen shot notification. In the Photos app, the images appear along with any photos you've snapped from the camera.

>> Some Samsung galactic gizmos use a Motion command to capture the screen: Hold your hand perpendicular to the touchscreen, like you're giving it a karate chop. Swipe the edge of your palm over the screen, right-to-left or left-to-right. Upon success, you hear a shutter sound.

>> Internally, screen shots are stored in the Pictures/Screenshots folder. They're created in either the PNG or JPEG graphics file format.

Chapter **26**

Ten Things to Set Up on Your New Phone

Upgrading technology keeps getting easier. It's not like the old days, back when you had to wire all those transistors, write an operating system, and then code all your own software. Those were fun times, but I'd rather enjoy a smooth upgrade process, like you get with an Android mobile gizmo.

Despite the quick transition from an old phone to a new one, a few items may need review. This chapter lists ten of them, settings and stuff you think might be copied from your new device but probably weren't.

Set Ringtones

Your new phone came with the default sounds set for the ringtone as well as the notification sound. If not, great! Otherwise, to get your familiar alerts back requires two steps:

1. Obtain the sound media from whatever source you originally obtained it.
2. Reconfigure the device to signal your familiar ringtones.

To start your journey, first check to see whether the old ringtone files were copied to the new device. If they were saved to cloud storage, you should have them. Otherwise, they must be transferred to the new Android or downloaded from cloud storage.

Refer to Chapter 21 for more details on setting the device's ringtone as well as other notification sounds, bells, and whistles.

Configure Volume Settings

One setting that doesn't get copied from your old device to the new one covers the volume levels you've set for specific Android squawks and squeaks. You can set these levels as you go by using the volume key, but you can also visit the Settings app.

In the Settings app, choose the Sound item or Sounds and Vibrations to adjust specific volume levels to your liking. See Chapter 21 for more details.

Activate Do Not Disturb Mode

Do Not Disturb mode is wonderful for a light sleeper such as myself. By activating this feature, I can blissfully sleep through the night or nap in the afternoon without the phone ringing away some notification or an incoming call. And, like other items in this chapter, your Do Not Disturb mode preferences aren't copied from your old device to your new one.

To activate Do Not Disturb mode, heed these steps:

1. Open the Settings app.
2. In the Search text box, type Do Not Disturb.

3. **Choose the item Do Not Disturb from the list.**

   Avoid selecting any related items. Though other Do Not Disturb settings are important, you want the main Do Not Disturb mode screen.

4. **Choose the Schedules item to set up this mode to activate at your preferred times.**

   For me, it's 10:00 PM to 7:00 AM.

5. **Peruse other settings on the Do Not Disturb screen to reconfigure this handy feature to your liking.**

   For example, allow exceptions for important or rational people, determine whether text messages can get through, allow alarms to sound (important for not missing a flight), and other options.

The good news about this item is that you're reminded right away when you forget to set it on the new phone. That's how I remembered to do it, with a drunk text message from a friend I didn't want to visit at 2 a.m.

Change Wallpapers

I'm sure Android device manufacturers are enamored with their selection of stunning wallpapers and lock screen backgrounds. I prefer my old standbys, which for some reason weren't copied to my new gizmo.

Ensure that your wallpapers are copied over from the old phone or tablet or otherwise available. Refer to Chapter 21 for details on resetting your Android's wallpaper or Home screen background.

Arrange the Home Screen

It was amazing to see that my new Samsung phone not only reinstalled all my old phone's apps but also arranged them the same way (in the same folders) on my new phone's Home screen. If your new Android was as kind, be thankful. Otherwise, you must re-create your Home screen.

I suggest that you snap a screen shot of your device's current Home screen arrangement: Press the Power/Lock and volume-down keys simultaneously. Share (save) the image to your Google Drive, changing the name to Home Screen or something equally obvious.

By saving your current Home screen as an image, you can better re-create your favorite layout should you need to when you upgrade to a new Android phone or tablet.

Assign Default Apps

This suggestion may not apply to a stock Android phone, where the only app options available are Google's. The default apps include the Contacts app, Messages (for text messaging), Chrome, the Calendar app, and more. Other device manufacturers (I'm looking at you, Samsung) may prefer to foist upon you their own versions of these popular apps.

Refer to Chapter 20 for details on setting default apps. Unfortunately, in some cases (my eye is still on you, Samsung) you can't remove or uninstall the similar apps. You must select a default and then use only one or the other app from this point onward.

TECHNICAL STUFF

>> The problem with duplicate apps is not only the similar-sounding names but also that some apps may not coordinate their contents with other services. For example, the phone manufacturer's Contacts app may not automatically synchronize new contacts with your Google account.

>> Because so many duplicate apps share the same name, the only way to know which are Google's and which belong to other developers is to visit the App's information card in the Play Store app. From your list of installed apps, choose both duplicate app names and see which is from Google and which was developed by someone else.

Peruse Notification Options

The latest version of the Android operating system (10.0) collects all notification options in one convenient place in the Settings app: Choose Apps & Notifications and then tap Notifications; on Samsung devices, choose Notifications.

The notifications screen displays a list of apps capable of generating a notification. Disable the master control by an app if its notifications bother you. Tap the See All item to view the entire list.

To control the variety of notifications, tap an app's entry on the notifications screen. For example, if you don't like Maps app asking if you know a place, disable the item Places You've Visited. The notifications relative to the item you disable no longer appear.

Configure Backups

Your Google account features synchronization options, which help keep a copy of many Android features on the Internet, sharable with your other Android devices, computers, or anywhere you can access your Google account. To confirm that synchronization is active, obey these steps:

1. Open the Settings app.

2. Choose Accounts.

3. Choose your Google or Gmail account.

4. Tap the Account Sync item.

5. Ensure that all the master controls are set to the On position.

   There! Everything is backed up — except for your pictures. Continue:

6. Open the Photos app.

7. Tap the Side Menu icon to view the navigation drawer.

8. Choose Settings.

9. Choose Back Up & Sync.

10. Ensure that the master control is on.

    With this feature active, your photos are backed up to your Google account.

One nifty thing about the Back Up & Sync option in the Photos app is that the screen graphically shows how much of your Google storage is available. If space is getting tight, you can disable this option. Otherwise, rest assured that the pictures you take are saved offline — and available to your next Android device.

Voicemail

Another feature not inherited from your old phone to your new one is voicemail — unless you use the same phone number. If so, the voicemail service is inherited, even an add-on service like Google Voice.

Just to be sure, check that your voicemail service is active: After upgrading to the new phone, have someone call you. Don't pick up! Instead, confirm that voicemail is active and set as you prefer. If not, refer to Chapter 6 for details on setting up voicemail.

Personal Safety

A new and welcome feature with the latest version of the Android operating system is personal safety. This feature is coupled with device security to ensure that both you and your information stay as private as you want when using your phone or tablet.

In the Settings app, choose the Security item; on Samsung devices, choose Biometrics and Security. Review the settings offered to ensure that everything presented is set according to your needs.

Next, choose the Privacy item in the Settings app. Browse the offering to see which may benefit you.

Finally, choose the About Phone option, which seems an odd place to locate emergency contact information, but now you know: Choose Emergency Information on the About Phone screen, and fill in the items presented as they relate to you. This information appears on the lock screen and is accessible when someone chooses the Emergency Call option.

For Samsung devices, open the Contacts app to review your emergency information: Tap the Side Menu item and choose Emergency Contacts from the navigation drawer. Choose Emergency Medical Information to provide medical details; tap the Edit (pencil) icon to create an Emergency Contacts group, to which you can add those people you want to bother in case of an emergency.

Refer to Chapter 5 for specifics on using emergency contact details in the Phone app or when using someone else's Android phone.

Chapter **27**

Ten Things to Remember

Have you ever tried to tie a string around your finger to remember something? I've not attempted that technique just yet. The main reason is that I keep forgetting to buy string and I have no way to remind myself.

For your Android, some things are definitely worth remembering. From that long, long list, I've come up with ten good ones.

Dictate Text

Dictation is such a handy feature — don't forget to use it! You can dictate most text instead of typing it. Especially for text messaging on an Android phone, it's just so quick and handy.

Just about any time you see the onscreen keyboard, you can dictate instead of typing: Tap the Dictation icon (shown in the margin) and begin speaking. Your utterances are translated to text. In most cases, the translation is instantaneous.

>> If you don't see the Dictation icon, tap the icon at the far left end of the predictive text list.

>> See Chapter 4 for more information on dictation.

Change the Orientation

The natural orientation of the Android phone is vertical — its *portrait* orientation. Larger-format Android tablets have a natural horizontal orientation. Smaller tablets beg to be held vertically. No matter what's natural, you won't break any law by changing the device's orientation.

Apps such as Chrome and Gmail can look much better in the horizontal orientation, whereas apps such as Play Books and Play Music can look much better in the vertical orientation. The key to changing orientation is to rotate the device to view the app the way you like best.

TIP

>> If you prefer a specific orientation, use the quick settings item that locks the orientation. See Chapter 3.

>> Some apps pop up the Rotation icon, which you can use to temporarily change's the app's orientation.

>> Not every app changes its orientation. Some apps — specifically, games — present themselves in one orientation only: landscape or portrait.

REMEMBER

>> eBook reader apps have screen rotation settings that let you lock the orientation to the way you want, regardless of what the Android is doing. Refer to Chapter 16.

Work the Quick Settings

Many Android controls are available at a single, handy location: the quick settings drawer. Use two fingers to swipe from the top of the screen downward, and behold the quick settings drawer.

Many common features sport quick settings icons: Wi-Fi, Bluetooth, screen orientation, and more. Using the quick settings drawer is far more expedient than visiting the Settings app.

Employ Keyboard Suggestions

Don't forget to take advantage of the predictive text suggestions that appear above the onscreen keyboard while you're typing text. Tap a word suggestion to "type" that word. Plus, the predictive text feature may instantly display the next logical word for you.

When predictive text fails you, keep in mind that you can use glide typing instead of the old hunt-and-peck. Dragging your finger over the keyboard and then choosing a word suggestion works quickly — when you remember to do it. Refer to Chapter 4 for details on enabling glide typing.

Avoid the Battery Hogs

Two items can suck down battery power on your mobile device faster than a massive alien fleet is defeated by a plucky antihero who just wants the girl:

>> The display

>> Navigation

The display is obviously a most necessary part of your Android — but it's also a tremendous power hog. To save power for the display, consider activating Dark mode or using the Adaptive Brightness (also called Auto Brightness) setting. See Chapter 21.

Navigation is certainly handy, but the battery drains rapidly because the touch-screen is on the entire time and the speaker is dictating your directions. If possible, plug the Android into the car's power socket when you're navigating.

See Chapter 24 for more tips on managing the battery.

Unlock and Launch Apps

The most common unlock and-launch feature is the Camera app. Swipe this icon across the locked touchscreen to quickly snap a picture or record a video. Many Androids let you add other lock screen launchers in addition to the Camera app. See Chapter 21 for the possibilities.

>> To unlock and launch an app, swipe the icon across the screen. That app instantly runs.

>> Depending on the screen lock that's installed, the app may run but the Android won't unlock. To do anything other than run the app, you must work the screen lock.

>> Lock screen launchers may not be available when the None or swipe screen lock is set.

Enjoy Phone Tricks

Most Androids sold are phones. They predate tablets by a few years. Still, it's possible to place phone calls on an Android tablet. That's just one of many phone tricks.

Locking the phone on a call

Whether you dialed out or someone dialed in, after you start talking, lock your phone. Press the Power/Lock key. By doing so, you disable the touchscreen and ensure that the call isn't unintentionally disconnected.

Of course, the call can still be disconnected by a dropped signal or by the other party getting all huffy and hanging up on you. But by locking the phone, you prevent a stray finger or your pocket from disconnecting (or muting) the phone.

TIP

If you like to talk with your hands, or just use your hands while you're on the phone (I sweep the floor, for example), get a good set of earbuds with a microphone. Using a headset lets you avoid trying to hold the phone between your ear and shoulder, which could unlock the phone or cause you to drop it or perhaps do something more perilous.

Making calls on a tablet

Yeah, I know: It's not a phone. Even Android tablets that use the mobile data network can't make phone calls. Why let that stop you?

The Skype app lets you place phone calls and video-chat with your friends. Boost your Skype account with some coinage and you can even dial into real phones. See Chapter 11 for details.

Avoiding roaming

Roaming can be expensive. The last non-smartphone (dumbphone?) I owned racked up $180 in roaming charges the month before I switched to a better cellular plan. Even though you might have a good phone plan, keep an eye on the phone's status bar to ensure that you don't see the Roaming status icon when you're making a call.

Well, yes, it's okay to make a call when your phone is roaming. My advice is to remember to check for the Roaming status icon, not to avoid it. If possible, try to make your phone calls when you're back in your cellular service's coverage area. If you can't, make the phone call but keep in mind that you will be charged roaming fees. They ain't cheap.

Use the plus (+) symbol when dialing internationally

That phone number may look like it needs the + symbol, and the Phone app's dialpad features a + key, shared with the 0 key, but don't use it unless you're dialing an international number. The + symbol prefix is the first part of any international phone number.

Refer to Chapter 23 for more information on international dialing.

Check Your Schedule

The Calendar app reminds you of upcoming dates and generally keeps you on schedule. A great way to augment the calendar is to employ the Calendar widget on the Home screen.

The Calendar widget lists the current date and then a long list of upcoming appointments. It's a helpful way to check your schedule, especially when you use your Android all the time. I recommend sticking the Calendar widget right on the main, or center, Home screen panel.

>> See Chapter 20 for information on adding widgets to the Home screen; Chapter 16 covers the Calendar app.

TIP

>> As long as I'm handing out tips, remember to specify location information when you set up an appointment in the Calendar app. Type the information as though you were searching in the Maps app. You can then quickly navigate to your next appointment by touching the location item when you review the event.

Snap a Pic of That Contact

Here's something I always forget: Whenever you're near one of your contacts, take the person's picture. Sure, some people are bashful, but most folks are flattered. The idea is to build up entries in the address book so that all your contacts have photos.

REMEMBER

When taking a picture, be sure to show it to the person before you assign it to the contact. Let them decide whether it's good enough.

>> Receiving a call on an Android phone is then much more interesting when you see the caller's picture, especially a silly or an embarrassing one.

>> Refer to Chapter 13 for more information on using the Camera app; Chapter 7 covers the address book.

Use Google Assistant

Google is known worldwide for its searching capabilities and its popular website. By gum, the word *Google* is synonymous with searching. So please don't forget that your Android, which uses the Google Android operating system, has a powerful search, nay, knowledge companion. It's called Google Assistant.

>> On many Androids, you access Google Assistant from the far left Home screen page.

>> The Google Search widget on the Home screen provides a shortcut to your Google Assistant.

>> The Google Assistant app is titled Google. (All the creative people were out sick that day.)

>> Review Chapter 16 for details on various Google Assistant commands.

>> Next to Google Assistant, you can take advantage of the various Search icons found in just about every app. Use this icon to search for information, locations, people — you name it. It's handy.

Index

apps icon, Home
    screen, 41
aspect ratio
    Camera app, 158
    cropping images, 167
attachments, email, 101
    receiving, 115
    sharing, 116
Audio settings
    ringtone, 267–268
    volume, 266–267
autocorrect, 63

B

Back button, 36
Back gesture, 35
backing up media
    overview, 294–295
    with Photos app, 169
    synchronization, 323
battery
    charging, 13–14
    display, 327
    extending life of, 299
    maintenance,
        296–299
    monitoring, 297
    navigation and, 327
    overview, 296
    troubleshooting, 305
    viewing battery usage,
        298–299
Bell, Alexander Graham, 67
Bixby app, 191
Bixby button, 16
blocking calls, 81
Blue Light filter, 261–262
Bluetooth
    activating, 216
    overview, 215–216
    pairing, 217–218
    unpairing, 218
bookmarks, online, 121
brightness, display, 263, 304
buying tips, 10

C

Calculator app, 184–185
Calendar app
    adding events, 186
    Calendar widget, 187
    categories, 188
    notifications, 187
    overview, 329–330
    Schedule view, 187
    travel plans, 288
    viewing events, 185–186
call forwarding, 79–81
Call in Progress notification icon, 70
call log
    adding contact from, 93
    blocking calls, 81
    overview, 82–83
camera
    front camera, 14–15
    rear camera, 15
    resolution, 10
    switching between cameras, 155–156
Camera app
    flash, 156–157
    location tag feature, 158–159
    overview, 151–153
    recording video, 154–155
    selecting shooting mode, 155
    self-timer, 157
    setting resolution and video quality, 157–158
    Single Shot mode, 153
    Still Shot mode, 153–154
    switching cameras, 155–156
    unlock-and-launch app, 328
cellular carrier
    cellular support, 302
    choosing, 12
charging battery, 13–14
Chevron icon, 49
Chrome app
    bookmarks, 121
    browsing tips, 118–119
    changing web's appearance, 126
    clearing web history, 126
    downloading

D

Dark Theme (Dark Mode), 262, 311
data roaming, disabling, 283
data usage screens, 311–313
Daydream feature, 313–314
default apps
  open-by-default apps, 250–252
  setting, 253–254, 322
Delete icon, 49
deleting
  Android icons, 49
  images and videos, 168
device status, Home screen, 40
dialing contact, 71
dictation
  overview, 325–326
  removing censorship, 314–315
Dictation icon, 49
dictionary, 315
Direct Dial widget, 316
Directions widget, 316
display
  battery use, 327
  Blue Light filter, 261–262
  brightness, 263, 304
  Dark Theme, 262
  defined, 2
  double-tap gesture, 34
  drag gesture, 34
  long-press gesture, 34
  Night Light filter, 262, 311
  overview, 14–15
  pinch gesture, 34
  rotate gesture, 34
  screen lock time-out, 263
  screen orientation
    changing, 39–40, 326
    setting, 262
    troubleshooting, 306
  Screen Saver, 264
  selecting multiple items, 35
  spread gesture, 34
  swipe gesture, 34
  tap gesture, 34

Do Not Disturb Mode mode, 320–321
Done icon, 50
Done key, keyboard, 53
double-tap gesture, 34
downloading
  apps from Play Store app, 196–198
  files, 124
  images, 124
  reviewing downloads, 125
  saving web page, 125
drag gesture, 34
Drive app (Google Drive), 228
Duo app, 134

E

earbud headset, 10
earphones, 16–17
eBook reader app, 188–189
eBook widget, 316
Edit icon, 50
editing
  contacts, 94
  image editing
    cropping picture, 166–167
    overview, 164–166
    rotating picture, 168
  text editing
    autocorrect, 63
    cutting, copying, pasting, 62
    moving cursor, 60–61
    selecting text, 61–62
    spell check, 63
email
  adding accounts, 110
  attachments, 101, 114–116
    receiving, 115
    sharing, 116
  composing, 113–114
  inbox, 111
  overview, 109–111
  reading, 111–112
  sending to contact, 114
  texting vs., 101

I

icons, Android
  Action Overflow, 49
  Add, 49
  Chevron, 49
  Close, 49
  Delete, 49
  Dictation, 49
  Done, 50
  Edit, 50
  Favorite, 50
  Refresh, 50
  Search, 50
  Settings, 50
  Share, 50
  Side Menu, 50
Image Settings control, Photos app, 165
images. *See also* Camera app; Photos app
  adding to contact, 94–95
  backing up in Photos app, 169
  downloading, 124
  image editing
    cropping picture, 166–167
    overview, 164–166
    rotating picture, 168
  sharing on Facebook, 131
  sharing on Instagram, 132
IMAP account, 110
inbox, email, 111
Incognito Tab, Chrome app,
    122–123
Instagram, 132
international calling, 283–285, 329
Internet
  bookmarks, 121
  browsing tips, 118–119
  changing web's appearance, 126
  clearing web history, 126
  downloading
    files, 124
    images, 124
    reviewing downloads, 125
    saving web page, 125

Incognito Tab, 122–123
multiple tabs, 121–122
navigating between web pages, 120
overview, 117
radio apps, 182
security settings, 127
sharing web page, 123
tab actions, 121
visiting web page, 119–120
Internet cafés, 290

K

keyboard
  accessing keyboard variations, 55
  Done key, 53
  feedback settings, 265
  glide typing, 266, 327
  Go key, 53
  Google Keyboard, 51
  layout, 264–265
  Next key, 53
  predictive text, 265–266, 327
  QWERTY layout, 52
  Return key, 53
  Samsung Keyboard, 51–52
  Search key, 53

L

launchers, 29
  adding, 242, 260–261
  in Favorites tray, 41
  on Home screen, 40
  moving, 244–245
  removing, 246
  starting apps, 45–46
layout, keyboard, 264–265
live wallpaper, 259
location
  hiding, 279
  location tag feature
    Camera app, 158–159
    Photos app, 164

resolution, camera, 10, 157–158

restarting device, 300

Return key, 53

Rich Communications Service (RCS), 99. *See also* texting

ringtone
  phone calls, 74
  setting, 267–268, 320
  texts, 106–107

roaming
  data roaming, disabling, 283
  defined, 281–282
  detecting, 282
  MMS, disabling, 282–283

rotating
  device orientation, 39
  pictures, 168
  rotate gesture, 34

S

S Pen, 16

Safety app, 71

Samsung devices
  Smart Switch app, 26
  unlocking, 28

Samsung Galaxy Store, 200

Samsung Keyboard, 51–52

Satellite view, Maps app, 142

screen caps (screen shots), 317

screen lock
  face unlock, 28, 274
  finding, 270
  fingerprint lock, 273
  launchers, 29
  lock screen apps, 29
  none, 270
  overview, 269
  password, 28, 270–272
  pattern, 28, 270, 272–273
  PIN, 28, 270–271
  removing, 271
  signature unlock, 29
  swipe, 270
  time-out, 263

screen orientation
  changing, 39–40, 326
  setting, 262
  troubleshooting, 306

Screen Saver, 264

screen saver, 313–314

screen shots (screen caps), 317

screencasting, 231–233

SD version, videos, 201

Search command, Play Music app, 175

Search icon, 50, 53

security
  adding owner info text, 275–276
  encrypting storage, 277–278
  factory data reset, 278–279
  Google Find My Device app, 277
  locating lost device, 276–277
  lock screen notifications, 274–275
  personal safety feature, 324
  screen lock, 28
    face unlock, 274
    finding, 270
    fingerprint lock, 273
    none, 270
    overview, 269
    password, 270–272
    pattern, 270, 272–273
    PIN, 28, 270–271
    removing, 271
    swipe, 270
  web browsing, 127

selecting text, 61–62

self-timer, Camera app, 157

Settings icon, 50

setup, device
  adding online accounts, 24–25
  configuring device, 22–23
  overview, 21–22
  upgrading device, 25–26

Share icon, 50

sharing
  email attachments, 116
  images, 131–132, 170
  locations, 145

About the Author

Dan Gookin has been writing about technology for nearly three decades. He combines his love of writing with his gizmo fascination to create books that are informative, entertaining, and not boring. Having written over 160 titles, and with 12 million copies in print translated into over 30 languages, Dan can attest that his method of crafting computer tomes seems to work.

Perhaps his most famous title is the original *DOS For Dummies,* published in 1991. It became the world's fastest-selling computer book, at one time moving more copies per week than the *New York Times* number-one bestseller (though, as a reference, it could not be listed on the Times' Best Sellers list). That book spawned the entire line of *For Dummies* books, which remains a publishing phenomenon to this day.

Dan's most popular titles include *PCs For Dummies, Laptops For Dummies,* and *Microsoft Word For Dummies.* He also maintains the vast and helpful website www.wambooli.com.

Dan holds a degree in Communications/Visual Arts from the University of California, San Diego. He lives in the Pacific Northwest, where he enjoys spending time annoying people who deserve it.

Publisher's Acknowledgments

Acquisitions Editor: Katie Mohr

Senior Project Editor: Paul Levesque

Copy Editor: Becky Whitney

Proofreader: Debbye Butler

Production Editor: Mohammed Zafar Ali

Cover Image: Robot © kirill_makarov/ Shutterstock, Phone © ExtraDryRain/ Getty Images, Android Icon © Courtesy of Dan Gookin

Leverage the power

Dummies is the global leader in the reference category and one of the most trusted and highly regarded brands in the world. No longer just focused on books, customers now have access to the dummies content they need in the format they want. Together we'll craft a solution that engages your customers, stands out from the competition, and helps you meet your goals.

Advertising & Sponsorships

Connect with an engaged audience on a powerful multimedia site, and position your message alongside expert how-to content. Dummies.com is a one-stop shop for free, online information and know-how curated by a team of experts.

- Targeted ads
- Video
- Email Marketing
- Microsites
- Sweepstakes sponsorship

20 MILLION PAGE VIEWS EVERY SINGLE MONTH

15 MILLION UNIQUE VISITORS PER MONTH

43% OF ALL VISITORS ACCESS THE SITE VIA THEIR MOBILE DEVICES

700,000 NEWSLETTER SUBSCRIPTIONS TO THE INBOXES OF

300,000 UNIQUE INDIVIDUALS EVERY WEEK

# of dummies

Custom Publishing

Reach a global audience in any language by creating a solution that will differentiate you from competitors, amplify your message, and encourage customers to make a buying decision.

- Apps
- Books
- eBooks
- Video
- Audio
- Webinars

Brand Licensing & Content

Leverage the strength of the world's most popular reference brand to reach new audiences and channels of distribution.

For more information, visit dummies.com/biz

PERSONAL ENRICHMENT

Staying Sharp dummies

9781119187790
USA $26.00
CAN $31.99
UK £19.99

Facebook dummies

9781119179030
USA $21.99
CAN $25.99
UK £16.99

Guitar dummies

9781119293354
USA $24.99
CAN $29.99
UK £17.99

Investing dummies

9781119293347
USA $22.99
CAN $27.99
UK £16.99

Beekeeping dummies

9781119310068
USA $22.99
CAN $27.99
UK £16.99

Digital Photography dummies

9781119235606
USA $24.99
CAN $29.99
UK £17.99

Meditation dummies

9781119251163
USA $24.99
CAN $29.99
UK £17.99

Pregnancy ALL-IN-ONE dummies

9781119235491
USA $26.99
CAN $31.99
UK £19.99

Samsung Galaxy S 7 dummies

9781119279952
USA $24.99
CAN $29.99
UK £17.99

iPhone dummies

9781119283133
USA $24.99
CAN $29.99
UK £17.99

Crocheting dummies

9781119287117
USA $24.99
CAN $29.99
UK £16.99

Nutrition dummies

9781119130246
USA $22.99
CAN $27.99
UK £16.99

PROFESSIONAL DEVELOPMENT

Windows 10 dummies

9781119311041
USA $24.99
CAN $29.99
UK £17.99

AutoCAD dummies

9781119255796
USA $39.99
CAN $47.99
UK £27.99

Excel 2016 dummies

9781119293439
USA $26.99
CAN $31.99
UK £19.99

QuickBooks 2017 dummies

9781119281467
USA $26.99
CAN $31.99
UK £19.99

macOS Sierra dummies

9781119280651
USA $29.99
CAN $35.99
UK £21.99

LinkedIn dummies

9781119251132
USA $24.99
CAN $29.99
UK £17.99

Windows 10 ALL-IN-ONE dummies

9781119310563
USA $34.00
CAN $41.99
UK £24.99

SharePoint 2016 dummies

9781119181705
USA $29.99
CAN $35.99
UK £21.99

Fundamental Analysis dummies

9781119263593
USA $26.99
CAN $31.99
UK £19.99

Networking dummies

9781119257769
USA $29.99
CAN $35.99
UK £21.99

Office 2016 dummies

9781119293477
USA $26.99
CAN $31.99
UK £19.99

Office 365 dummies

9781119265313
USA $24.99
CAN $29.99
UK £17.99

Salesforce.com dummies

9781119239314
USA $29.99
CAN $35.99
UK £21.99

Coding dummies

9781119293323
USA $29.99
CAN $35.99
UK £21.99

dummies.com

dummies
A Wiley Brand